D0310064

PERSPECTIVES AND POLICIES ON ICT IN SOCIETY

IFIP – The International Federation for Information Processing

IFIP was founded in 1960 under the auspices of UNESCO, following the First World Computer Congress held in Paris the previous year. An umbrella organization for societies working in information processing, IFIP's aim is two-fold: to support information processing within its member countries and to encourage technology transfer to developing nations. As its mission statement clearly states,

> *IFIP's mission is to be the leading, truly international, apolitical organization which encourages and assists in the development, exploitation and application of information technology for the benefit of all people.*

IFIP is a non-profitmaking organization, run almost solely by 2500 volunteers. It operates through a number of technical committees, which organize events and publications. IFIP's events range from an international congress to local seminars, but the most important are:

- The IFIP World Computer Congress, held every second year;
- Open conferences;
- Working conferences.

The flagship event is the IFIP World Computer Congress, at which both invited and contributed papers are presented. Contributed papers are rigorously refereed and the rejection rate is high.

As with the Congress, participation in the open conferences is open to all and papers may be invited or submitted. Again, submitted papers are stringently refereed.

The working conferences are structured differently. They are usually run by a working group and attendance is small and by invitation only. Their purpose is to create an atmosphere conducive to innovation and development. Refereeing is less rigorous and papers are subjected to extensive group discussion.

Publications arising from IFIP events vary. The papers presented at the IFIP World Computer Congress and at open conferences are published as conference proceedings, while the results of the working conferences are often published as collections of selected and edited papers.

Any national society whose primary activity is in information may apply to become a full member of IFIP, although full membership is restricted to one society per country. Full members are entitled to vote at the annual General Assembly, National societies preferring a less committed involvement may apply for associate or corresponding membership. Associate members enjoy the same benefits as full members, but without voting rights. Corresponding members are not represented in IFIP bodies. Affiliated membership is open to non-national societies, and individual and honorary membership schemes are also offered.

PERSPECTIVES AND POLICIES ON ICT IN SOCIETY

An IFIP TC9 (Computers and Society) Handbook

Edited by

Jacques Berleur
Institut d'Informatique
Facultés Universitaires Notre-Dame de la Paix
Belguim

Chrisanthi Avgerou
London School of Economics
United Kingdom

 Springer

Library of Congress Cataloging-in-Publication Data

A C.I.P. Catalogue record for this book is available from the Library of Congress.

Perspectives and Policies on ICT in Society, Edited by Jacques Berleur and Chrisanthi Avgerou

p.cm. (The International Federation for Information Processing)

ISBN-10: (HB) 0-387-25587-7
ISBN-13: (HB) 978-0387-25587-3
ISBN-10: (eBook) 0-387-25588-5
ISBN-13: (eBook) 978-0387-25588-0
Printed on acid-free paper.

Printed in the United States of America.

9 8 7 6 5 4 3 2 1   SPIN 11415114 (HC) / 11416487 (eBook)
springeronline.com

Content

SUBJECT INDEX

Introduction

Jacques BERLEUR and Chrisanthi AVGEROU (Eds.)
IFIP-TC9 Past Chair and Chair
jberleur@info.fundp.ac.be, c.avgerou@lse.ac.uk

'Information Society?' 'Knowledge Society?' 'Networked Society?' Whatever expression we may prefer, aren't we at risk of playing with buzzwords instead of deepening the meanings that are slipping into our mind? Are these expressions equivalent? And if they are taken as such by many authors, or if we use the general denomination popularized by Manuel Castells' trilogy *Information Age*, is it true, and what does it imply?[1]

In any case, a multidimensional approach is surely necessary to understand the multifaceted characteristics of this society. It is surely a technological phenomenon: the developments in the last fifty years appear as overcoming the imagination, from the ENIAC (Electronic Numerical Integrator and Computer) of 1946 to the PDA (Personal Digital Assistant) of today. It is also clearly an economic challenge: the globalization of economy has created a real impulse of huge telecommunication investments, of the merging of gigantic businesses, which imperatively require a return.[2] It has also helped to develop a service society, when the western societies were facing a ceiling, if not saturation, of their industrial activity.[3] In other words, from the technological and economic point of view, there is such a radical change than many people call it easily a 'revolution.' Businesses and financial institutions are surely accrediting such a thesis where they find it fitting with their interest. Public authorities are not far from advancing at the same pace, and emphasizing the rhetoric of the inevitable and inescapable destiny.[4] But, as stressed by Frank Webster about the 'Information Society', if something "cannot be accurately distinguished, then it is accordingly rather difficult to assert that it is novel." (...) "If there is more information around, but this information remains under the control of long-established forces, then there are surely good reasons to doubt claims that we are entering a new era. Accordingly, such sceptical reasoning may lead people to resist endorsing the argument that we live now in an 'Information Age', and - more serious still – to doubt its corollary, that adaptation to this novel situation is a necessity."[5] Even when not adopting such a radical statement, we are led to think that the concept of *Information Age*, or whatever we may call it, is anything but clear and therefore needs a deeper reflection. We must go further than the technological and economic vision.

What about the cultural vision of the *Information Age*? There are domains, such as music, where the diversity is dominated by USA and UK way of life! But there are also claims for favouring multiculturality at large, and multilingualism. This is the quasi-permanent discourse of UNESCO. There are also challenges in terms of thinking of life and society. The virtual world is raising concerns, and people make claims for "grounding the 'virtual' life in the physical realm": "Many people are concerned that the increasing importance of 'virtual life' will have serious psychological and social implications. Proposals have been made to encourage the use of computing to support rather than supplant real life. For example, 'community nets' are geographically based networks that help enhance real participation within a specific locality (e.g. neighbourhood, village)."[6]

Common sense requires a balance between the different dimensions of the Information Age. The development of ICT must be thought of in terms of *appropriate use by all*. But then, immediately, the question is raised: appropriate to what? To economic growth, to particular interests, to political and democratic concerns, to social values, to cultural identity, to social organization, to justice? It is up to us to decide, to us all, and not only to the happy few who are today fixing the goals and purposes of what they decide to be sustainable development or common good.

*

* *

The origin of this book is a discussion that took place at a gathering of information and communication technology (ICT) professionals and academics for a business meeting of the Technical Committee 9 (TC9) of the International Federation for Information Processing (IFIP) in Stockholm in 1999. TC9 is concerned with the relationship between computers and society, and more largely between ICT and society. Its membership consists of representatives of national computer societies and chairpersons of working groups specializing in the study of particular issues of social concern regarding ICT, which include: computers and work; social accountability; ethics of computing; home oriented informatics; ICT in developing countries; ICT misuse and the law; history of computing; and ICT, women and work.

The trigger for the discussion was an expression of apprehension about the technocratic nature of various 'Information Society' policies by Jacques Berleur, the chair of the committee. His concerns were reinforced in the course of the discussion, as participants drew from the preoccupations of the working groups they represented or the specific experiences of their countries.

This book reflects the spirit of the concerns that were articulated in that event and the synthesis of the forum that created it. First, it contains mainly – though not exclusively – critical voices on the nature of and the social consequences of the emerging global 'Information Society'. Second, it is structured in two parts, one reporting on Information Society policy initiatives pursued in various countries and regions, and another focusing on a number of relevant issues, and thematic policies by drawing upon the specialist knowledge of the working groups of TC9.

The chapters vary in style: some have a clear academic orientation, and make use of theory to propose and support their arguments; while others have a professional tone, highlighting and discussing issues, policies and initiatives in a direct way without making explicit theoretical connections. The editors felt it is inappropriate to use a common template in the production of this book. Indeed, they believe that one of its most significant and valuable characteristics, as is true for most of the work of the IFIP teams, is that it brings together analysts from diverse backgrounds who have diverse points of view and ways of expressing them.

*

* *

Part 1, on Information Society Policies, contains chapters on initiatives and experiences in Africa, China, the European Union, India, Australia, Central and Eastern Europe, the United States and Hungary.

Jonathan Miller outlines the main policy initiatives intended to promote the exploitation of the developmental potential of ICT in Africa and discusses some of the outcomes of these efforts. Specifically, Miller highlights the inadequate supply of telecommunications that hinder not only the development of a modern business environment, such as e-commerce, but also improvements in such crucial areas for the development of the continent as health and education. This chapter concludes with the identification of four areas that need attention in any inquiry of the African Information Society: physical resources, digital resources, human resources and social resources.

Xinxiang Chen, Jiaqing Gao, and Wenda Tan outline China's ICT strategy as part of a broader industrialization and informatization effort for economic and social development. This effort includes the following: the search for a new industrialization mode with high technology content, sound profits, lower resource consumption, reduced environmental pollution and adequate use of human resources; the boosting of sciences, education and sustainable development; the use of IT to enhance industrialization levels and to reconstruct traditional industries through informatization; the use of the advantages of a late starter to develop IT; the development of an IT industry and the application of IT in all aspects of social and economic fields.

Jacques Berleur and Jean-Marc Galand trace the history of ICT policies of the European Union (EU) and unravel their logic, objectives, changing emphasis, and achievements. The authors structure their study in two periods of policy making: 1994-1999 that was initiated with the adoption of the Bangemann report, and 1999 and beyond that was initiated by the formation of the DG 'Information Society' and the launching of its eEurope action plans. In their discussion of the policy initiatives during these two periods, the authors note two tensions manifested in the succession of policy declarations and actions of the EU: the tension between technologically deterministic visions and socio-political realities and the tension between pursuing social objectives and strengthening the market. Overall, the authors voice concern about the technocratic nature of the policy process and content and a bias towards market issues despite a rhetoric suggesting an orientation towards 'people'. Yet, in their conclusions the authors point out that the EU Information Society and eEurope policies should be appreciated as a valuable forum of vision and continuous discourse on the challenges of contemporary ICT mediated society.

Sowmyanarayanan Sadagopan and John Weckert consider two countries in the Asia-Pacific region, India and Australia. Policies are outlined that show how the governments in these countries are attempting to encourage the IT industry, e-business and e-government, to address problems of Internet access, and to regulate Internet content. The authors conclude with the optimistic observation that the continuing policy efforts of both these countries 'appear to be bearing fruit'.

Niko Schlamberger and Franci Pivec describe a new regional initiative born in collaboration with some national computer societies in Central and Eastern Europe and IFIP. A new rather informal regional body has been set up – Information Technology Standing Regional Committee for Regional Collaboration (IT STAR). Its purpose is to facilitate common performance of IT professionals regardless of their momentary employment or any other kind of affiliation. The prerequisite is a professional capacity and wish to take part in certain kinds of projects. The authors point out that this initiative has triggered wide attention and may hopefully be adopted as a paradigm to be used elsewhere where regional collaboration is appreciated.

John A.N. Lee examines some issues associated with the Internet that emerged in the cultural context of the United States and describes measures taken to address them. Specifically, Lee describes the attention given to the regulation of the Internet, privacy, and the digital divide. He outlines Presidential initiatives towards a policy for the use of ICT to improve society and discusses the significance of federally funded research. Finally, Lee notes that the culture of the USA promotes policies that favour non-governmental control mechanisms. He points out some of the most salient characteristics of American culture within which the country's Information Society policy is shaped.

László Z. Karvalics starts by reviewing the roots and the current situation of an unevenly information-intensive global society in the early high cultures to the middle of the 20th century. As a 'prehistory', the author outlines the emergence of the Information Society and its uneven development to a competition problem: principally the movement of the American-Japanese tandem (1961-1978) and 'the pursuing bunch' (1978-1991). He then focuses on the decade 1992-2002, which is characterised by comprehensive national information strategies, and demonstrates that in the measurable domain of Information Society there are winners and losers, thus arguing that systematic Information Society development programmes have tangible outcomes. Karvalics is concerned that the information gap is widening as the developed countries, engaging in a mutually competitive race, are winners every time.

*

* *

Part 2 focuses on specific issues of the Information Society, or better said, on issues of major concern.

Peter Mambrey outlines the work of the working group WG 9.1 on computers and work and explains its focus on issues of the design of technology that determine the relationship between ICT users and their work place. Furthermore, he positions the interests of the working group against a review of the main themes of research in the vast area of the impact of ICT on work. The author identifies two broad questions of great concern in this area, namely whether technologies destroy more jobs than they create, and the effects of ICT on democracy and quality of life in the work place. He traces the main debates in the literature of the field and points out the issues associated with the relatively new challenges of telework and networked work.

Jan Holvast, Penny Duquenoy, and Diane Whitehouse, remind us of the debate that gave rise to and accompanied the emergence of the 'Information Society'. They start with the seminal publication of Joseph Weizenbaum's *Computer Power and Human Reason* in 1976, which raised concerns about the social and ethical challenges posed by developments in the field of artificial intelligence. The authors review a stream of important publications on IT and society and conclude that the development of the technologies of the Information Society results from an evolutionary rather than a revolutionary process, the social consequences of which it is possible to control. The authors identify three forms of control mechanisms: reactive control oriented towards protection from the potentially damaging effects of a technical innovation; participatory control dealing with active involvement of citizens to safeguard their interests and form appropriate regulatory regimes; and anticipatory control, which consists of procedures for predicting social economic and political consequences of new scientific and technological advances.

Geoff Busby looks briefly at the historical development, the contemporary status, and the future possibilities of ICT to assist people with impairments live fulfilled lives. Busby is cautiously optimistic about the way ICT developments in corporations address disabilities. Nevertheless, he is concerned that the private sector on its own is not going to exploit the full potential of ICT for disabled persons and he points to the need for relevant legislation and government action.

Penny Duquenoy's paper, on the ethics of computing, begins with a review of the early discussions concerning ethical aspects of computer technology and the identification of three dimensions of ethical issues that continue to be relevant today: those stemming from the technical characteristics of the technology, those referring to the application of computers and those concerning the environment of use of the technology application. Duquenoy points out the emergence of a broad range of ethical concerns, including issues of professional responsibility, privacy, security, and quality of working life, since the 1980s. She then focuses on the current debates on moral responsibility of the technological experts and moral choices in their use of technologies, and argues that the most challenging ethical issues in the foreseeable future are associated with the capabilities of the Internet and its governance.

Jacques Berleur discusses a number of ethical questions implicated in governance of the Internet. This chapter starts with a brief history of IFIP initiatives on ethics of computing and outlines the lessons learnt from an analysis carried out in 1996 by an IFIP task force of the codes of ethics for professional conduct of member societies and their mechanisms of enforcement. Subsequently, J. Berleur focuses on questions of ethics regarding the governance of the Internet, drawing from research conducted by the IFIP Special Interest Group SIG9.2.2. He points out the emphasis given to self-regulation across a spectrum of international institutions concerned with the governance of the Internet and he notes the prevalence of corporate actors over public authorities, highlighting the risk of neglecting issues of common good and of serving too solely commercial interests. The chapter concludes with a list of recommendations to address questions of ethics in the governance of the Internet.

Andy Sloane looks at the position occupied by the home as the central focus of the Information Society. A working definition of the home is used and various interactions and activities that take place in the home are discussed in relation to its changing role in the move towards an Information Society. The chapter also discusses various information activities that impinge upon the function of everyday life in the home including the use of information and information systems. Finally Sloane outlines some of the consequences of the move to an information-based model of the home.

In the chapter on 'Information Society and the Digital Divide Problem in Developing Countries', Chrisanthi Avgerou and Shirin Madon critically discuss the current view of Information Society as a strategy for socio-economic development. They question the way the discourse on the 'digital divide' problem has identified the needs of developing countries in universalistic techno-economic terms, with little attention to the historically formed circumstances within which ICT and information resources acquire meaning. They argue for an approach that associates the developmental potential of ICT with local social circumstances. To that end, they suggest the following areas of research that will contribute to policy makers' ability to draw contextually relevant and effective Information Society initiatives: attention to issues of social exclusion and cultural hybridization, and attention to 'knowledge' as distinct from the a-contextual notion of 'information' and as a concept associated with the local dynamics of culture and power.

Albin Zuccato and Simone Fischer-Hübner examine the effects of the Internet on privacy. Drawing upon concepts from sociology, they describe the effects that technology has on society as structuring or symbolic. They analyze these effects of technology on privacy and thereby demonstrate the potential of Internet technology and its effect on our life in society.

John Impagliazzo, John A.N. Lee, and David C. Cassidy suggest a method to integrate computing history in the computing curriculum and to elevate the awareness of the social context of the subject. They propose ways in which instructors can enrich the curriculum by including history in the subjects they teach, even though they may not have had formal education in computing history or the history of science. The authors argue that using history in computing stimulates discussion and dialogue among students and makes them aware of the social consequences of the computer systems they will use, design, or create. They point out that instructors can enrich the courses they now teach by integrating social and historical interludes within them.

Ronald E. Anderson provides a critical appraisal of the role and impact of the Information Society model in the United States educational system. Anderson begins with a discussion of three dominant paradigms: 'automation', 'Information Society,' and 'mind tools'. He then traces the history of ICT in education in the United States, describing how ideas intertwined with the concepts of the Information Society led to distractions that have impeded vigorous development of ICT to improve education. These distractions included the claim that schools should take up the responsibility of training all students in ICT for the so-called information workforce. Promoters of the Information Society model together with the marketing arms of the IT industry have perpetuated the adoption of ICT as an end in itself rather than as a means of improving the main business of education, learning. The author argues that these pressures over the past three decades have left ICT in education in a state of confusion, lacking adequate support and, in many instances, the infrastructure to adapt to the demands of the twenty-first century.

Dick Sizer examines the notion of 'professionalism' and discusses the development of IS professional responsibilities in information systems. In particular, Sizer describes the efforts of the British Computer Society to promote professional responsibility through the elaboration of a 'code of conduct'.

Finally, Pertti Järvinen starts with the observation that most problems associated with IT in organizations and society at large require knowledge drawn from multiple sciences and therefore research in this field requires careful choice of method. Järvinen outlines eight examples of such research to demonstrate the variety of theoretical and methodical requirements and suggests a taxonomy of methods to clarify the possibilities and help in the making of sound decisions of appropriate research method.

*
* *

During the recent WITFOR (World IT Forum) held in Vilnius (Lithuania), Commission 8, devoted to the social and ethical issues of the ICT, and which was animated by Working Groups members of IFIP-TC9, stressed the following emergent issues as an agenda to be tackled without delay: "Among the social and ethical concerns we strongly suggest a focus on professional ethics; access to content and technology for all; education, literacy and public awareness; multilingualism, cultural concerns; influence of globalization; regulation, self-regulation, governance and democratic participation; intellectual property rights; specific digital policies such as eHealth, eWork, eGovernment ....; privacy; protection of human and civil rights; protection of the individual against surveillance; develop quality of life and well-being; combating social exclusion; computer crime, cyber-attacks and security; employment and participative design at work; risk and vulnerabilities."[7]

Others, like Kari A. Hintikka, advised us that the debates related to the Information Age cover four major domains: the debate on the grounds ('Grundlagen') of human thinking and social life – distinction between information/knowledge, role of networks, information which can be treated and processed by machines, and knowledge which is proper to humankind; the debate about the network economy, and the changes in working life; democracy, daily life and continuous learning; finally the debate about the knowledge and communication 'markets'.[8] Accents should be put also on the relationship to culture through, among others, a debate on real/virtual, the social dualization, and the ethical question of the technological innovation.

We are ourselves convinced that we cannot escape a debate about the roots of our conception of space and time, and the way we try to master them.

This book is a first attempt to make the point on several of those questions, without pretending to be the best views! It is an attempt to propose a reflection on the future of our so-called Information Age, through the continuous work of the TC9 Working Groups.

Let us conclude with an address of the Director-General of UNESCO, Mr Koichiro Matsuura, at the Special Session on Global Divide Initiative at the Annual Meeting of the World Economic Forum (Davos, Switzerland, 29 January 2001): "If the knowledge societies are ever to take proper root and gain global acceptance, we must look beyond the technical and gadget appeal of ICTs and home in on the human dimensions of the digital divide: cultural and linguistic diversity of contents, empowerment of civil society, privacy and ethical issues, and access, especially by safeguarding the public domain. There will be *no information for all* without *education for all*. This is top priority for the public and the private sectors alike. The business community is increasingly concerned about the future of education systems. The Education for All agenda, adopted last year in Dakar, aims at combating poverty and ensuring development and growth through an expansion of educational attainment and quality. UNESCO is the UN system's lead agency here. We are determined to harness ICTs to the full in translating the lofty political goals into practical and tangible progress on the ground."[9]

Paraphrasing Mr Koichiro Matsuura, who was speaking in the domain of competence of UNESCO, we could broaden the scope to the different dimensions of society, asking: Information Society, Knowledge Society, Network Society, Information Age for all? This means *for the whole person, for the integral person, and for all human beings (pour tout l'homme et pour tous les hommes")*, - as emphasised by the economist François Perroux in all his work.[10]

May we also suggest that the sphere of information technology and society pervades many areas: it is involved in working life, in the accountability of social and ethical issues, in daily and home life, caring for both developing countries and deprived people, grounding the virtual in the physical realm, being aware of the misuse and the capacity of the law, putting these issues with an historical perspective, and being sensitive to gender balance ... just to mention specifically the direct concerns of IFIP-TC9 and its working groups!

---

[1] Manuel Castells, 1996-1998: *The Rise of The Network Society. The Information Age: Economy, Society and Culture,* 3 vol., Oxford: Blackwell.

[2] For instance, in February 2004, Cingular, the number 2 in the USA mobile telephony, acquires AT&T wireless for US$ 40,5 billions!

[3] *Eurofutures. The Challenges of Innovation,* The FAST Report, Commission of the European Communities in association with the journal *Futures,* Butterworths, 1984, Table 2.1, p. 96.

[4] Jari Aro, Narratives and Rhetoric of the Information Society in Administrative Programs and in Popular Discourse, in: *Informational Societies. Understanding the Third Industrial Revolution,* Erkki Karvonen, Ed., Tampere University Press, 2001, pp. 69-84.

[5] Frank Webster, Global Challenges and National Answers, in: *Informational Societies. Understanding the Third Industrial Revolution,* Erkki Karvonen, Ed., op.cit. p. 260.

[6] *Ethics and the Governance of the Internet,* Jacques Berleur, Penny Duquenoy and Diane Whitehouse, Eds., IFIP-SIG9.2.2, September 1999, IFIP Press, Laxenburg - Austria, ISBN 3-901882-03-0, 56 p. This monograph may also be found on the SIG9.2.2 website:
http://www.info.fundp.ac.be/~jbl/IFIP/Ethics_and_Internet_Governance.pdf

[7] WITFOR, Commission 8, Social and Ethical Aspects of ICT, Jacques Berleur, H.E. Vigdis Finnbogadottir, Prof. Klaus Brunnstein, Ed., in: *WITFOR 2003*

White Book, Dipak Khakhar, Ed., IFIP Press 2003, pp. 259-339, ISBN 3-901882-18-9

[8] Quoted by Jari Aro, Narratives and Rhetoric of the Information Society in Administrative Programs and in Popular Discourse, art. cit.

[9] UNESCO Director-General: Education and Cultural Diversity are Key to Bridging Digital Gap,
http://www.unesco.org/webworld/news/2001/010131_davos.shtml

[10] See, for instance, François Perroux, *La coexistence pacifique,* 3 vol., Paris, Presses Universitaires, 1958, 666 p., *Le pain et la parole,* Paris, Ed. du Cerf, 1969, 334 p., or, *L'Économie du XXème siècle,* 2de édition, Paris, Presses Universitaires, 1964, 690 p.

PART 1 – POLICIES ON INFORMATION AND COMMUNICATION TECHNOLOGY IN SOCIETY

Perspectives and Policies on ICT in Africa

Jonathan MILLER
Trigrammic
Hout Bay, South Africa
jonmil@icon.co.za

*"While there has been great value in focusing on the profound digital
differences between developed and developing countries, the
downside has been a potential and insidious distinction between
civilized tool-users and uncivilized non-users. What is missing is a
deeper focus on the "true" knowledge needs of particular cultures
and communities, and the relevance of ICT to individual social
contexts."*

Key words: Information technology, telecommunications, ICT, Internet, policy, digital divide, Africa, development, social norms.

To understand ICT in Africa, one must first understand Africa: a continent comprising fifty-four countries showing extreme diversity, in most cases grinding poverty, high levels of public debt, unhealthy dependence on international donor funding, vast geographic dispersion and low population densities, a multiplicity of languages and very low levels of literacy, and a continent ravaged by HIV/AIDS. Africa is also characterised by political turmoil, endemic warfare, an agrarian society and a generally very weak private sector. In all, Africa comprises 10% of the world's population but only 1% of world GDP.

Despite the gloomy picture this paints, there are signs of significant improvements in prospects for the continent. Peace appears to be breaking out, with recent agreements between warring nations and troop withdrawals in the Great Lakes region in particular. There is more evidence of working democracies. In 2002 the moribund and ineffective Organisation of African Unity was replaced by the African Union. The New Partnership for African Development (NEPAD) was launched with great fanfare and, despite hitches, seems to be establishing itself as the continent-wide mechanism to build political and economic stability.

While the continent battles with the social and economic circumstances outlined above, it is also caught up in the burgeoning field of telecommunications, the Internet and ICT. International agencies are strongly encouraging African governments to launch themselves into the Knowledge Era and see ICT as an essential component of their economic and social resurgence. One of the outcomes is seen in African leaders' response – the NEPAD programme – which identifies ICT as one of its four pillars and has formed the eAfrica Commission to spearhead ICT activities. Some say ICT is the last hope for Africa to participate effectively in the global economy.

Any discussion of ICT in the developing world inevitably addresses the so-called "digital divide" between the developed and developing world. Definitions vary, but essentially this notion refers to the huge, and widening, gap between developed and developing world as regards availability and cost of computer hardware, software and access to telecommunications facilities, including telephones and the Internet. It also refers to indigenous capabilities to use the telecom infrastructure for socio-economic development. It is argued that the gap will continue to widen – especially in Africa – unless the continent makes heroic efforts.

There are, indeed, innumerable efforts to "narrow the divide" and, as discussed below, some notable successes. The process seems to be taking a long time, however, and many examples of well-meaning efforts have failed dismally. New terms are being invented such as "digital opportunities" and suggestions that there is no such thing as a digital divide, but rather a "development divide." In fact, recently, there have been calls to re-conceptualise the Digital Divide in ways that will redirect efforts towards more effective solutions.[1] We return to this topic later in the chapter, but first we flesh out the top level initiatives designed to better exploit ICT in Africa and discuss some of the outcomes to date.

TOP LEVEL INITIATIVES

Despite the awesome challenges facing the continent – arguably needing attention before even contemplating a focus on the information society – there is an impressive array of policies, programmes, projects designed to apply the benefits of ICT to Africa. Most of those activities originated in 1995 with a key speech by South Africa's then deputy-President Thabo Mbeki to the Brussels G7 Conference on the Information Society, in which he challenged the developed world to engage the developing world on the issue of the Information Society. A direct outcome of that intervention was the so-called ISAD (Information Society and Development) Conference that took place in South Africa in 1996, for the first time engaging the developed and developing world in a debate about the information society and development.

Among several resolutions passed and announcements made at ISAD, perhaps the one of most relevance for this chapter was that by the UN Economic Commission for Africa that launched the African Information Society Initiative (AISI). The AISI comprised an action plan "to build Africa's information and communications infrastructure (NICI)."
The action plan calls for

"the elaboration and implementation of national information and communication infrastructure plans involving development of institutional frameworks, human, information and technological resources in all African countries and the pursuit of priority strategies, programmes and projects which can assist in the sustainable build up of an information society in African countries."

In the ensuing years many African countries embarked upon ICT policy and planning processes. As of 2002 some twenty-seven countries claimed to be at various stages in building national ICT infrastructures. For example:

- In Mozambique lengthy consultative processes since the mid-90s led to the Government adopting an ICT policy in 2000.[2] There are six priority areas: Education, Health (with a priority on HIV/AIDS), Human Resource Development, Infrastructure, Access and Governance. In place is an ICT Policy Commission in the Prime Minister's office, but to date there is little evidence of tangible outcomes.

- Tanzania has also seen the need to develop a policy that addresses the ICT Sector as a whole. Unusual is the emergence of a strong forum of businessmen, government employees, academics and donor organisations called "eThinkTank," a group that engages in vigorous debate on ICT matters via an electronic list server. In October 2001 the group held a public forum where it tabled Terms of Reference for the development of an ICT policy. This triggered the formation of an official government group to carry the ICT policy process forward. The Tanzanian Government adopted the proposed policy in 2003 and is proceeding to form a top level implementation body.

- Rwanda first engaged in ICT policy formation in 1998. By 2001 there was a report presented to the President, entitled: *An Integrated ICT-led Socio-Economic Development Policy and Plan for Rwanda 2001 - 2005.* The document suggests a budget of US$ 500 million together with broad timeframes and responsible government departments. To date, however, there has also been little tangible action, possibly since there have been delays in constituting the planned implementing agency.

There was an important opportunity to reflect on progress in ICT in Africa at the first African Development Forum in Addis Ababa in 1999. The overall theme was *Globalisation and the Information Economy: Challenges and Opportunities for Africa.* Four priority sub-themes emerged:
- Creating the Enabling Policy Environment,
- ICT, Youth and Education,
- ICT and Health, and
- Electronic Commerce.

Subsequently the ECA AISI group issued a "Common Position for Africa's Digital Inclusion" elaborating on these recommended sub-themes, which now enjoys wide acceptance. The eAfrica Commission mentioned above is the natural body to carry forward the recommendations, but remains at an early stage of development.

This is not the place to offer a comprehensive analysis of all the elements of the various policies in place or in process, but it can be stated that most of the real activity in ICT policy making throughout Africa remains at the level of formation of national ICT commissions and central implementation agencies, establishment of telecom regulators and moves towards telecommunications liberalisation and privatisation. Most countries have yet to translate their policy proposals into action on the ground.

In addition to the initiatives described above, there are many others involving bilateral and multilateral organisations, the donor community and the countries themselves. The Appendix lists several with weblinks. One of the most popular projects receiving funding from such entities nowadays is the so-called "eReadiness" assessment. Many African countries have been subject to such assessments – sometimes more than once – where consultants carry out quantitative assessments of telecom infrastructure, ICT-related education and training, diffusion of ICT into government, business and civil society in general, and policy and regulatory issues. The crucial question is to what extent the numerous top-level, well-funded projects and programmes have helped Africa. Certainly, despite the AISI and ADF '99, much needs to be done in order to achieve higher order goals, such as application of ICT to health and education, promotion of eCommerce and eGovernment, let alone achievement of the overarching notion of an Information Society.

ICT SUPPLY AND DEMAND

Supply

There is abundant evidence that the supply of telephones and the Internet in Africa is growing at a rapid rate. Any assessment, however, has to be seen in light of aspects such as:

- *The extremely low base from which the continent is developing.* For instance, while all are aware that the number of telephones per hundred people in Africa is far lower than that for typical developed countries, it is salutary that the ratio of perhaps 1:100 persons is five times worse even than the average "low income" country. The number of Internet users is estimated at between 1:250 and 1:400 persons, compared with the world average of 1:13 and that for North America of 1:2.
- *Disparities between countries.* Overall averages for Africa conceal major differences within Africa, whether between capital cities and the rest of the country, or between the better endowed countries like South Africa, Egypt, Morocco and Nigeria, and the least well-endowed like Eritrea, Somalia, Central African Republic, etc.
- *The importance of the overall context for ICT equipment and applications.* The growth of ICT is severely hampered by poor and fluctuating electricity supply in most of Africa; very unreliable and costly transportation via road, rail and air links; time-consuming and unpredictable procedures at border posts; tax regimes that consider computers to be luxury goods; very low levels of education and literacy and the growing brain-drain of those that do gain superior qualifications.

Nonetheless there are notable advances in the availability of information and telecommunications technologies in Africa. While fixed line telephony is minimal and growing only at about 6% per annum in real terms (i.e., taking into account population growth), there has been a veritable explosion in mobile telephony. There are now some 100 GSM networks in 48 African countries providing service to 14 million customers (plus a further 10 million in South Africa). This subscriber base is well in excess of fixed lines and is made even more surprising by the high cost of mobile calls: 20-40 US cents a minute. Such rapid growth underlines a fundamental demand, supported by an open competitive market for mobile telephony characteristic of virtually all African countries, and the highly successful pre-paid business model that attracts well over 80% of all subscribers.[3]

Internet growth is rapid as well, although outside of North and South Africa, there are currently perhaps only two million Internet users. On the positive side the Internet market is generally competitive with some 560 Internet Service Providers on the continent serving individuals, business and government via dialup and leased lines. International bandwidth is growing rapidly (e.g., 700-1500 Mbps from 2001 to 2002), but not as rapidly as the world as a whole (174%) and Latin America in particular (479%). Again, while prices for international connectivity are declining and many African countries are rolling out Points of Presence (POPs) in secondary towns, and a price structure that permits all Internet calls at local prices, the cost of Internet access remains relatively very high. Most access via the public telephone system is charged per minute (which is known to severely inhibit usage) and typical monthly Internet subscriptions run at US$60. Given relative purchasing power, this makes Internet access at least ten times more expensive than in a typical developed country.

Significant in Africa is the prevalence of public access points for telecommunications and in particular the Internet. While early models focused on so-called multi-purpose telecentres that might offer business, training, telephony, computing and Internet facilities, the somewhat smaller and simpler "cybercafés" offering Internet access and perhaps some secretarial services, have become very popular[4]. For instance it is estimated that there are several hundred such cybercafés in Tanzania alone. While 80%+ are in the main city of Dar es Salaam, there is a growing incidence of such facilities in secondary towns, as telecom infrastructure spreads into the regions and local districts. Other models include the several thousand phoneshops in Senegal. Overall, given the relatively high cost of a domestic telephone and Internet service in Africa (as well as long waiting lists for service and subsequent maintenance and service problems), different models of public access points such as cybercafés and phoneshops, and public access points in schools, police stations, clinics, hotels etc. can be expected to proliferate over the coming years.

Related to this phenomenon is that of Internet Telephony, or "Voice over IP." VOIP enables voice communications by digitising analogue signals and transmitting the resultant data packets using the Internet protocol. While in many cases the quality of the voice transmission remains poorer than the analogue equivalent, this is changing. Indeed many public telephone companies are now contracting with backbone providers to transmit their own international traffic using VOIP. The use of VOIP by individual Internet users, ISPs, mobile operators etc., is, however, illegal in most countries of the world. This because it enables anyone with Internet access to bypass the licensed telephony operators (often still a government monopoly), depriving them of revenue in the process. This in turn challenges the typical country telecom policy and regulatory environment, especially in Africa. On the other hand Africa is characterised by its large Diaspora. Many families have members overseas with whom they wish to stay in touch. VOIP avoids the – typically extremely high – international telephone costs (which subsidise local calls and rentals) that such contact would imply. Some say the business model for cybercafés relies heavily on VOIP, which is very difficult to police. Thus we see more and more country governments and telecomm regulators tackling the issue and essentially preparing the way to legalise VOIP.

Outside a few countries like South Africa, there are virtually no computers other than PCs. Estimates of PCs vary from 1:100 to 1:500 persons. Most of those will be found in private businesses as opposed to government offices or homes and will most likely be running the Windows operating system and applications software. The major PC suppliers generally have a presence in African countries via agents and distributors rather than country offices. For this reason among others, technicians are in very short supply and support and maintenance is very difficult. Where PCs are present in larger firms and government departments they are much less likely to be linked in a LAN than in a developed context.

ICT technical and professional training and education is minimal in Africa, but is attracting a lot of international interest lately. Donors are funding training institutes and programmes for computer technicians and to impart entry level computing skills, and tertiary institutions, with and without funding support, are launching and growing advanced telecom and ICT professional training programmes.[5] The numbers of graduates of most of these programmes remains very small, however, and there is widespread concern that many of those who graduate join the brain-drain. Clearly this inhibits the demand for, and application of, ICT in Africa.

Demand

As mentioned previously in this chapter, at the African Development Forum (ADF) 99, education, health and eCommerce were identified as key application areas for ICT. To date, however, there is but a smattering of such activity in Africa.

- Despite the many offers of donor funding and awarded contracts, access to computers and the Internet in schools and universities remains confined to a tiny proportion of African institutions. The presence of active SchoolNet NGOs in several countries and the recent launch of SchoolNet Africa to coordinate those initiatives may augur well for more rapid incorporation of computers and the Internet into school curricula. To date, however, there is certainly no evidence of a changing culture of learning, for instance, applying distance learning protocols, This is not surprising, given the paucity of other facilities such as teachers, electricity, water and classrooms that characterises education in Africa.

- The health sector also suffers under the burden of a desperate lack of medical professionals, drugs, consumables and medical facilities – all in the face of the catastrophic rise in HIV/AIDS and other diseases like malaria. While there are long-standing electronic communications networks such as HealthNet linking medical professionals in Africa, and a rapidly increasing emphasis on the use of the Internet and the Web to support health initiatives, the potential benefits of approaches such as telemedicine have yet to be tapped.
- Electronic commerce too is at a nascent stage. There are some (and a growing number) of examples of African entrepreneurs using eCommerce facilities, but in almost all African countries, fundamental aspects such as cash-based economies, primitive banking systems, very poor and expensive logistics and concerns about corruption severely inhibit this sector.

A brief review of recent content of a popular electronic newsletter on ICT in Africa reveals an interesting collection of real applications of ICT in Africa. There are agricultural applications including web sites offering current weather conditions, research data and information relevant to local fishing companies, as well as access to produce prices via SMS messages on mobile phones. There are attempts to provide guidance for starting up small and micro enterprises, enabling bill payments over mobile phones and smart cards to pay for usage in Internet cafés. There are references to healthcare applications, use of ICT in electoral administration, and provision of information to help teachers,[6] but such examples are few and far between. Noticeable is the absence of applications, for instance, to provide language translation, innovative user interfaces to allow people with low levels of literacy to access useful information, implementation of wireless application reaching into remote rural areas, etc.

Towards an African Information Society

The previous sections of this chapter offer abundant evidence of top level commitments to building ICT infrastructure in African countries, applying ICT to directly address profound problems such as the burden of disease, realising the benefits of ICT for education and assisting African entrepreneurs to enter the global marketplace. Does this mean that Africa has become an Information Society? Certainly not. Is ICT being appropriately applied to serve the developmental needs of the poorest countries? Hardly. There is a concern that the notion of ICT for development has assumed a narrow and possibly inappropriate meaning. It may simply be encouraging all countries to emulate the patterns of use of ICT in industrialised countries, "catching up" by following in their footsteps of technology and socio-economic innovation and thereby avoid marginalisation in a global economy.

As was briefly presented in the previous section, the benefits of ICT are starting to be seen in the growing number of ICT applications in key sectors of African economies. However, this is only part of the story. The thrust of almost all top-level interventions by government and international donors and today's application of ICT in developing countries is largely in the hands of the minorities – whether in the public or private sector – who find its global symbolic and material value meaningful in their way of living and therefore are willing and able to acquire the skills and attitudes required to exploit its potential. This bias comes out in most discussions of the so-called Digital Divide, where the emphasis remains on the supply side: install sufficient telephone lines (or mobile phones), provide sufficient computers, make the Internet widely available, and the rest will follow. While there has been great value in focusing on the profound digital differences between developed and developing countries, the downside has been a potential and insidious distinction between civilized tool-users and uncivilized non-users.

What is missing is a deeper focus on the "true" knowledge needs of particular cultures and communities, and the relevance of ICT to individual social contexts. This aspect is receiving more academic and practitioner attention nowadays with a shift in perspective from the digital divide to "ICT for social inclusion." Here social inclusion may be achieved when *"individuals, families, and communities are able to fully participate in society and control their own destinies, taking into account a variety of factors related to economic resources, employment, health, education, housing, recreation, culture, and civic engagement.[7]"* The criteria to achieve such a condition are much broader than simply making computers and the Internet available. Warschauer proposes four areas of attention useful to frame the enquiry. These are listed below with brief commentary on the general situation in Africa.

(1) *Physical Resources,* encompassing access to computers and telecommunication connections. As discussed earlier in this chapter, this has been the area of most activity in ICT in Africa and its impact cannot be overstated. The last few years have seen a profound upgrading of basic telephony, an explosion in mobile services, and rapidly growing access to the Internet. There can be little doubt that this has had, and is having, a beneficial impact on the economies of many African countries. It is also noteworthy that despite an order of magnitude difference in price between fixed line and mobile telephony in most African countries, the local populace appears to have a great propensity to consume mobile minutes. But still missing is the provision of voice and data access in most secondary

towns and villages throughout Africa, thus forcing large numbers of rural inhabitants to travel long distances to exchange messages.

(2) *Digital Resources.* This addresses the provision of digital material online. If we view such resources as necessary for commercial activity and streamlining the provision of government services then we need to consider the widespread transfer of tacit knowledge into information systems, giving countries access to new process technologies and products developed in the industrialised countries, both rapidly and at low cost. This is happening to a degree and certainly the focus on eGovernment is growing apace.

But are Africans developing their own ICT materials? To what extent is access to ICT tailored to uniquely African social contexts? How relevant is ICT to the way Africans live their lives? Are Africans using computing devices and connectivity to engage in *meaningful social practices,* or simply to meet imported visions of modernity stressing decontextualised, formal knowledge as opposed to local formal and tacit knowledge? In the end, how relevant is ICT to the way Africans live their lives? There is very little evidence of appropriate user interfaces, web pages in local languages, etc. that would allow the broad mass of urban and rural populations to use ICT in ways meaningful to themselves.

(3) *Human Resources,* dealing with issues such as literacy and education (including the particular types of literacy practices that are required for computer use and online communication). Does ICT enable Africans to have "mastery over the processes by means of which culturally significant information is coded?" Is ICT providing access to information sources and communications media that are useful for learning and innovation? Despite valiant attempts to introduce computers and connectivity to schools, even in South Africa, the most connected of African societies, school computer laboratories and facilities for distance learning and training in information literacy are almost non-existent. There is much talk about cybercafés as valuable entities for public access. While true, again the incidence is minimal and the uses to which such facilities are put have more to do with western models than to serve indigenous tasks and pastimes.

(4) *Social Resources,* facilitating the community, institutional, and societal structures that support access to ICT. Are the settings such that young ICT learners are surrounded by people who support them in the ICT learning process, e.g., parents that help them with computers, to schoolmates that work on computer projects together, to village elders that value ICT in community life? Who are the intermediaries influencing ICT projects, such as public servants, NGOs, community-based organisations or private sector organisations? How are they helping adapt and shape ICTs, mediating or negotiating between the familiar and the new? Is the impact of the information society vision that drives policy initiatives in most developing

countries limited to the minorities who find its global, symbolic and material value meaningful in their way of living and therefore are willing and able to acquire the skills and attitudes required to exploit its potential?

Conclusions

ICT in Africa is clearly at a very early stage. Rightly it is being driven by lofty visions of the potential of ICT to transform essentially agrarian economies into knowledge societies, visions of dramatically improving the learning conditions for millions of African students who cannot afford books, of a health system that can exploit international best practice to come to terms with rampaging diseases, and of enabling countless African entrepreneurs to enter the global marketplace. For many obvious reasons this process of transformation must take a long time. Indeed, given the history of Africa, political and technological progress on the continent has been quite impressive. It will be many years, though before the vision of an African Information Society is realised.

APPENDIX

The Acacia Initiative: www.idrc.org/acacia
The African Connection: www.africanconnection.org
The African Information Society Initiative: www.uneca.org/aisi
Building Digital Opportunities: www.dfid.org.uk
Francophonie Information Highway Fund: www.francophonie.org
IICD ICT Activities: www.iicd.org
ITU's Internet Training Initiative: www.itu.int
Leland Initiative: www.usaid.gov/leland
Regional Information Network for Africa:
www.unesco.org/webworld/informatics/rinaf.htm
UNDP Initiatives: www.undp.org
Digital Opportunity Task Force: www.dotforce.org
UN ICT Task Force: www.unicttaskforce.org
The French reader will take advantage of consulting: *Enjeux des technologies de la communication en Afrique. Du téléphone à Internet*, sous la dir. d'Annie Chéneau-Loquay, Paris, Khartala 2000, Coll. Regards. He will find inserted a CD-ROM 'Internet au Sud' edited par Pascal Renaud. (*Note of the editor*)

[1]   Warschauer, M. Reconceptualizing the Digital Divide. First Monday Peer-reviewed Journal on the Internet

[2]   www.infopol.gov.mz

[3]   The pre-paid model obviates the need for subscribers to take out long term contracts. Users acquire a mobile handset by whatever means and then purchase a SIM card plus a "starter kit" that includes a mobile number plus a number of "minutes." Thereafter they can recharge their phones with additional minutes as and when they choose, exercising direct control over their expenditures. It is estimated that well over 80% of mobile usage is based on this model.

[4]   Indeed recently the ITU proposed changing its definition of public access to telecom services from telecentres to cybercafés.

[5]   A well-known computer technicians' certification is A+ (see www.comptia.org). The dominant international certification for basic user computing skills, covering word processing, spreadsheets, presentation graphics, data base usage and Internet usage is the International Computer Driving License (see www.ecdl.org)

[6]   www.balancingact-africa.com

[7]   Warschauer, M. op. cit.

ICT in China: A strong Force to Boost Economic and Social development

Xinxiang CHEN, Jiaqing GAO, and Wenda TAN
Capinfo Company Limited
xxchen@capinfo.com.cn

Key words: Development strategy, industrialization and informatization, liberalization, ICT and economic growth, social economy.

Further development of science and technology in the 21st century, especially IT and life sciences, will exert a profound influence on politics, economies and cultures around the world. In the opinion of experts, digitization in the early years of the 21st century will give new impetus to IT development: integrated circuits will enter into a new phase of integrated system development, transmission capacity of the DWDM (Dense Wavelength Division Multiplexing) communication system will be improved dramatically, and the technology and capacity of personal mobile communications and the Internet will also be enhanced to a great extent. The constant development of intellective and technological innovations, as well as combinations of material object production and intellectual production, hardware and software manufacture, traditional economies and IT technologies, will form a strong force to boost economic and social development in the 21st century.

ICT DEVELOPING STRATEGY IN CHINA

President Jiang Zemin, delivering a keynote speech during the opening ceremony of the 2000 World Computer Congress, emphasized the importance of IT for the country's economic development and social informatization. China's ICT strategy is: utilizing IT in the process of industrialization to enhance industrialization levels, utilizing IT in the process of informatization to reconstruct traditional industries, using IT to propel industrialization itself and, lastly, striving to realize "great-leap-forward" development and better use of IT for human well-being, taking advantage of China's position as a late starter. This implies that the government regards ICT as a strategic measure for national economic development. Further rapid growth of information and communication industries would make them pillar industries in the Chinese economy and an accelerator and amplifier for the development of other industries.

The above strategy has been formally integrated into state policies. It is clearly stated in the 16th Communist Party Congress that "centering on economic construction and liberalizing and developing social productive forces is essential to build a comprehensively well-off society. According to the latest developing trend of the world economy and technologies as well as the situation in the new phase of economic development of China, the main tasks in economic development and reforms in China for the first twenty years of this century are: perfecting the socialist market economic system; boosting strategic adjustments to economic structures, generally realizing industrialization; a greater effort to promote informatization; speeding up modernization; maintaining the sustainable and healthy development of the national economy and constantly improving the people's life". The Chinese government is attaching much importance to the IT industry and is engaged in a great effort to boost the national economy and social informatization, centering on the grand objectives laid down in the 16th Communist Party Congress.

Realizing that China is a developing country facing the arduous tasks of achieving both industrialization and informatization at the same time, we established the following development strategy: to search for a new industrialization mode with high technological content, sound economic profits, lower resource consumption, reduced environmental pollution and adequate use of human resources; to enforce the strategies of rejuvenating the country through sciences, education and sustainable development; to make use of IT to propel industrialization and, in turn, stimulate informatization; to utilize IT in the process of industrialization, in order to enhance industrialization levels, as well as employing IT in the process of reconstructing traditional industries through informatization; to make use of our advantages as a late starter, in order to develop IT by leaps and bounds; and meanwhile, give a priority to IT industry, applying IT in all aspects of social and economic fields.

IMPACT OF WTO ACCESSION ON ICT POLICIES AND ADMINISTRATION IN CHINA

With the unparalleled challenges and opportunities brought about by China's accession to WTO, the Chinese telecom market will become a focus of future global competition. Figure 1 provides the basic framework and schedule for China's gradual liberalization of the telecom service market, in accordance with China's accession commitments.

Figure 1: Gradual Liberalization of the Chinese Telecom Market After China's Accession to WTO

Type of Services	Time	Liberali- zation Ratio	Cities to be liberalized
Value-added services	2001	30%	Beijing, Shanghai, Guangzhou
	2002	49%	Beijing, Shanghai, Guangzhou, Chengdu, Chongqing, Dalian, Fuzhou, Hangzhou, Nanjing, Ningbo, Qingdao, Shenyang, Shenzhen, Xiamen, Xi'an, Taiyuan, Wuhan
	2003	50%	The whole country
Mobile data services	2002	25%	Beijing, Shanghai, Guangzhou
	2004	35%	Beijing, Shanghai, Guangzhou, Chengdu, Chongqing, Dalian, Fuzhou, Hangzhou, Nanjing, Ningbo, Qingdao, Shenyang, Shenzhen, Xiamen, Xi'an, Taiyuan, Wuhan
	2006	49%	The whole country
Fixed services	2004	25%	Beijing, Shanghai, Guangzhou
	2006	35%	Beijing, Shanghai, Guangzhou, Chengdu, Chongqing, Dalian, Fuzhou, Hangzhou, Nanjing, Ningbo, Qingdao, Shenyang, Shenzhen, Xiamen, Xi'an, Taiyuan, Wuhan
	2007	49%	The whole country

To confront these challenges, ICT governmental organs and the ICT circle have made some adjustments in the areas of laws and regulations, organization structures and regulatory roles.

During recent years, obvious progress has been made in telecom legislation and the regulatory system. In 2000, the State Council promulgated the Telecommunications Regulation of the People's Republic of China, which is the major regulation for defining juristic relationships among parties with different interests in the telecom sector. Another instrument of equal importance is the Radio Administrative Regulation jointly published by the State Council and the Central Military Committee in 1993. In the past several years, competent authorities, such as the Ministry of Posts and Telecommunications and the Ministry of the Information Industry successively enacted many rules and regulations, involving many aspects such as: Internet connections, authentication of equipments for accessing networks and Internet access service. At present, we hope that the Telecommunication Act will, after multiple rounds of negotiation, be adopted as soon as possible, in order to provide a more stable legal framework for the Chinese telecom industry, one which is beneficial to investment, commercial development and technical advances.

Currently, the Ministry of the Information Industry acts as a decision developer as well as a regulator, mainly responsible for developing and enforcing development and regulatory policies relating to information and communications policies (ICT), covering the electronic industry and the communication service sector. Generally speaking, the objective of Chinese telecom policies and regulatory system is to promote the ICT industry in China and provide a fair competitive environment for all companies entering the Chinese market, based on the principle of market orientation and compliance with the WTO Agreement. As a regulatory organ, the Ministry of the Information Industry is independent from any telecom operators, and administers the information sector according to principles of fairness, transparency, independence, specialty, consistency and accountability. In terms of organizational construction and competence development, telecom administrative bureaus are set up within the Ministry of the Information Industry, and there is a telecom bureau in each province that is directly accountable to the Ministry. This kind of vertical incorporated organization structure is quite unique among the sector regulatory systems of China.

ICT POLICIES ENCOURAGE COMPETITION IN THE TELECOM SECTOR

Considering current competitive situation and opportunities brought about by technical advances, the telecom circle and policy researchers have reached a consensus that more competition should be introduced into the Chinese telecom sector. Quite especially since China's accession to WTO, the country should open telecom services to enterprises under different ownerships as soon as possible.

Figure 2: Market Shares of the Turnover of Major Telecom Operators in China in 2002

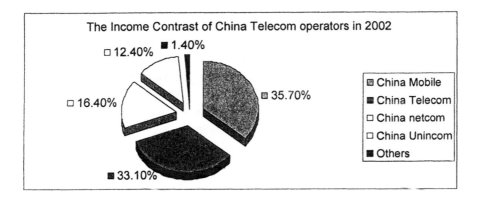

As a public utility, the telecom sector has a certain natural monopoly. As a result, telecom service sectors in a majority of countries of the world were owned and operated by the government for most of the last century, and China was no exception. In making the transition from planned economy to market economy in China, most sectors have undergone drastic market-oriented reforms since the beginning of the 1980's, reforms which have been quite effective and fruitful. However, due to its natural monopoly and its strategic importance in the economy, market-oriented reforms in the telecom sector fell behind other sectors. The establishment of China Unicom ended the monopoly status of the telecom department subsidiary to the Ministry of Posts and Telecommunications. Compared with European countries such as Germany and France, such reform in the telecom sector was relatively early. Introduction of competition to the telecom sector has exerted an obvious influence on the attraction of investment, technical innovation, reduction of operational costs and the improvement of service quality, as well as has greatly boosting the development of the Chinese telecom sector, in particular mobile communications.

Confronted with new challenges after China's accession to WTO, the Chinese government conducted in-depth reforms in telecom systems in 1998, including the separate operation of posts and telecom, separation of telecom enterprises from government organs, company-oriented reorganization of enterprises and the establishment of the Ministry of the Information Industry, etc.

In 1998, the former Ministry of Posts and Telecommunications completed the separation of postal operations from telecom operations, as well as the separation of telecom enterprises from governmental organs. China Telecom, China Unicom and other telecom enterprises became real commercial entities via company-oriented reorganization. China successfully introduced competition into the telecom sector in a period shorter than ten years. Up to now, China has six basic telecom operators namely: China Telecom, China Netcom, China Mobile, China Unicom, China Railcom and China Satellite Communications, and has over 4400 companies offering telecom value-added services and non-basic telecom services. China Unicom operates two mobile communication networks: a GSM network with 70 million users and a CDMA (Code-Division Multiple Access) with 15 million users (December 2003). China Mobile is now the mobile communication operator with the most users in the world, mainly providing vocal and data mobile communication services. Its users currently exceed 140 million. China Telecom and China Netcom are two major providers of fixed telephone services. Meanwhile China Railcom and China Satellite Communications have in recent years marked their fastest development.

IMPACT OF ICT ON THE NATIONAL ECONOMY

In China, great things have been achieved in informatization construction in recent years. ICT has an increasingly significant influence on the national economy and social life as the share and importance in the national economy of industries involving ICT has gradually advanced year by year. Added value in IT represented 4.66% of GDP in 1998, while in 1993 the ratio was 2.45%. IT industry growth contributed 11.00% to the expansion of GDP in 1998, while in 1993 its contribution was 4.22%. In 1999, the contribution ratio of IT output value to GDP exceeded 10%, while within the 7.1% of growth, the IT industry contributed approximately 1%. The export value of IT products accounted for 20% of total export value of China. The IT industry has maintained an average growth rate of 32% each year in the last 10 years, nearly 18% higher than the average growth rate of all industries combined in the same period.

The Chinese communication sector has kept up such high-speed consecutive annual expansion throughout more than a decade, and already as far back as 1984 its growth had begun to pull ahead of that of the national economy. From 1989 till 2001, the business income in the communication sector grew 36% each year on average, with the highest growth exceeding 50%.

The percentage of the telecom service sector in all other service sectors increased by 2.9%, from 3.8% in 1995 to 6.7% in 2000. Such rapid development has promoted the manufacture of communication equipment. Many big multinational communication equipment suppliers entered the Chinese market and set up their own equipment manufacturing bases in China. Yet some domestic equipment suppliers such as Huawei, ZTE and CATT have emerged in this severely competitive environment. Based on a better understanding of domestic telecom markets, these elite domestic companies are thriving, both in competition and cooperation with multinational firms, representing a greater and greater market share and expanding abroad. With regard to the contribution of ICT to socio-economic development, the electronics industry (i.e. ICT and hardware, including communication equipment) contributed 4.9% to manufacturing sector output in 1995, while in 2001 the ratio reached 8.02%, representing an increase of 3.12%.

Under the 10th national five-year plan, our industry objective is: the gross output value in the electronic industry is to reach RMB2500 billion Yuan, with an average annual growth rate of 20%; sales revenue is to reach RMB 1500 billion Yuan, an increase of 20%; and the productivity of all those working in the IT industry is to reach RMB180,000 Yuan per capita per annum (calculated on the basis of added value).

ICT AND PEOPLE'S LIFE IN CHINA

China's ICT policies highlight the principle "putting people first and serving the people". As described by the International Telecommunications Union (ITU), the information-based society is comprised of two parts: the social economy and the industries (see Figure 3).

Figure 3: Correlations among various parts of information-based society (ref.7)

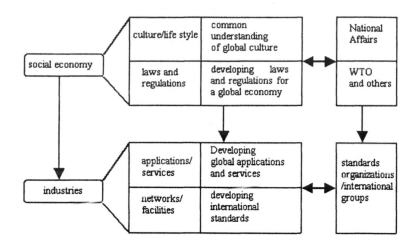

"Social economy" includes: establishing new life styles (such as online shopping, virtual reality, etc.), creating new cultural and artistic patterns (such as multimedia books, distance music listening, etc.), developing laws, regulations and rules (such as medical care law for telemedicine) and so on. "Industries" involves: the creation of new applications and services (such as eCommerce and video services), setting up of information networks (such as telecom networks, cable TV networks and satellite networks) and the manufacture of equipment (such as terminals, transmission systems and servers). In this way the information-based society will be one in which people are put first and cultures and the environment are better protected. In such a society, the keywords will be: humanity, environment and information – as each and every person becomes able to create, acquire, use and share information and knowledge, and individuals, communities and the wider community in every country will be in a position to exercise their potential to the fullest, to boost sustainable development and the improvement of life quality.

Realization and development of the information-based society is inseparable from the ICT and IT industry. In the 21st century, humans will create new modes of working, management, trade, finance, communications, education, medical care, etc., as well as new modes of consumption and lifestyle. Thus ICT will inevitably take a lead in the process of sustainable development.

According to the Statistical Survey on Internet Development in China, published by China Internet Network Information Center ("CNNIC") in January 2004, the number of internet users, computer hosts, domain names registered under ".cn" and websites in China reached 79.5 million, 30.89 million, 340,000 and 595,500 respectively, while total bandwidth of leased international connections reached 27,216M. More and more "netizens" log onto the Internet at home, the percentage of these netizens represented 66.1% of all netizens in China; dial-up is still the dominating method for logon, but broadband users have grown rapidly, reaching 17.40 million. Meanwhile, 32.2% of netizens log on for leisure and fun.

"Logon by households" is an important project in the process of community informatization. The overall objective of "logon by households" is: in 2004, community information chain stores are to cover all cities at or above prefecture level in the country; and 20% of communities in China's major cities are expected to become eCommunities; by 2005, the number of Internet users around the country is supposed to reach 150 million, over 30% of households will have access to the Internet through various terminals, and 80% of information flows in the area of urban family and individual life, as well as community services, are expected to be achieved through networks.

eCommunity construction is speeding up in large and medium-sized cities in China. Education and training, culture and entertainment activities, medical consulting, housekeeping services, governmental services and logistics and commercial services based on eCommunity networks are becoming available; more and more websites are providing agricultural information, professional, technical and distance education. ICT is influencing all aspects of people's life not only in major cities, but also in rural areas of China.

With regard to the businesses of China Telecom, in 1990 less than 1% families in China owned fixed-line telephones. After over a decade years' development, in 2002 over 13% families owned fixed-lined telephones. China now owns the biggest fixed-line communication network and mobile phone network in the world. By the end of December 2003, the number of fixed telephone and mobile phone users hit 264 million and 269 million respectively.

At the same time, IT applications represented by Golden Taxation, Golden Customs and Golden Card provided a broad range of IT applications; IT applications in companies, such as CAD and CIMS technologies have made obvious progress; and eGovernment, eCommerce, distance education and telemedicine are also undergoing further development.

In a word, ICT has penetrated into all fields of society and is affecting all aspects of people's lives and habits. ICT will bring people into an information-based era, and help them to accommodate to and enjoy this era. A typical example was shown in the way the sudden attack of SARS highlighted the value of ICT and communication service providers. Indeed, as SARS prevented people from normal social and interpersonal relations, they chose to keep in touch more by phone and short message services, and began to get used to acquiring information and conducting online education and commercial activities through Internet, some even worked at home through the Internet, becoming real members of the SOHO group.

In conclusion, we have seen, and will continue to see, the alteration and improvement of people's lives through the development of ICT, under the guidance of China's ICT policies. And ICT will certainly have an increasingly significant influence on both economic and social development in China.

REFERENCES

1. *Opening Address by President Jiang Zemin on the 16ᵗʰ World Computer Congress,* August 21, 2000
2. *Report of the 16ᵗʰ Communist Party Congress of China,* by President Jiang Zemin
3. *Current Status of Chinese Telecom Industry,* by Lin Jintong from Beijing Posts and Telecommunications University
4. *Calling for and Taking Actual Measures to Narrow "Digital Gap",* by Ma Songde from the Ministry of Sciences and Technologies of China
5. *2003 Statistical Survey on the Internet Development of China,* CNNIC
6. *Information Technologies and Sustainable Development,* by Lei Zhenzhou from Scientific and Technological Information Institute under the Ministry of the Information Industry
7. *Information Communication Technology and the Consistent Development,* by Lei Zhenzhou, from China communication net (www.cl14.net), 14ᵗʰ May 2004.

ICT Policies of the European Union: From an Information Society to *eEurope*. Trends and visions

Jacques BERLEUR
IFIP-TC9 Chair, IFIP-SIG9.2.2 Chair
University of Namur (Belgium)
jberleur@info.fundp.ac.be
and Jean-Marc GALAND
University of Liège, Belgium
jean-marc.galand@ckfin.minfin.be, jmgaland@ulg.ac.be

Keywords: Information Society, policy, eEurope, action plan, benchmark, European
Commission, social issues, People first, IS for all, assessment

TOWARDS AN INFORMATION SOCIETY?

An official presentation of the European history "Towards an Information Society" can be found on the ISPO archives website (Information Society Project Office – 'Project' becoming 'Promoting' in 1998).[1] It covers the period 1993-2000. This 'history' is just a sequence of documents, plans, events, and programmes, drawn from different initiatives within the European Commission, and which do not necessarily follow the same objectives and goals. The logic needs to be restored! The first part of this history has to be complemented by what is now under the responsibility of the European Commission General Directorate 'Information Society'.[2]

We can distinguish two periods in which we note a clear discontinuity, even in the names of the programmes, although no one would believe that the second is a complete re-build of the first! Two periods that may be associated with two names: the first with the former Commissioner Martin Bangemann[3] and the second with the former President of the Commission, Romano Prodi.[4] When referring to 'policy', the official presentation opens with the second period, although some documents of the first are still mentioned. In other words, for people acquainted with the history, the ISPO site is today no longer considered as anything other than archives.

Is it a "European way for the Information Society"? That was, at least, the conviction of the Information Society Forum in its 1999 Report.[5] We shall assess the answers.

FIRST PERIOD: 1994-1999

The first period of European policies is surely rooted in the decision of the European Council (Corfu, June 1994), which adopted the Bangemann report. But the main events and documents that accompany it are as famous too: the July 1994 *Europe's way to the information society, An Action Plan*. The report to the July 1996 Dublin Council meeting, *Information Society: From Corfu to Dublin - The new emerging priorities* that resulted, in November 1996, in a new *Rolling Action Plan*.[6] Four other major initiatives shaped the landscape of the emerging European Information Society: the February 1995 Brussels G7 Conference on the Information Society, the Report *Building the European Information Society for Us All, First Reflections of the High Level Group of Experts* (HLEG) (Interim Report in January 1996, Final Report in April 1997), the 3 annual Reports (1996, 1997 and 1999) of the Information Society Forum, and also the Green Paper *Living and Working in the Information Society: People First*. Finally, other policies also emerged to support the development of the European Information Society, namely the Research Programmes of the Commission (Framework Programmes) where large funds were allocated to the field of information and communication technologies – it is still the case in the current (sixth) Programme.

The Bangemann Report

There is no doubt that the Report *Europe and the Global Information Society, Recommendations to the European Council*, known as the Bangemann Report (1994) is one of the major signposts in the landscape of the European Information Society.[7] But we should remember that this report was already requested by a so called 'high-level group of experts' (it would be better to say a high-level of industrialists among whom the future President Romano Prodi) as a follow-up to the 1993 President Jacques Delors' White Paper on *Growth, Competitiveness and Employment: The Challenges and Courses for Entering the XXIst century*.[8]

This Report is also clearly an answer to the U.S.A. *National Information Infrastructure: Agenda for Action* of President Bill Clinton and Vice-President Al Gore whose announcement was made in September 1993.[9]

It is worth noting that where the USA speak of 'infrastructure', the Europeans seem to prefer a more global approach: *A global Information Society*. Six chapters: 1. The information society - new ways of living and working together, 2. A market-driven revolution, 3. Completing the agenda, 4. The building blocks of the information society, 5. Financing the information society a task for the private sector, and 6. Follow-up. Some of the pervasive ideas that could not be missed: A challenge for the deciders. All together for employment! A social challenge: improve the quality of life, improve the efficiency of our social and economic organisation. Urgent? A market-driven revolution. New markets? But, more seriously, it is important to have a look at Section 22, 'Blazing the Trail - Ten Applications to Launch the Information Society.' Those applications and their objectives should be compared later to those of the eEurope initiative:

-   Teleworking - More jobs, new jobs, for a mobile society;
-   Distance Learning – Life-long learning for a changing society;
-   A Network For Universities and Research Centres - Networking Europe's brain power;
-   Telematic Services for SMEs – Re-launching a main engine for growth and employment in Europe;
-   Road Traffic Management - Electronic roads for better quality of life;
-   Air Traffic Control - An electronic airway for Europe;
-   Healthcare Networks - Less costly and more effective healthcare systems for Europe's citizens;
-   Electronic Tendering - More effective administration at lower cost;
-   Trans-European Public Administration Network - Better government, cheaper government;
-   City Information Highways - Bringing the information society into the home.

In an IFIP-WG9.2 Working Conference (Corfu, 1997), where we intended to discuss the 'Culture and Democracy revisited in the Global Information Society,' we had made a rough statistic of the interests of the Bangemann report and associated documents about such themes, in terms of wording. The result: Democracy is not mentioned; Culture is present 7 times, but about the cultural industries; language, linguistics are not worth noting, whilst 'market' is present 110 times. It has even a chapter about it: Chapter 2 is 'A market-driven revolution'![10]

Later our Technology Assessment research team (CITA) went further in this first perception. We elucidated some indicators on the basis of the occurrence of associated keywords. For instance we derived the indicator 'Public sphere' from the occurrences of words such as public, administration, government, citizen, city, local, etc. The result is confirming our first perception, as stated in Table 1.[11]

Indicators	Ranking
Economic Values	21.7
Information and Communication Technologies	17.3
Information/Knowledge Society	14.2
Public Sphere	10.8
Actors	10.7
Uses	9.5
Methodology	7.1
User's representation	6.0
Social Values	5.3
European Values	2.5

Table 1: Indicators in the Bangemann Report

Observing the ranking of these "European Values", we may have some doubts about a specific 'European way for the Information Society'!

From an Action Plan to a Rolling Action Plan

The 1994 Action plan covered 4 areas: the regulatory and legal framework (54 actions); the Networks, Basic Services, Applications and Content (27); the Social, Societal and Cultural Aspects (5); and some Promotion Activities (11).[12]

The main area was that of the regulatory and legal framework, but in domains where the economic aspects were prevalent: a competitive environment; standardisation, interconnection and interoperability; tariffs, intellectual property rights; electronic protection, legal protection and security; media ownership; privacy. Whereas the actions related to the social, societal and cultural aspects included orientations towards the flexible firm, proposals for the language industries, and agreements of regional cooperation for promoting a common information society approach, that is to say, with very loose link to real social, societal and cultural aspects.

The 1996 Rolling Action Plan tried to balance the trend, and to build the church in the middle of the village, or as underlined by many documents of the time "People at the Centre".[13] It covered four areas: Improving the Business Environment, Investing in the Future, People at the Centre, and

Meeting the Global Challenge. Area 1 included, in July 1997, 45 actions; area 2, 13; area 3, 26, and area 4, 16. The weight is still on the same side, but it seemed that some new balance was being sought. Unfortunately, it was purely a game of shifting some action from one category to another. Many of the actions of the area 'regulatory and legal framework' of the Action Plan had been shifted, in the Rolling Action Plan, to the area 'People at the Centre'. It would have been more honest to consider that they might have been better suited to the area 'Improving the Business Environment'!

Other major initiatives

G7 Conference on the Information Society – Information Society and Development (ISAD) Conference

Following the G7 Naples Summit in July 1994, Ministers from the G7 countries and Members of the European Commission met in Brussels on 25 and 26 February 1995 in the G7 Ministerial Conference on the Information Society.[14] In their conclusions, eight core principles were endorsed for promoting new computer, telecommunications and media networks. The G7 identified 11 international pilot projects whose aim was to demonstrate the potential of the Information Society and stimulate its development.[15]

The Brussels conference emphasised the need for all countries, including developing nations, to be integrated. President of the Republic of South Africa, Nelson Mandela, and Executive Deputy President, Thabo Mbeki, convened the "Information Society and Development conference (ISAD)" in Midrand, South Africa, on 13-15 May 1996.

Sentences of the keynote address of Executive President Thabo Mbeki to the G-7 Conference remain in all our memories: "There are more telephone lines in Manhattan than in all of sub-Saharan Africa", and "half of humanity has never made a telephone call."

Social Issues? The High Level of Experts and the Information Society Forum

Mentioning the Bangemann report and the efforts directed by the techno-economic paradigm without paying attention to other directions with more specific social accents cannot be a well-balanced presentation of the European way towards the Information Society. Among these other directions, we should mention first the so-called *High Level Group of Experts* (HLEG) established by Padraig Flynn, Commissioner for Employment and Social Affairs – i.e. another Directorate General (DG5) than the DG in charge of the 'Information Society' programme. We should also mention the *Information Society Forum*.

The Executive Summary of the HLEG "Interim Report" mentioned: "Social policy therefore merits equal if not more weight than economic policy in formulating our approach to the Information Society (IS). We believe that the Commission has paid insufficient attention to these issues so far, and in the following sections we elaborate these arguments in more detail." (...) "The Group welcomes the Commission's initiative to provide a major impulse into the broader policy debate surrounding the emerging IS, by setting up the HLEG. So far, the IS policy debate has been dominated by technological issues and, more recently, the appropriate regulatory economic environment, neglecting by and large some of the broader issues implicit in the 'society' notion."[16]

A set of 12 recommendations structures the final report, touching all the questions which are still prominent in the building up of the Information Society: education, regulation, efficiency of public services, development of flexible working arrangements, managing time, reprioritising 'full' employment, including everyone, European diversity, democracy.

Another initiative must be mentioned: the *Information Society Forum*. Its main purpose was to "provide the opportunity for representatives from a variety of different groups, including the social partners, to contribute to open debate and reflection on the challenges of the Information Society, including the social and societal aspects, as well as to raise the level of public awareness. The Forum will work on the framework for implementing the Information Society. The Forum should also indicate to the Commission the priority projects that need to be implemented...".[17] The Information Society Forum has published 3 reports (1996, 1997, 1999).[18] The recommendations encompass Internet for all, economic, framework for the information society, global governance, consumers and citizen rights, cultural sustainability, the role of the public sector, environmental sustainability. "The ISF proposes that there is *a distinctive European Way* which has much to offer the world in meeting the challenges of the global information society. This is rooted in the search for *dynamic equilibrium between different and sometimes competing concerns and goals*. Its principles could be summarised as liberty, equality, fraternity, solidarity, and sustainability." (We underline)

The idea of a 'European way' may be found again in the last part of the Green Paper 'Living and Working in the Information Society: People First' (July 1996).[19] "The Member States have developed social models with many common features including strong social rights and independent social partners, able to take responsibility for working conditions and for fair distribution." (...) "The European social model is built both on competition between enterprises and solidarity between citizens and Member States. The European Information Society must draw strongly from this economic, social and cultural strength, linking technological, economic and social aspects together in the creation of new opportunities for all its citizens."

Supporting Research Programmes and Promotion Activities

Information and Communication Technologies (ICT) have always received the lion's share of funding in the Research Programmes initiated by the European Commission, namely in the Framework Programmes (FP). Everybody calls to mind ESPRIT (European Strategic Programme for Research and Development in Information Technologies) or RACE (Research and Development in Advanced Communications Technologies for Europe). ICT Research Programmes counted for 42% of the budget in the 2nd FP (1987-91, 5,400 millions ECU), 39% in the 3rd FP (1990-94, 5,700 millions ECU), 39% in the 4th FP (1994-98, 12,300 millions ECU). The programme 'User friendly Information Society' (IST) has been funded up to 3,600 millions Euros during the 5th FP (1998-2002), out of a total budget of 13,700 millions Euros. It first covered 4 key actions: systems and services for the citizen, new methods of work and electronic commerce, multimedia content and tools, essential technologies and infrastructures. After this came research and technological development activities of a generic nature: future and emerging technologies; and finally the support for research infrastructures: research networking. Information Society Technologies (IST) priority of the 6thFP is funded at a level of 3,984 millions Euros out of a total of 17,883 millions Euros. But there are also other IST related activities that can be funded by other budgetary lines.

On the side of the supporting promotion activities, in November 1998, ISPO, the Information Society Project Office, became the Information Society Promotion Office.

Finally, among the promotion activities, let us mention that, on 30 March 1998, the multi-annual Community programme (1998-2002) to stimulate the establishment of the Information Society in Europe was adopted. The programme Promoting the Information Society (PROMISE) was launched.[20] The programme aimed at: increasing public awareness and understanding of the potential impact of the Information Society; optimising the socio-economic benefits of the Information Society in Europe; and enhancing Europe's role and visibility within the global dimension of the Information Society. We shall see later that this programme is still waiting for a "successor" in the new European policies.

SECOND PERIOD: FROM 1999 AND BEYOND, *eEurope*

eEurope, An Information Society for All

eEurope was initiated in 1999 by the new DG, *Information Society*, directed by the Finnish social-democrat commissioner Erkki Liikanen, under the then Commission presidency of Romano Prodi. Rather than a document derived from long-lasting stakeholders viewpoint confrontation, eEurope initiative presentation was written by three executives attached to the new DG. The arrival of a new commission team naturally raises the opportunity and the 'necessity' for the launching of such ambitious global policy documents, belonging to the category of visions more than to that of programmatic policies.[21] eEurope is a remainder of the Bangemann Report and of all the other documents that preceded it. Furthermore, at a more basic level, those few years around the turn of the century were also years of significant Internet growth among the public at large. Thus, in order to avoid uncontrolled, anarchical or undesired development, public authorities felt it necessary to transform their vision of the Information Society, becoming increasingly conscious of the fact that, regardless of the importance you may give to the term, the Information Society was becoming reality and no longer just a dream for the future.

eEurope was adopted at the European Council of Lisbon in March 2000. The declared purpose was to take a unique opportunity to shape the Information Society, with respect to *specific* European values, principles and strengths.[22] The overall and declared objectives of the eEurope initiative were:
- to bring every individual, household, school, enterprise and administration into the digital age, put prosaically, online;
- to create a digitally literate Europe sustained by an entrepreneurial culture ready to finance and develop new ideas;
- to ensure that the programme as a whole is socially inclusive, builds consumer trust and strengthens social cohesion.[23]

The initial eEurope document stated ten priorities for the implementation of this ambitious project that are worth being compared to the objectives of the ten applications of the Bangemann Report, which we mentioned earlier: bring European youth into the digital age; ensure cheaper Internet access; accelerate electronic commerce; provide researchers and students with high-speed Internet access; ensure secure electronic access through the use of smart cards; make risk capital readily available for high-tech SMEs; increase the eParticipation of disabled people; maximise the use of digital technologies for healthcare; develop intelligent transport; and boost on-line government.

The programme presented targets associated with deadlines ranging from March 2000 until the end of 2003. So, despite its characteristic of being a visionary plan more than a very pragmatic policy, eEurope endeavoured to define and consolidate a procedure of benchmarking.

eEurope 2002, An Information Society for All, Action Plan

As was the case for the Bangemann report, an Action Plan was produced immediately after the release of the original eEurope. The necessity for writing and adopting such a plan had been stressed during the first hasty evaluations, and officially requested by the Lisbon summit. Prepared in cooperation between the Council and the Commission and adopted during the European summit of Feira in June 2000, it was called *An information society for all*. The declared aim of this Action Plan was to define measures to achieve the goals that were set in Lisbon.

Some of the initial objectives present in the original eEurope document were modified, some withdrawn, and some added: the concept of 'working in the knowledge-based economy', as well as the idea of 'European digital content for global networks'. All objectives underwent a cosmetic change and were classified under more generic titles and presented in an "*e-manner*": eHealth, eLearning, eWorking, eInclusion, etc. All the major actors were identified for each action line and the final term was reduced to end 2002.

More importantly, eEurope 2002 was a more precise document than the initial version of eEurope. The sought-after logic was to evoke the policy as a dialogue between challenges posed and answers carried out. Three working methods were implemented to achieve the goals: the building of an appropriate legislative framework, the support to selected new services and infrastructures, a coordination and a comparative benchmarking of State performances (with a dedicated Council which should be held each spring).

eEurope 2002 reinforced the will present in eEurope of a strong benchmarking procedure. Commission and Council together defined a list of indicators.[24] These were designed for both calibrating changes and measuring the impact of the application of eEurope.

The Evaluation of the *eEurope 2002 Initiative*

In December 2000, the European Council in Nice adopted an update of *eEurope 2002*. While noting the progresses made in different fields of the eEurope policy, the document formalised the concept of benchmarking and proposed structural indicators in order to make performance comparison possible between Member States, and to underline best practices. At the occasion of the Nice Council, it was asked that a first assessment of the impact and priorities of this programme should be presented at the spring 2001 Stockholm European Council.

During the Stockholm summit, the report *eEurope 2002: Impacts and Priorities* was presented. This summit also gave the opportunity to ask for eEurope to be raised to a higher priority level within the political agenda. But why this sudden preaching, since eEurope had already been ennobled one year before as the 'knowledge-based economy credo'? The truth is that at the March 2001 Council meeting in Stockholm, eEurope was already no longer "flavour of the month", according to Frank Mather, a member of the DG Information Society and one of the three authors of the eEurope document.[25] In a few months, priorities had radically changed. Since the breakdown of the so-called new economy, the assertion was severely countered that it might one day provide a solution to almost every economic and social woe in Europe. Whereas this assertion had a central role in the eEurope reasoning, did this contribute to a renewed and more mature eEurope policy? We will analyse this question later. As one could have expected, the Stockholm evaluation gave a high satisfaction note to the completion of the first main tasks assigned to eEurope.

The next intermediary evaluation was undertaken in February 2002[26] and the final evaluation of the eEurope 2002 process took place in February 2003, while the new eEurope process (*eEurope 2005*) was launched in June 2002 in Sevilla.

Which are the most significant points in this evaluation? Among the 11 action areas and the 64 targets to be achieved before the end of 2002, the Commission points out a rapid growth of Internet connectivity, concerning "more than 90% of schools and businesses [...] and more than the half of Europeans".[27] This fact would be linked to the decrease in access prices (considered as another satisfactory point), the establishment of the widest and fastest research backbone in the world (called GEANT) and the availability of basic eGovernment services in each Member State. Another satisfactory element, according to the Commission, lies in the implementation of a complete legislative regulatory framework for electronic communications and commerce – even if we personally would not give the main credit of this performance to eEurope.[28] We shall return to this subject in the conclusion.

"The goal of a competitive knowledge-based economy is still some distance away, but eEurope has laid solid foundations."[29] The main declared dissatisfaction in the assessment of the eEurope 2002 action plan comes from the remaining differences in connection rates between social groups (for instance, the gap between men and women remained proportionally constant) and Member States, from a stagnation of digital literacy among work forces or from a disappointing use rate of ICT and eBusiness by European SMEs.

eEurope 2005 Action Plan – An Information Society for All

The new action plan, adopted at the Sevilla Summit in June 2002, is focused on five main issues:
- Modern and on-line public services (eGovernment, eLearning, eHealth) to strengthen their productivity and accessibility;
- The promotion of a dynamic environment for eBusiness;
- A secured information infrastructure (eSecurity);
- Substantial availability of broadband access with competitive prices;
- Comparative benchmarking and the diffusion of best practices.[30]

This new action plan, covering the period 2003-2005, focuses on a more limited number of actions and targets. These remain clearly located in the Lisbon strategy of making Europe the most competitive and dynamic knowledge-based economy by 2010. The credo is clear: there is a great but uncultivated potential lying in the Information Society, to improve competitiveness and quality of life. And broadband as well as multi-platform access is considered as the key factor to enlarge this potential. The task to be assigned to eEurope is to stimulate service and infrastructure creation and development, to create a favourable environment for private investment, capable of creating and sustaining a reciprocal positive feedback effect.[31]

So, the purpose is to stimulate services (eGovernment, eLearning, eHealth, eBusiness) as well as the necessary infrastructure for them (available and affordable broadband access, security). Four intervention tools are privileged to achieve this general goal: general policy measures of legislative nature, measures aimed at facilitating good practices exchanges, comparative benchmarking and an overall coordination of existing policies (led by a steering group).

As far as services are concerned, the accent given is on the production of (relevant) content in order to get people interested. In this regard, *eEurope 2005* is going to pursue the eContent programme initiated with *eEurope 2002*. Its purpose is to support "the increased availability, use and distribution of European digital content" and to improve "access for all to high-quality digital content on the global networks, in a multiplicity of languages", including – and above all – governmental content, but excluding massive digitisation of already existing content.[32] The budget to be requested for years 2003 and 2004 from the European Parliament is envisaged as 51.5 million Euros.

What about social inclusion issues? Whereas eEurope 2002 underscored the problem of extending Internet connectivity across Europe, this connectivity seems to be considered as granted, in the reasoning of eEurope 2005. In the Action Lines, very little is currently said about support or measures favouring social inclusion! Even the fundamental concern of digital literacy is hardly mentioned, no more than either Public Internet Access Points (PIAPs) or public websites accessibility. So, although Erkki Liikanen stated as a principle petition that every eEurope 2005 action had to be *"integrative* in order to be efficient" and that "every citizen no matter his personal or geographical situation should benefit from opportunities offered by the knowledge-based society", our concern is that there is a clear mismatch between declared goals and chosen action tools.[33] The *Information Society for All* concept is viewed almost entirely through support to broadband and multi-platform access - the latter justified by the assertion that not everyone will be able to buy and use a PC, though eEurope 2005 mid-term revision, which occurred in 2004, seems to pay more attention to this inclusion aspect, according to the conclusions of various ad hoc consultations.

The evaluation paper of the eEurope 2002 initiative itself declared that "increasing effective use of the Internet is the focus of the next step, eEurope 2005": more eCommerce, more *effective* use in the classroom, more use by governments, etc.[34] This argumentation about *effective* use is quite curious and disturbing.[35] Can we imagine countries pushing the equipment of households in television sets and then asking people to *really* use them? We must realise, that since eEurope deliberately chose to be a market-push initiative, this reasoning is anything but logical: if you want the industry to develop and promote new uses, whatever the final goal may be (employment, competitiveness, social inclusion, or all three), you merely have to pay to help the content pipes fill up.

This is currently an axial argumentation in eEurope 2005: a more effective use of computers requires the improvement of education and skills in order to improve productivity and competitiveness in the EU economy as a whole. The ultimate goal of the eEurope policy clearly remains mostly mechanical and economic, but in no way directly political: it is to improve the competitiveness of Europe.[36]

eEurope 2005 Updates

As we have elucidated here, there was a lack, in terms of cohesion, of an integrated IS European policy, as well as in terms of financial pan-European support for the eEurope Action Plan. A 2003-2005 programme called

MODINIS has been launched, which is intended to provide "financial support for the implementation of the eEurope 2005 Action Plan."[37]

The MODINIS program also appears as an attempt to complete the benchmarking procedure with more qualitative indicators; such an observation was also made by the Commission (and endorsed by the Council in February 2004), in recognition of a relative weakness in the benchmarking procedure in the eEurope mid-term evaluation, at least with regard to a weak linkage between indicators and the objective completion evidence of the eEurope 2005 measures.

However, we regret the absence of a general questioning of the initial eEurope 2005 objectives. Open consultations that were undertaken should have observed the lack of such a will. Thus the 'Update' of the Action Plan is officially limited to a 'Readjustment'. Yet writing the contrary would have sounded like a disavowal. It is also true that this Update remains an update, being only "a series of preparatory steps towards the establishment of a new policy framework for ICT policy in Europe."[38]

The Update contains a formal switch in the rhetoric: it proposes the adoption of a demand-based approach, in addition to stating the will to measure the impact of the Information Society in terms of efficiency gains as well as of quality of work ... and life (including citizenship and governance aspects).

Let us hope that their concept of demand and eInclusion will not remain too instrumental in the future. For instance, there is talk in the mid-term evaluation of sustaining demand shortages in rural and isolated regions by measures appealing to EU structural funds, in a curiously Keynesian-like approach... Even if we agree that taking inclusion for a goal in itself makes no sense we may still wonder whether the Lisbon strategy is the most comprehensive, socially-oriented approach to dealing with such inclusion and demand...

The new policy fragments finally seem to reinforce the role and the presence of multi-level stakeholders in the definition of policies, in a so-called tradition within our *European way to the Information society...* The eEurope Advisory Group should work as such a gathering place, as well as the MODINIS programme, which should concentrate on spreading good practices and building stakeholders networks.

Overall Appreciation of the eEurope Assessment Process

Concerning the evaluation of eEurope 2005, we note that the European Telecom Council of December 2002 has adopted the renewed methodology and the list of benchmarking indicators proposed by the Commission. Compared to the eEurope 2002 indicators, the new ones seem to be more precise.[39] They also include direct comparison with countries outside the EU. As in the past, benchmarking and yearly assessments are intended to take place each spring.

As a general consideration, a significant flat note to this evaluation process comes from the fact that these indicators cannot properly be linked to eEurope actions.[40] They are general indicators, insufficiently well-designed to provide a satisfactory benchmarking of directed policies: the proper influence of measures deriving from the eEurope action plan can in no way be isolated from other major factors, such as economic issues of purchasing power or inflation. For instance, it seems difficult to link in any real way the percentage of individuals regularly using the Internet with any single item of the eEurope action plan. Using such generic, one-dimensional tools may lead to over-subjective interpretation.

Furthermore, the fact that the main controller is the controlled person itself (the Commission), rather than research institutes or independent public bodies, raises questions. The Council should engage in promoting and committing rigorous control, such as could be achieved by delegating the control power − including the definition of the benchmarking indicators − to an independent committee. A strengthened *eEurope steering group* − the group to which eEurope has given the charge of coordinating existing policies about Information Society − could be the basic core from which to derive a specific assessment organisation. This steering group is a concrete application of what political scientists have called 'new governance': it involves representatives from official instances and from so-called interested groups, or 'civil society' − even if it has no deep democratic legitimacy. This should be scrutinised carefully.

A very good score should nevertheless be given to the eEurope evaluation process, since exchange of good practices and comparative benchmarking are simply added to the action tools of eEurope among two far more classical tools (policy measures and overall coordination of existing policies). According to the action lines, selected good practices would be enhanced to broaden their applicability, transformed into guidelines, analysed and disseminated.[41] Well-functioning benchmarking would ease the making of this selection.

Information Society: How to Achieve a Well-Balanced Diffusion Across all Member States and Candidate Countries?

No specific action has been carried out by the successive versions of the eEurope action plans to ensure their harmonious development and expansion among the different Member States. Indeed, we have to acknowledge the existence of a centre and of a periphery concerning the extent of the deployment of the Information Society. Greece, and to a lesser extent Spain, Portugal, Italy and France, are far from presenting the same figures as the Netherlands, Sweden, Denmark, or Ireland.[42]

At least this problem is mentioned in the eEurope 2005 Action Plan: the Member States should support broadband deployment in less favoured areas. We will add no comment to this, except that broadband is really considered in eEurope 2005 as a universal panacea.

The European Regional Development Fund (ERDF) has developed a policy for boosting regional competitiveness – besides the structural funds that might be awarded to some *eProjects*. For the period 2000-2006, the ERDF decided to support measures relating to one or more of three specific domains: knowledge-based regional economies and technological innovation; eEuropeRegio: the information society and regional development; regional identity and sustainable development.[43] Some 400 million Euros are planned to be budgeted until 2006, mainly in co-financing regional projects and in respect of the subsidiarity principle. The emphasis, according to Commissioner Barnier, is clearly set on competitiveness and sustainable development. Peripheral regions – both geographically and in terms of their position on an eDevelopment level – should feel concerned.[44]

As regards new Member States to be integrated in 2004, an important measure was announced in Stockholm in June 2001: the launching of the eEurope + 2003 Action Plan.[45] It claimed to "mirror the priority objectives and targets of eEurope", but to "provide for actions which tackle the specific situation of the Candidate Countries". It seems evident that there is an important emphasis on liberalisation and implementation of the already acquired EU legislative framework. The accent is on the initial eEurope priorities: cheaper – some price regulation would be allowed – and faster Internet access, skills development and use stimulation. Since the funding that these countries could provide to such policies is not necessarily high, they are encouraged to seek funds in the PHARE programme and support from the international financial institutions. A progress report has been made public in June 2002 and it brought to light crucial disparities between joining Member States (and candidate countries such as Bulgaria, Romania and Turkey) in terms of inclusion in an Information Society – or whatever we want to call it. A fundamental problem is the cost of telephone calls and the reliability of traditional analogical connections, added to the fact that no other massive connectivity infrastructure has yet been developed or even planned. Among others, Lithuania, Latvia, Slovakia and Hungary also present dramatic figures on access costs as well as on digital literacy or computer penetration in schools. One may pretend that there are more important and urgent matters than this. But without taking a position on this assertion, this situation is nonetheless symbolic of the challenges that the enlargement process will have to cope with.[46]

The EU policy towards peripheral States may be considered as a subsidiarity action and as a legitimate worry about foresight and cohesion since important gaps – in various policy areas – may hinder the continuation of the enlargement process. But, while enthusiastic literature has given credit to the idea that the arrival of the Information Society should solve regional disparities, some rudimentary or elementary political economy principles and market realities demonstrate this is far from being the case: oligopoly structures, cultural, legal or economic barriers, play a negative role. Paschal Preston pleaded for less "economism" in EU strategy. Have such voices been heard?[47]

The Information Society: Policy Elements Besides eEurope

To whom are documents of so-called policies such as eEurope addressed? They challenge Member States to make ambitious commitments. They address invitations to the private sector to collaborate with the Commission and the Member States to share the same objectives. They indicate the initiatives the Commission will take or is willing to take. And, finally, they describe a kind of idealistic coordinated approach to European policies on the so-called Information Society.[48]

But no specific fund is directly allocated to eEurope! The vocation of successive eEurope plans has voluntarily remained general policy documents aimed at underlining certain European priorities. But they have to be put in concrete form by specific research programmes, initiated by a European DG other than the Information Society DG, the Member States or other decision levels, so that European-wide actions may derive from existing programmes or programmes to come.

Concerning eEurope 2005, new programmes will be proposed and fund-raised by the Commission. The Action Plan also counts on programmes that are likely to be continued and that the Commission will sustain for that purpose. This, for instance, is the case of eContent.[49] The eTEN programme initiated in 1997 is also mainly aimed at helping launch and develop eServices – mainly public services – for trans-European goals and on a socially inclusive basis.[50] This programme is derived from the Trans-European Network policy. The IDA programme, devoted to interoperability between different administrations, is another major programme which has been launched and which will continue to be used to put eEurope into concrete actions. The eEurope 2005 Action Plan also expects to keep the heritage of the 1998-2002 PROMISE programme which aimed, as we mentioned in the analysis of the first period, at promoting and stimulating the Information Society and its most promising applications among the public at large, at analysing relationships between all the Information Society tenants (societal, economic, legal), and at working on collaborations between different levels of governments and private partners.

The new (sixth) Framework Programme of the European Union (FP6) presents an ambitious Information Society Technologies (IST) priority and programme, which will be endowed with no less than 3,984 million Euros. This thematic priority will in a large part be dedicated to the implementation of European Information Society policies. Its ambition is even to go far beyond the eEurope 2005 priorities. This kind of programme is helpful to gain the lasting support of industrial sectors as it favours major partnerships included in broad and firm concepts and tools like integrated projects and so-called *networks of excellence*. The global objective of the IST thematic priority of the FP6 seems even more comprehensive and ambitious from the societal point of view than the eEurope Action Plan itself. Reality will show us how these good intentions translate into projects and practices, but the goal of strengthening social cohesion appears at the same level as growth and lasting competitiveness and not as an estimated and hoped for consequence of the invisible hand as it is the case in eEurope.[51]

And, importantly, besides these trans-European programmes, eEurope 2005 has to rely on its persuasive power and on a large-scale adoption of its beliefs and objectives to become reality. Most Member States have already adopted national plans that are more or less based on eEurope ideology, and this is also the case for all 10 new Member States.

Besides all these elements linked to eEurope, the Information Society landscape in Europe is shaped by a consequential legislative framework which has – or is going to have – a deep impact on European, national and sub-national policies and actions.[52] The purpose for developing an appropriate legislative framework is to ensure harmonious development and the expansion of policies – such as eEurope – throughout all Member States. In that respect, we have to acknowledge a particular efficiency of the European Union. It has succeeded in developing a complete regulatory framework that is far more integrative than the American one.[53] The latter – as with almost every American legislation, because they are by nature reactive – was underpinned by a confrontational logic and has therefore encountered far more resistance. So far, the European approach has demonstrated better and more long-lasting results than the American one in issues such as telecom liberalisation, privacy or intellectual property, although the European approach may be felt as formal. This is probably partly due to the nature of European legislation, which is more accompanying than binding or forbidding.[54] But this does not mean that critical voices are not heard, to which we shall return later. Let us note that the tragic 9/11 tragic terrorist attacks on the USA have led to still more non-constructive legal developments – such as, for instance, those included in the "Patriot Act".

A TENTATIVE ASSESSMENT: WHICH POLICIES AND FOR WHAT?

General Philosophy

As it emerges from our analyses, the Information Society has been conceived from the start with very little concern for cultural, social, and even governmental, political, and societal aspects. It has been mostly a market-push initiative or, as we have observed, mostly technological, mechanical, and economic. A group of CEOs of computer firms in the USA declared just before the 1995 Brussels meeting: "Let's put the private sector in the driver's seat."[55]

There is also a belief that the 'digital age' or the 'Information Society' is inevitable, inescapable: we have to lead people into it, and it is their interest for the future. The eManner is the law: eEducation, eLearning, eHealth, eWorking, eGovernance,... are the buzzwords which dominate current rhetoric!

At the same time, we have noted the weakness of social indicators in the benchmarking. Everything is thought of in terms of markets, and expansion of the economic model, even given the lukewarm economic improvement we have mentioned.

We could say the same of the regulatory framework.[56] Let us briefly evoke the logic of development of the European Regulatory Framework. It is said to build confidence, but in what and in favour of whom? The first legal intervention was to protect intellectual property and related rights, or as said by the Bangemann report itself, it was about protecting the agreed investments by those who tomorrow will become the providers of services and information. Protecting investors guarantees the presence of content on the Internet. The transactions still have to be developed, between professionals (B to B) or with consumers (B to C). To do this, the issue is one of reassuring partners about the identity of their opposites in a transaction, about the authentication of messages and the assurance of confidentiality. The legislation, as on the subject of electronic signatures, granting them the same value as written signatures and granting electronic documents the same value as written ones, answers this concern. Next step: the protection of investments and transactions, this equally demands the possibility of detecting illicit schemes on the Internet and of efficiently punishing their perpetrators. The Convention on Cybercrime adopted by the Members of the Council of Europe, as well as by Australia, Canada and the USA makes the Internet more reliable and confident![57]

The biggest differences between Europe and the USA could be on the questions of freedom of expression and on privacy protection.

First Reflections on the First Period: A Market Europe

The first five years of the so-called Information Society Programme have been decisive in shaping our European Society of today. Alvaro de Miranda and Morten Kristiansen analyse them in terms of tension between 'Social Europe' and 'Market Europe'.[58] We share their analysis not only for the first period, but also for what we have called the second one. The Bangemann report, from a pure lexicographic point of view, is an argument, as we have shown earlier. The analysis of eEurope programmes reinforces the result. But more than words are at issue. Europe has chosen to speak of 'the global information society' whereas others (USA and G7) were mentioning 'national or global information infrastructure'. The pace to 'Society' indicates a kind of technological, mechanical, and economic determinism that everybody has to face. If not, we are at risk, even promised, to a quick societal decline. The Bangemann report title itself makes explicit the link between the concept of 'Information Society' and 'global' (in French 'planétaire').[59]

As soon as the concept of information society is accredited, the next message, on the role of the private sector, affects the role of the social, societal, and public authorities. A. de Miranda et al. insist on the decisive character of the 1993 White Paper of Jacques Delors on growth, competitiveness, and employment, which in their view is the most influent paper on the Information Society, a paper which is the source of "all the documents to come".[60] This White Paper faces the dramatic rate of unemployment in Europe, but answers that unemployment is essentially due to social policies (regulation and protection of the labour market, welfare policies,...) that reduce European competitiveness. Therefore, liberalisation has become the major keyword.

Social policies will no longer be at the forefront of Information Society policies, and reports such as of the High Level Group of Experts (HLEG) or of the Information Society Forum (ISF) are initiatives "from outside" or "snatched" as the opportunity presented. Curiously, the HLEG and the ISF have disappeared from the scene of the new eEurope. As stressed by Bernard Cassen, eEurope was destined to mean 'Europe, Inc.': he was commenting a paper of the Financial Times *A corporate Plan for Europe, Inc.*[61] Although the HLEG and the ISF have insisted on the choices to be made, it seems that the Commission is now just offering 'to adapt ourselves' to that situation.

In official documents the words *People First*, or *People centred* are a tissue of misleading metaphors, which hide underlying interests behind particular policies. It is ideology that now justifies policies. The traditional *Social Europe* has largely opened the doors to the *Market Europe*, without keeping the usual balance between both. The current debate on the European constitutional treaty reinforces our perception.

About the Legitimacy of *eEurope*

Europe is now equipped with a general Information Society policy mainly through the succession of the eEurope Action Plans. We have to wonder where the legitimacy of such a policy lies, a policy that claims to cause a profound change in the life of all the European citizens.

Why does Europe's Information Society policy remind us of modern States from the 1930's with their Keynesian entrepreneurial attitudes? Have the markets failed to provide an autonomous and self-regulated solution to these concerns of societal adoption of ICTs (partly due to problems of scale)? And must the EU then be forced to act as the most appropriate political level to make things change? Has Europe become, like others, a political system where intervention in technological development is considered unnatural, because each political trend tries to position itself as an outside bidder to the others on such subjects? Is Europe a system captured by power groups or class interests?[62]

The EU policy is a logical consequence and continuity of traditional European research, competition and industrial policy initiatives. We consider that it is also an heir of what has become a real European way of doing politics: strong law building, prospective policy with hard agenda setting and calendars, binding political commitment.

Is there any democratic control? No more than in other aspects of European policies. In the first months of eEurope, the DG "InfSo" let visitors to its website review eEurope and give their comments. Unfortunately, it was a clumsy attempt to involve citizens – or at best users or concerned people. Beyond the fact that this looked more like a way to give oneself a good conscience than a democratic measure, no procedure had really been foreseen to evaluate and use this feedback. Few reports start to be published for assessing, for instance, the impact of eEurope strategy on growth and employment.[63]

Thus legitimacy cannot lie in the assessment procedures that have been implemented, since these are not known or public. While assessment is not an ancient tradition in the European Commission – there has for instance been no official assessment of the Bangemann report – methods and indicators have in all seriousness been built in order to evaluate the effects of eEurope action plans. Furthermore, there is a clear formal continuity between the two plans in terms of concepts and benchmarking methods employed, of seemingly continuous guidelines. Nevertheless, not enough lessons are taken from all the benchmarking and assessments, as if most of the commitments taken in eEurope 2002 were considered as definitely in place at the moment of writing eEurope 2005.

One may also have one's own appreciation of the benchmarking indicators. Do they go further than an evaluation of the penetration rate of Information Society policy? Adoption, penetration, connection are not primary concepts for appropriation! Moreover, it seems as if every new policy statement gives rise to a switch to a next and subsequent point in a reasoning that should have been decided from the start and which should mechanically be followed. So, even if one accepts the assertion developed in Lisbon that we are on "the way to the most competitive knowledge-based economy", is it a reason not to question the methods that are chosen and the resulting societal evolution? Should we not also question the timing, as well as the effect these policies have on ICT take-up? As Ducatel, Webster and Herrmann stated already three years ago, "if we want the 'society' in Information Society to be more than a rhetorical device, [it is necessary] to develop a more sophisticated appreciation of these social issues". And thus we must accept lessons and failures from the past, instead of repeating over and over that this time, conditions are really different.[64] This means than the social and societal aspects should be reflected in the indicators.

As stressed before, the first period of the Bangemann report was already 'Market Europe oriented', but the HLEG and ISF reports, for instance, still manifested a preoccupation with social values, social challenges, social policies, etc. In short, the insistence on People First, People Centred policies, showed, at least in words, the conviction that a *European Social Model of the Information Society* was possible, that the emphasis could be put on Society rather than on Information. But was social cohesion never a genuine concern? Today, even the so-called 'socially inclusive issues' seem to have disappeared from the action lines of eEurope 2005.

One might argue that legitimacy comes from the kind of a 'natural balance' included in EU policies: although the Commission (the European bureaucracy) is quite monolithic and may seem to function as an autonomous power, there is plenty of national and external influence in its decisions. Furthermore, the Commission is far from being the single centre of political forces in European decisions. Every EU presidency (rolling every 6 months to another Member State) wants to leave its own mark in each policy domain, though this does not necessarily work in favour of the coherence and permanence of such a policy.

Anyway, it is true that a large number of interests are represented in the decision process and, moreover, that a certain common ground of European political culture exists, which works in favour of non-openly competitive decisional processes. The latter is usually based on achieving satisfactory compromise even before the political issue treated gets formally discussed. While one could argue that this way of acting rather diminishes both the transparency of the process and the inclusion of interest groups, we nonetheless observe that in the eEurope initiative – originally prepared by three experts – the Commission's impulsion has never been seriously disputed or challenged.

One lesson from such an evaluation of EC-policy as ours is that academic people and EC decision-makers seem to live in two separate worlds.[65] While the former "have repeatedly observed that discourses about ICT are driven by technological determinism", the latter do not seem to bother about such ivory tower appreciation, or to question their beliefs in this, or in other external regards. Maybe a disenchanted vision of things does not suit the political discourse, aimed as it is at pushing forward 'positive' visions.[66] Another way of seeing things is that we enter the Internet galaxy at full speed, but fully confused, as Manuel Castells describes: evolution has been so fast that research has struggled to keep up and been unable to produce enough empirical on about the how, the what and the why, leaving empty spaces for futile discourse.[67] This way of thinking cannot satisfy scientific requirements, neither does it accord with the democratic principles which characterise Social Europe, as long, that is, as it is not pervaded by the laissez-faire of Market Europe.

About European Policies at Large

On a wider basis, all this raises questions on the nature of mostly proactive European policies, which do not benefit from strong popular adherence. With Dominique Wolton, we would like to highlight the paradox between, on the one side, all these policies that work for more and more communication between peoples and between groups and, on the other, the fact that the ongoing trend of more communication and information in no way eases the rise of a unified European conscience.[68] Policy makers and citizens do not share the necessary minimal common representations for a dialogue to be initiated and built. And this is even truer when information and communication are co-substantial to discourses on Europe. Indeed, as Wolton points out, from a certain point of view, information and communication *are* Europe. Yet the more it seems technically easy to build a communication-Europe, the more the difficulty appears on the actual content level of this Europe.[69] The effort the European Union has to make on its communication should, according to Wolton, polarise in two dimensions: a more explicit - and transparent - communication on the forces and weaknesses of Europe and European policies; a less institutional, formal, promotional communication than demonstrated by previous models of the last thirty-five years. If identity may have been, for past decades and centuries, a precondition of communication, communication must nowadays help to strengthen identity.[70] From a more prosaic standpoint, does the eEurope jargon and its 'Information Society' sound good – or even sound at all – to the lambda citizen?

On the Nature of the eEurope Initiative

1999 and eEurope has meant a gearshift to a greater density and political consistence of the European discourse on Information Society. While the market aspect of eEurope is seemingly less pregnant than in its predecessors, we cannot avoid thinking that social and societal considerations have been sprinkled on what mainly remains a market-driven plan. In our opinion, the market-driven option has never been questioned since it was chosen as a central pivot in the Delors White Paper. Indeed, some statements clearly show an in-depth, long-lasting inclination of policies that will remain difficult to change. As a piece of evidence, we notice that the matter of efficient uses comes in every official reasoning, far after questions concerning the 'critical mass' of users and the availability of broadband pipes.[71] It seems as though mass ICT adoption is the only way to be considered for the only problem that would really be handled: escaping from the 'classic chicken-and-egg scenario' and entering *the Internet economy*.[72]

The latest elements of European policy on Information society maintain the same convergent discourse. eEurope shares with its predecessors – which were in a certain measure, as shown, linked to US discourses – a common cognitive map.[73] Do we remain in the same main trend that characterised the 90's, the building of large-scale infra-structural projects at the inter-sectoral level, which followed another trend consisting of political intervention in meso-industrial development?[74] Anyway, beyond the fulfilment of the Lisbon strategy, our point is that eEurope has failed to formulate a clear political and citizen-oriented strategy. We see eEurope heading for something, but what precisely? Some even claim that eEurope would be a 'Commission's brand' rather than a strategy...[75]

Despite regretting some significant elements, this policy is above all a discourse that has to exist in order to pose a welcome European vision and challenge. Few would want it to remain merely 'flavour of the month'. This is even more true, now that we must acknowledge a heavy trend to *immaterialisation* of everyday activities, backed by an accumulation of knowledge, an increase of electronic devices, interconnectivity and accelerating diffusion of digital technical applications across an increasing panel of sectors.[76] So there is indeed a crucial role for technical progress – which we certainly do not restrict to so-called technological determinism! And thus there is an even more crucial need for (adequate) *policies* on these concerns.

To recapitulate, the nature of eEurope action currently remains modelled by the obstinate classicism of a vision generated within inner administrative circles and seeking legitimacy through reliance on chosen expert groups, a vision translated into vague action plans and embellished with some social or democratic concerns. And despite a will to make things change on a wider level, despite ambitious and various action plans, the range of ground-level action remains tight and often limited to small-scale demonstrators.[77] The relevance of this policy will be shown at the *local* level, while on the other side it will have also to work for harmonious *global* development. Regarding this, it may be less appropriate to set up a number of new international instances, than to buttress those already existing with clear, sustainable rules and guidelines.

---

[1]   History, Towards the Information Society,
      http://europa.eu.int/ISPO/basics/i_history.html , updated on 02/03/01.

[2]   The Information Society Homepage, http://europa.eu.int/information_society/

[3]   Commissioner from 1989 to 1999.

[4]   President from 1999 to 2004.

[5]   Information Society Forum, A European way for the Information Society, 3rd annual report, 1999, http://europa.eu.int/ISPO/policy/isf/i_documents.html

[6]   Communication from the Commission to the Council, the European Parliament, the Economic and Social Committee and the Committee of the Regions - The Information Society: From Corfu to Dublin "The new emerging priorities"; COM(96)395 final of 24 July 1996. Europe at the Forefront of the Global Information Society: Rolling Action Plan"; COM(96)607final; 27 November 1996, http://europa.eu.int/ISPO/policy/i_rollingaction.html

[7]   Europe and the Global Information Society, Recommendations to the European Council, Corfu (Greece), June 1994,
      http://europa.eu.int/ISPO/docs/basics/docs/bangemann.pdf

8   White Paper. on growth, competitiveness, and employment: The challenges and ways forward into the 21st century COM(93) 700 final. Brussels, 5 December 1993.

9   The National Information Infrastructure: Agenda for Action, http://www.ibiblio.org/nii/NII-Table-of-Contents.html

10 Jacques Berleur and Diane Whitehouse, Eds., *An Ethical Global Information Society: Culture and Democracy Revisited*, Chapman & Hall, 1997 (now available at Kluwer Academic Publ., Boston), p. 8.

11 Béatrice Van Bastelaer, eEurope ou les cohérences et incohérences de la Société européenne de l'Information, Working Paper of the COST 269 Group " User Aspects of ICTs ". See: http://www.info.fundp.ac.be/~cita/publications/e_Europe.pdf

12 Requested by the European Council during its Corfu meeting and approved in the Essen Council (December 1994) : Europe's Way to the Information Society - An Action Plan, COM(94)347 final, Brussels 19 July 1994, http://www.europa.eu.int/ISPO/docs/htmlgenerated/i_COM(94)347final.html

13 A Rolling Action Plan, COM(96)607, Brussels 31 July 1997 (version 1.3; version 1 in 1996), http://europa.eu.int/ISPO/policy/i_rollingaction.html

14 G-7 Information Society Conference, http://www.europa.eu.int/ISPO/intcoop/g8/i_g8conference.html

15 The pilot projects were : Global Inventory Project, Global Interoperability for Broadband Networks, Transcultural Education and Training for Language Learning, Electronic Libraries, Multimedia Access To World Cultural Heritage, Environment and Natural Resources Management, Global Emergency Management Information Network Initiative, Global Healthcare Applications, Government On-line, Global Marketplace for Small and Medium Enterprises, and Maritime Information Society.

16 Building the European Information Society for Us All. First Reflections of the High Level Group of Experts (HLEG), Interim Report, January, 1996. Final Report, April 1997 http://europa.eu.int/ISPO/docs/topics/docs/hlge_final_en_97.rtf

17 Mission and Role of the Information Society Forum, http://www.europa.eu.int/ISPO/policy/isf/i_mission.html

18 Information Society Forum documents, http://www.europa.eu.int/ISPO/policy/isf/i_documents.html

19 Green Paper - Living and Working in the Information Society: People First; COM(96)389, July 1996, http://europa.eu.int/comm/off/green/index_en.htm#1996

20 Council Decision 98/253/EC of 30 March 1998; Official Journal, L107 of 07 April 1998.

21 eEurope Initiative: http://europa.eu.int/ISPO/basics/i_europe.html

22 eEurope. An information Society For All. Communication on a Commission Initiative for the Special European Council of Lisbon, 23 and 24 March 2000. http://europa.eu.int/information_society/eeurope/news_library/pdf_files/initiati ve_en.pdf

23 eEurope, an Information Society for All, Initial document on the web site of the Commission, http://www.europa.eu.int/information_society/eeurope/2002/news_library/docu ments/text_en.htm

24 Benchmarking eEurope : http://europa.eu.int/information_society/eeurope/2002/benchmarking/index_en. htm

25 Interviewed by Béatrice van Bastelaer.

26 Communication from the Commission to the Council, the European Parliament, the Economic and Social Committee and the Committee of the Regions, eEurope Benchmarking, Report COM(2002) 62, http://europa.eu.int/eur-lex/en/com/cnc/en_cnc_month_2002_02.html

27 Commission of the European Communities, eEurope 2002, Final Report, Communication from the Commission to the Council, the European Parliament, the Economic and Social Committee and the Committee of the Regions, February 2003, http://europa.eu.int/information_society/eeurope/news_library/documents/acte_ eEurope_2002_en.doc

28 New Regulatory Framework for electronic communications infrastructure and associated services, http://europa.eu.int/information_society/topics/telecoms/regulatory/new_rf/text _en.htm and eCommunications Networks and Services, EU Policy and Regulation, http://europa.eu.int/information_society/topics/ecomm/text_en.htm

29 Commission of the European Communities, eEurope 2002 Final Report, doc. cit.

30 Commission of the European Communities, eEurope 2005: An information society for all, Action Plan to be presented in view of the Sevilla European Council (June 2002), Com(2002) 263 final, May 2002, http://europa.eu.int/prelex/detail_dossier_real.cfm?CL=fr&DosId=173882

31 Ibid.

32 Commission of the European Communities, DG Information Society, eContent. A multiannual Community programme to stimulate the development and use of European digital content on the global networks and to promote the linguistic diversity in the Information Society. Work Programme 2003-2004, 2002, ftp://ftp.cordis.lu/pub/econtent/docs/work_programme_2003_2004_en.pdf

33 Liikanen Erkki, "Priorités pour l'eEurope", in Le Soir, Brussels, 15 mars 2002.

34 Ibid.

35 For instance, "schools not only connected but also making full use of the Internet in class" (ibid.).

36 Ibid.

37 The MODINIS Programme, http://europa.eu.int/information_society/eeurope/2005/all_about/modinis/text_en.htm

38 eEurope 2005 Action Plan : an Update.

39 Commission of the European Communities, eEurope 2005: Benchmarking indicators, Communication from the Commission to the Council and the European Parliament, COM(2002) 655 final, November 2002, http://europa.eu.int/eur-lex/en/com/cnc/2002/com2002_0655en01.pdf

40 Besides the difficulty, here maybe more than in other policy domains, of having recent data at disposal as well as sufficiently defined statistics between Member States to ensure the homogeneity of the indicators.

41 Commission of the European Communities, eEurope 2005, doc. cit.

42 Gallup Europe, Flash Eurobarometer 125: Internet and the Public at Large, May-June 2002, and Commission of the European Communities, eEurope 2002 Final Report, Communication from the Commission to the Council, the European Parliament, the Economic and Social Committee and the Committee of the Regions, February 2003, COM(2003) 66 final, http://europa.eu.int/prelex/detail_dossier_real.cfm?CL=en&DosId=180710

43 INFOREGIO, The regions and the new economy - Guidelines for innovative actions co-funded by the European Regional Development Fund 2000-06, http://europa.eu.int/comm/regional_policy/innovation/pdf/sheet/inforegio_en.pdf

44 Inforegio Panorama, Politique de Cohésion: quel avenir dans une Union élargie?, Nr.3, Communautés Européennes, 2001.

45 The Candidate Countries with the assistance of the European Commission, eEurope+2003. A cooperative effort to implement the Information Society in Europe. Action Plan, June 2001, http://europa.eu.int/information_society/topics/international/regulatory/eeuropeplus/doc/eEurope_june2001.pdf Please also note that eEurope 2005 plans to integrate smoothly, step by step, new Member States into its policy and benchmarking.

46 Central and Eastern Europe Information Society Benchmarks, Summary Report, September 2004 http://europa.eu.int/information_society/eeurope/2005/all_about/benchmarking/index_en.htm

47 Preston Paschal, "The Information Superhighway and the Less Developed Regions/Smaller Entities: Implications for Policy in the EU", in Kubicek Herbert, Dutton William H., Williams Robin (eds.), *The Social Shaping of*

Information Superhighways. European and American Roads to the Information Society, Campus Verlag, St. Martin's Press, Frankfurt/New York, 1997, pp. 277-297.

[48] Commission of the European Communities, eEurope 2005, doc. cit.

[49] See http://www.content-village.org/. A working programme for years 2003 and 2004 has been adopted last year.

[50] eTen, Deploying Services for an Information Society for All (eServices), http://europa.eu.int/information_society/programmes/eten/index_en.htm

[51] Commission of the European Communities, Information society Technologies. A thematic priority for Research and Development under the Specific Programme "Integrating and strengthening the European Research area" in the Community sixth Framework Programme, 2003-2004 Working programme, 2002, ftp://ftp.cordis.lu/pub/ist/docs/wp2003-04_final_en.pdf For an accurate view on societal strengths, weaknesses and challenges of each aspect of this thematic priority, see Internal Reflection Group (IRG) Report, Major Societal Challenges in the IST Programme of the Sixth Framework Programme, 8 May 2002. ftp://ftp.cordis.lu/pub/ist/docs/irg-msc-eport-v6(final).doc

[52] As it is not the purpose of this paper, we will not emphasise international level policies and relations. But it is worth noting that agreements like WTO GATS (General Agreement on Trade in Services) as well as other multilateral or bilateral dialogue between Europe and all its partners have an important role to play in the definition of the European policies.

[53] Six European Directives and one decision have been published in the recent times: a Framework Directive, an Access Directive, an Authorisation Directive, a Universal Service Directive, a Directive on privacy and electronic communications, and a Radio Spectrum Decision, Official Journal of the European Communities of April 24, 2002 (L108, volume 45, pp. 1-77) and July 31, 2002. Member states are awaited to have these directives transposed on national grounds not later than July 24, 2003.

[54] As pointed out in 1999 by Catinat Michel, Entrer dans la société de l'information. L'enseignement américain, in *Futuribles*, Nr. 242, May 1999, pp. 19-42.

[55] The 'Computer Systems Policy Project', an affiliation of chief executive officers of the 13 largest American computer companies, were advocating a strictly business perspective on development of the Global Information Infrastructure, together with a tough negotiating posture. FINS Special Report February 21, 1995.

[56] New Regulatory Framework for electronic communications infrastructure and associated services, doc. cit.

[57] Council of Europe, Convention n° 185 on Cybercrime, http://conventions.coe.int/Default.asp

[58] Alvaro de Miranda and Morten Kristiansen, Technological Determinism and Ideology: The European Union and the Information Society, Paper delivered at the 3rd Policy Agendas for Sustainable Technological Innovation (POSTI) International Workshop, London, U.K., 1-3 December 2000, http://www.esst.uio.no/posti/workshops/miranda.pdf

[59] A. de Miranda et al. note that the link was first made by American presidential adviser, Zbigniew Brzezinski in his 1969 book *Between Two Ages, America's Role in the Technetronic Era* (quoted from A. Mattelart, Archéologie de la "Société de l'Information", in *Le Monde Diplomatique*, August 2000).

[60] European Commission, White Paper on growth, competitiveness, and employment: The challenges and ways forward into the 21st century, COM(93) 700 final, Brussels, 5 December 1993, http://europa.eu.int/en/record/white/c93700/contents.html

[61] Bernard Cassen, Naissance de l'Europe S.A., in Le Monde Diplomatique, Juin 2000.

[62] Volker Schneider proposes an interesting review of these hypotheses and others in: Schneider Volker, Different Roads to the Information Society? Comparing U.S. and European Approaches from a Public Policy Perspective, in Kubicek Herbert, Dutton William H., Williams Robin (eds.), *The Social Shaping of Information Superhighways*, opacity, pp. 339-358.

[63] European Commission, *Facing the challenge. The Lisbon strategy for growth and employment*, Report from the High Level Group chaired by Wim Kok. Luxembourg: Office for Official Publications of the European Communities, 2004 - 51 pp., ISBN 92-894-7054-2

[64] Ducatel Ken, Webster Juliet, Herrmann Werner, Information Infrastructures or Societies?, in Ducatel Ken, Webster Juliet, Herrmann Werner (eds.), *Praise for The Information Society in Europe. Work and Life in an Age of Globalization*, Rowman & Littlefield, Lanham, 2000, p. 9.

[65] van Bastelaer Béatrice, eEurope and User Aspects of ICT, COST Working Paper No. 1, June 2001. She was research assistant at the CITA, FUNDP Namur, and is currently associate project leader at the eGovernment team of the Walloon Region, Belgium.

[66] Although a traditional European (French?) trend of considering IT as creating more problems than it solves, we can say that EU rallied the US position which is more confident about the potential of technologies to boost growth.

[67] Castells Manuel, *La galaxie Internet*, Fayard, Paris, 2001, 370 pp.

[68] Wolton Dominique, *Naissance de l'Europe démocratique*, Champs, Flammarion, Paris, 1997, 460 pp, p. 360.

[69] Ibid., p. 373, 385.

[70] Ibid., p. 381.

[71]   The word 'critical mass' is taken from the conclusions of the eEurope+2003 progress report.

[72]   Ibid.

[73]   Breton, quoting Proulx. Breton Philippe, *Le culte de l'Internet. Une menace pour le lien social?*, La Découverte, Paris, 2000, 130 pp.

[74]   Schneider Volker, Different Roads to the Information Society?, op. cit., p. 340.

[75]   Alabau Antonio, Understanding the eGovernment Policy of the European Union. A comparative analysis with the eGovernment policies of some supra-national organizations, working document, Universidad Politecnica de Valencia, Valencia, 2003.

[76]   Dalloz Xavier, Portnoff André-Yves, La prolifération numérique: ressorts et impacts. Repères pour "années chien"" in *Futuribles*, Nr. 266, July-August 2001, pp. 23-40, p. 24.

[77]   Ducatel Ken, Webster Juliet, Herrmann Werner, Information Infrastructures or Societies?, op. cit.

The Information Society in the Asia-Pacific Region India and Australia

Sowmyanarayanan SADAGOPAN
Indian Institute of Information Technology, ss@iiitb.ac.in
and John WECKERT
Centre for Applied Philosophy and Public Ethics, Charles Stuart University,
JWeckert@csu.edu.au

> *"In both India and Australia, Governments are keenly interested in information technology, and have introduced new policies in order to encourage acceptance ... and to stimulate ICT development."*

Abstract: This chapter considers just two countries in the Asia-Pacific region, India and Australia. Policies are outlined that show how the governments in these countries are attempting to encourage the IT industry, eBusiness and eGovernment, address problems of Internet access, and regulate Internet content.

Key words   Information Technology (IT), information and communication technology (ICT), eBusiness, eGovernment, digital divide, Internet content

INTRODUCTION

There are a large number of countries in the Asia-Pacific region, ranging from tiny island nations to the country with the largest population on earth. It also includes economically very poor countries together with one member of the G8 group. Given this vast diversity, there can be no one "typical" country, but looking at India and Australia can be instructive. Neither India nor Australia is in the G8, and both are geographically remote from the economic centres of North America and Western Europe. Both have also enthusiastically embraced information technology.

INDIA

Preamble

A number of developments over the past two decades have moved ICT to centre–stage in India. There have been some Indian IT companies that have attained notable success in the global software development arena (Infosys and Wipro); some IT professionals of Indian origin made headline news in the global IT scene: Gururaj Deshpande (Founder CEO of Sycamore Networks), Arun Netravali (Head of Bell Labs), and Sabeer Bhatia (Founder of HotMail) - building on the earlier success stories of people like Vinod Khosla (Co-Founder of Sun Microsystems), and Vinod Dham (Chief Architect of Pentium Microprocessor at Intel). The Indian software and services industry achieved some major milestones in *quality*, with more than 70% of the SEI Level 5 quality level companies – considered the highest process quality attainment – located in India, and *quantity*, about half a million IT professionals in India generated business worth ten billion dollars in 2001. Of this sum, more than six billion dollars is in export. Software services export alone is expected to exceed fifty billion dollars by the year 2008. In turn, Indian IT received global attention, so much so that IT has caught the imagination of the average Indian – from the Prime Minister of the country to the man or woman on the street.

Policy in India

Until the early nineties when the central Government and the State Governments started liberalizing the economy, the Indian Republic was overly centrally administered by the Planning Commission, and that too in a socialist manner - where private sector, market economy, competition, service quality, service charges etc., had practically no place. Naturally, Government Policy played a dominant role. Unlike other industries, ICT was relatively new in India until the eighties and most of the policies of that decade aimed at freeing the industry from the control of the bureaucracy and enabling it to grow, through liberal fiscal, labour and company policies. With the industry growing in size, recent policies have been aimed at promoting sustained growth, taking IT to the masses, drawing up sector–specific policies, creating infrastructure, attracting FDI (Foreign Direct Investment) and even addressing sensitive issues, such as Public Sector Unit (PSU) privatisation; in the process many other issues have been addressed too, for example: liberalized foreign exchange, people exchange, labour laws, technology inputs to Government, and legislative and administrative support for wider use of IT by Government, Corporations and citizens through the IT Act, Public Key Infrastructure (PKI), Certificate Authority, De-materialization of share certificates, Transparent Electronic Stock Market, Corporate Governance, eGovernance, Government Citizen Interface and enabling wider usage of e Commerce. Based on this, the broad ICT related policies can be categorized as follows:

Free Industry from shackles

- The New Computer Policy (1984) and the earlier Computer Policy (1978), that permitted the private sector to enter computer manufacture, removed the prior permission needed for the import of computers from abroad, and drastically scaled down the duty structure to make computers affordable, so that end users could easily and affordably buy computers from both Indian and foreign manufacturers. These policies also levied "Zero duty" on software, permitting the later spectacular growth of this industry (50% Compounded Annual Growth Rate (CAGR) over the years 1995-2000)
- Removal of the VSNL monopoly in the ISP business; prior to 1997 this was the public sector long-distance and international carrier of voice and data and the only Internet service Provider. Open the multiple Internet Gateway, including private Gateways (1999) and later the privatisation of VSNL (2000). In turn a number of private ISP's were born
- Awarding of Cellular Licenses for the private sector (1992), permitting Basic Telephony from private operators (1994) and introducing competition in the national long-distance telephony (1999). These in turn led to a healthy growth in telephone density from 0.9 in 1991 to nearly 6.0 by the year 2002 with nearly nine million cellular phone subscribers as of October 2002.

Promote Sustained Growth

Develop Infrastructure (Software Technology Parks of India): In order to get the right push for this sunrise industry the Government of India set up an autonomous body in the form of Software Technology Parks of India (STPI) with a mission to provide single point service to software and services companies in the form of data circuits, local "last mile" connection through radio lines, Internet Connection, International data circuits (shared and dedicated), duty exemption for import of equipment, certification for Income Tax exemption etc. It proved to be a big hit; with full income exempted from Income Tax (which is very high in India) and the STPI Registration guaranteeing it, the growing software industry got a significant cost advantage in the export market (reduced cost of infrastructure, savings in import duty, savings due to Income Tax exemption). At a later date (1994), STPI took the "virtual" view of the enterprise – any enterprise located anywhere in the identified cities (more than dozen of them) could be a Software Park (and not limited to those located in the physical premises of Export Exemption/Processing Zones, Software Parks etc).

Fiscal Incentives: Income Tax Exemption - under Sections 80HHE, 10A and 10B of the Income Tax Act provided a strong incentive for corporations in the IT arena to perform better, by way of freeing them from payment of very high and even cumbersome Income Tax (and the attendant paperwork, litigation and wasted management time). Also, the concept of Bonded Warehouse permitted IT equipment within identified STPI premises to be imported from anywhere in the world without payment of Import Duty (that could be high as 150%) leading to considerable cost savings.

Other Issues: In recent years Governments (both central and state) have been formulating policies to increase the use of IT within the administration. Notable among them is the IT Act 2000 that legalized Electronic Signatures (leading to widespread PKI Infrastructure) and permitted electronic storage of documents (increased use of document management systems). Through a plan to allot 3% of the Budget of all Government Departments (since 2000), there is now an indirect incentive for the Governments to use IT. Through a merger of the Telecommunications and IT Ministry (in the year 2001) there is better coordination between the Infrastructure Provider and the IT user interests. With increased outsourcing of ITES (IT-enabled services such as Call Centres, Back Office Processing (BPO), Medical Transcription etc.) to India, several State Governments (Karnataka, Kerala, West Bengal, Tamil Nadu) have passed legislation that frees the BPO organizations from the rather stringent labour laws, particularly in the areas of employment of women. In addition, there is competition among the states to attract BPO operations from the major world companies like GE, HSBC, Citibank etc.. There are also well-defined fiscal incentives for investment in FDI (for example, the state of Karnataka provides a fixed amount cash incentive for BPO operations reaching a size of 1000-seater). A number of Hi-Tech Parks (with several million square feet of world-class working space in terms of connectivity, power availability and even the sheer elegance of the ambience) have been developed with participation from private sector parks.

Many states and the central Government have even established Institutions of Higher Learning under the banner of Indian Institutes of Information Technology (IIIT's), hoping to build on the track record of the earlier string of institutions under the tag of Indian Institutes of Technology (IIT's).

AUSTRALIA

Like India, Australia is a large country, but unlike India, it has a relatively small population, and that population is concentrated along the coast, particularly in the south-east corner. This creates transportation and communication problems, and the new Information and Communication Technology (ICT) is seen by many as a way to alleviate the problem. This technology introduces a problem in itself too, in the form of fair access. With vast distances and extremely uneven population distribution, it is important to ensure that the digital divide between metropolitan and remote areas is not too great. The Australian Government and the various state and territory governments have a variety of policies, strategies and initiatives to develop the infrastructure for ICT, to encourage its use, particularly in government and business, to bridge the digital divide between city and country, and in some instances to regulate its use.

At the Australian Government level, the Department of Communications, Information Technology and the Arts [5] has responsibility for ICT. The Department provides strategic advice and professional support on information and communications technology and telecommunications, and also administers legislation, regulations, grants, and incentives to industry and the wider community.

The infrastructure and the digital divide

In 1997, the Australian telecommunications market was opened to full competition. Previously the government-owned Telstra supplied this service to all Australians. Also in 1997, the partial sale of Telstra began, and currently it is 51% government owned. Its full sale is planned but no timeframe has been mentioned. Even though the market has been opened, the government has a policy framework for supporting and encouraging the growth of telecommunications. There is also a range of laws designed to ensure the availability, quality and reasonable pricing of fixed telephones (for example, the Universal Service Obligation and the Customer Service Guarantee). The Australian Communications Authority [1] enforces these obligations. The mobile phone sector is also being supported, both with land-based, cellular networks, and satellite systems, with most of the population already having coverage.

This infrastructure enables all Australians to dial-up at least one ISP at un-timed local call rates (although of course, not all do this). This Internet access is narrowband, though there are also efforts to develop broadband. Currently these services are available primarily in metropolitan areas and larger rural towns.

Because of its size and uneven population distribution, the "digital divide" between rural and metropolitan areas has been a concern. Various initiatives are in place around Australia that are designed to encourage Internet use in rural areas. For example, at the National level, Government, through the Department of Transport and Regional Services has established the Rural Transaction Centres Program [6]. This programme is designed for communities with populations under 3000, to help them establish centres that "provide access to basic transaction services, such as banking, post, phone, fax, the Internet, Centrelink Services and Medicare Easyclaim".

One of the most important initiatives by the Commonwealth Government was the Networking the Nation (NTN) programme and the Regional Telecommunications Infrastructure Fund [11]. NTN was "a Commonwealth grants program providing over $400 million in funding to not-for-profit organisations to support activities and projects designed to address a range of telecommunications needs in regional, rural and remote Australia", and in general to improve the quality of telecommunications services in rural Australia. (This is put in the past tense because on the NTN website it says that nearly all funds have been committed.)

In New South Wales, the CTC@NSW programme is a major NSW/Commonwealth Government initiative to establish Community Technology Centres (CTCs) throughout regional NSW. CTCs in New South Wales provide a wide range of services, programs and facilities designed to support the social economic, cultural and educational life of people in small rural NSW towns. The home site CTC@NSW is managed by the NSW Office on Information Technology and is funded by the NSW Government and Networking the Nation. CTCs are located throughout NSW targeting areas that need them most, small communities with less than 3000 people. CTCs give people in rural communities: access to the latest information via the Internet, email, and videoconferencing; access to on-line government and non-government services; access to on-line education and training courses; IT enabled facilities that enable the development of programs that contribute to their social and cultural development into total communities [4].

For Victorians who are hardest to reach, the government has the Connecting Communities strategy. This is a framework to use technology to create and strengthen communities, and to provide the context for existing and new Internet access and training programs. It operates throughout Victoria's library branches through the Libraries On-line program. The access@schools program provides the wider community with access to Internet-equipped workstations in schools, including schools in rural and remote areas. The Victorian Government is also working on other programmes to increase Internet in rural areas uptake, including the Regional Connectivity Project, and Skills.net, a programme to ensure that everybody is able to access the resources of the Internet. Skills.net provides free or affordable Internet training and access to those Victorians who would not otherwise have such access. In particular, Skills.net is assisting technologically disadvantaged communities, including those in rural and remote Victoria [7].

This is only a small sample of Government activity designed to increase Internet use in rural areas of Australia. All State Governments are involved in some way in projects similar to those mentioned here.

eBusiness

eBusiness is being actively promoted, particularly through the National Office for the Information Economy (NOIE) [8], established by the Government in 1997. A current priority focus is the promotion of the uptake of electronic procurement and broader electronic business processes, especially by small and medium enterprises. eBusiness is seen by the Government at national level as being vital for the future economic prosperity of Australia, and is one of the main drivers for ICT policy.
Currently NOIE aims to accelerate the uptake of electronic-business tools and practices by:
- Working with industry and government to facilitate the development of collaborative eBusiness solutions;
- Identifying and influencing how standards, technology and market forces are shaping the rate at which economy-wide benefits from eBusiness are being achieved;
- Identifying and promoting the business case for the adoption of eBusiness at the firm level, within supply chains and throughout industry sectors; and
- Establishing specific strategies designed to encourage small and medium enterprises (SMEs) to get online and more deeply engaged in the use of eBusiness tools. [9]

eGovernment

The government sees itself as having an important leadership role in enhancing the extent to which businesses and the community takes full advantage of the opportunities provided by the information economy. It is attempting to do this by maximising the opportunities provided by technology to help transform government activities. This transformation, it is hoped, will have a significant 'demonstrator' and 'pull-through' effect on Australia's wider information economy. There is an EGovernment strategy that will involve the transformation of government service delivery through the use of new technologies. It is hoped that this will provide better customer focus and access, greater availability of information, improved business processes, and efficiencies. Current NOIE projects in this area include, an eGovernment benefits study, a study regarding Access to Government Information, and an examination of Government eProcurement [10].

Internet content regulation

While the Governments in Australia are committed to encouraging and promoting ICT, there is concern about some of the material available on the Internet. As a consequence of this concern, Internet content is regulated by both the Australian and South Australian governments. On the 1st January, 2000, the Broadcasting Services Amendment (Online Services) Act 1999 [3] of the Australian Government, came into effect.

The law defines *Internet content* as stored information accessed over an Internet carriage service, including material on the World Wide Web, postings on newsgroups and bulletin boards, and other files that can be downloaded from an archive or library. The Act does not include ordinary email or information that is accessed in real time without being previously stored, for example chat services and voice over the Internet.

The following categories of Internet content are prohibited:

– Content which is (or would be) classified RC or X by the Classification Board.

  Such content includes:
  - material containing detailed instruction in crime, violence or drug use;
  - child pornography;
  - bestiality;
  - excessively violent or sexually violent material.
  - real depictions of actual sexual activity; and

– Content hosted in Australia which is classified R and not subject to a restricted access system which complies with criteria determined by the Australian Broadcasting Authority (ABA).
Content classified R is not considered suitable for minors and includes:
- material containing excessive and/or strong violence or sexual violence;
- material containing implied or simulated sexual activity;
- material which deals with issues or contains depictions which require an adult perspective.[2]

The ABA was established by the Broadcasting Services Act 1992, and began operations on 5 October 1992. The Act defines the role of the regulatory authority, gives the ABA a range of powers and functions, and sets out explicit policy objectives.

CONCLUSION

In both India and Australia, Governments are keenly interested in information technology, and have introduced new policies in order to encourage acceptance of the technology, and to stimulate ICT development. To the extent that ICT development and acceptance is a feature of both countries, those policies appear to be bearing fruit.

REFERENCES

References to Indian IT policy

Most of the references can be seen in far greater detail at NASSCOM (National Association of Software & Services Companies) site (http://www.nasscom.org) The Ministry of Information Technology site gives lots of details too (http://www.mit.gov.in/). Earlier, it had the name of Department of Electronics and is often referred to as DoE; there is even a DoEACC Society focusing on IT Education (http://www.doeacc.org.in/); naturally many Policy Documents would refer to DoE. Typical State Level Policies can be looked up at http://www.bangaloreit.com site that keeps Karnataka Policy as well as pointers to policies of other States in India. STPI site is another store of information (http://www.stpi.soft.net)

1. Semiconductor Integrated Circuits Act 2000
2. Information Technology Act 2000
3. Telecom Regulatory Authority of India (Amendment) Act 2000

4. Foreign Exchange Management Act 1999 (allows software firms to freely undertake transactions on current account)
5. Telecom Regulatory Authority of India Act 1997
6. New Telecom Policy 1999 (and 1994)
7. Export Import Policy 1997-2002 (provides for license free import of computers, imports of second-hand equipment no older than 10 years and sales of up to 50% by revenue, by units under Software Technology Park, Electronic Hardware Technology Park, Export Oriented Unit, Export Processing Zone Schemes)
8. Securities and Exchange Board of India (Venture Capital Funds) Regulations 1996
9. Software Technology Park Scheme 1991
10. Computer Software Export, Development and Training Policy 1986
11. New Computer Policy 1984
12. Income Tax Act 1961, Sections 80HHE, 10A and 10B (deduction of profits from export of computer software)
13. Indian Copyright Act 1957 (amended in 1995, makes copyright infringement of computer software an offence)

References to Australian IT policy

1. Australian Communications Authority, http://www.aca.gov.au
2. Australian Broadcasting Authority http://www.aba.gov.au/aba/index.htm. For a summary of prohibited Internet content see http://www.aba.gov.au/internet/complaints/complaints.htm#what
3. Broadcasting Services Amendment (Online Services) Act 1999 http://www.aph.gov.au/parlinfo/billsnet/main.htm
4. CTC@NSW, http://www.ctc.nsw.gov.au
5. Department of Communications, Information Technology and the Arts http://www.dcita.gov.au/
6. Department of Transport and Regional Services' Rural Transaction Centres Program http://www.dotars.gov.au/rtc/
7. Multimedia Victoria – Connecting Communities, 2002. Available at http://www.mmv.vic.gov.au. See also http://www.skills.net.about/default.
8. NOIE, National Office for the Information Economy, http://www.noie.gov.au/
9. NOIE Business, http://www.noie.gov.au/projects/ebusiness/index.htm
10. NOIE Government, http://www.noie.gov.au/projects/egovernment/index.htm
11. Networking the Nation. available at http://www.dcita.gov.au/Article/0,,0_1-2_3-4_106337,00.htm

IT STAR in Central and Eastern Europe – A Synergy of a Goodwill

Niko SCHLAMBERGER
Slovenian Society INFORMATIKA, niko.schlamberger@gov.si
and Franci PIVEC
IZUM, Maribor, franci.pivec@izum.si

> *"...within IFIP a new kind of integration has emerged that deserves attention and is worthy of being copied. The initiative was born in Middle Europe, which throughout history has been characterized by a vast diversity of all kinds, but also by an intense common communication. In this region there were always connections that have overcome whatever partitions were current to the times."*

Abstract: The contribution describes a new regional initiative born in collaboration between certain national computer societies and the International Federation for Information Processing. A new, rather informal, regional body has been set up – the Information Technology Standing Regional Committee for Regional Collaboration. Its purpose is to facilitate the cooperative interaction of IT professionals regardless of their momentary employment or any other kind of affiliation. The prerequisites are a professional capacity and a wish to take part in certain kinds of projects. This initiative has attracted rather wide attention and, hopefully, may also be adopted as a paradigm to be used elsewhere wherever such regional collaboration is appreciated.

Key words: Regional cooperation, IT STAR, IFIP, paradigm

THE HISTORY

IT STAR (Information Technology STAnding Regional) Committee has grown from an initiative that was "engineered" by the president of the Slovenian computer society, Niko Schlamberger, and IFIP executive director Plamen Nedkov. They also came up with the much appreciated name of the committee. It all started some thirty years ago at a Slovenian annual computer conference that has been organized by various entities in collaboration, but, since 1993, is organized by the Slovenian Society INFORMATIKA (SSI), as it is officially called. The conference has seen its revival under the name "Days of Slovenian Informatics" as a national meeting of computer professionals and users from business, universities and administration. Since one ambition was to compare domestic achievements internationally, notable professionals from abroad were invited as guest speakers. In 1998, after SSI became a member of CEPIS and IFIP, the conference was seen as a possible platform for the launching of a more systematic international collaboration. The fact that Slovenia was at the time one of the countries hoping soon to become a European Union member state, where regional cooperation is appreciated, provided an additional stimulus to the idea. Beyond any doubt, the merit for the success of the initiative goes also to former IFIP president Peter Bollerslev who has understood its potential and has taken an active part in preparation for the first meeting.

The official constitutive meeting of the IT STAR took place in Portoroz, Slovenia, in April 2001, as one of accompanying events of the conference. Next to SSI and IFIP representatives who were the initiators, representatives of national computer societies from Austria, Italy, and Hungary were also present at this first meeting. The event was rather appreciated nationally, as the presence of Slovenian Deputy Minister of Information Society Dr. József Györkös bears witness. During the meeting the participants adopted a statement, which was later published and distributed (Fig. 1: Copy from the IFIP web site).

The Regional meeting, jointly chaired by the IFIP Executive Director and the President of the Slovenian Society "Informatika", adopted the following Statement:

MEETING OF REPRESENTATIVES OF THE COMPUTER SOCIETIES OF AUSTRIA, HUNGARY, ITALY AND SLOVENIA

Portoroz, 18 April 2001 - The Computer Societies of Austria, Hungary, Italy and Slovenia met today in Portoroz, Slovenia to inform each other of their national IT priorities, activities and initiatives and to explore areas of common interest for future regional and international cooperation.

The participating societies recognize IFIP's authority and potential to initiate important international activities and are grateful to IFIP for providing its auspices to the meeting and for its willingness to continue supporting the efforts of its members in establishing closer regional links.

The meeting agreed to establish an IT STAnding Regional (IT STAR) Committee for cooperation of the participating societies. Its function would be to assess the current contacts and to assist and monitor the development of bilateral and regional programs for scientific and technical cooperation. IT STAR membership shall consist of one representative of each participating society and IFIP. It will remain open for other societies from the region.

Signed:

For OCG-Austria by V. Risak, Past President

For NJSZT-Hungary by B. Domolki, Honorary President

For AICA-Italy by G. Occhini, Board Member

For SSI-Slovenia by N. Schlamberger, President

Figure 1: IT STAR comes into life

The next meeting, at which the Slovak and Czech national computer societies joined IT STAR, was held in September 2001 in Como, Italy, under the auspices of the Italian computer society AICA. During the Como meeting, the participants further elaborated the outline and organization of collaboration, including a joint information and communication platform, publication of a newsletter, regional workshops during annual conferences, contributions to national journals, and other matters of common interest. After that, meetings were held in November 2001 in Bratislava, Slovakia, and again in Portoro, Slovenia, in April 2002, to which the Croatian computer society was admitted. A further meeting took place in June 2003 in Opatija, Croatia, which was hosted by the Croatian computer society. By then the IT STAR initiative had become popular, and those national societies that had previously expressed an interest were invited to join, with a special mention for the Lithuanian computer society, which filed a formal request to be adopted. In Opatija the Greek, Rumanian, Bulgarian, Yugoslavian, Macedonian, and Lithuanian national computer societies were invited as new members of IT STAR, and Yugoslavian, Macedonian, and Lithuanian national computer societies were admitted.

The key issue of the Bratislava meeting was a proposal for an IT STAR Professional Pool of Experts (IT PP) with the objective of developing a regional database of information technology experts. The idea was to set up a data base containing those experts who are qualified and willing to take part in national or international projects for non profit-making entities such as governments, societies, universities, international organizations, such as the United Nations and its affiliated bodies, the European Union and such-like.

Membership

Members of the pool are individual IT professionals. All members should apply for membership voluntarily and their request must be supported by their national computer society. They must provide a minimum of personal data listed below. They must agree to comply with the purpose of setting up the pool and with the rules governing its functioning and operation as well as with using the data provided by them for the purpose of setting up and operating the pool.

Data
- name
- family name
- home address
- email
- affiliation(s)
- degree and institution
- skills
- references
- preferences
- languages
- other relevant useful information

Database system

The national databases would be operated by the national member societies who have agreed to join the project under central guidance and operational oversight by an entity, as agreed by IT STAR, preferably with or close to the IFIP Secretariat. This entity would be authorized to investigate programs, projects and activities for which there would be a need of expertise from IT STAR countries, to dispatch inquiries and gather inquiries for expertise.

Two levels of database are considered: national and international, both to be maintained by the national computer societies. The national database will be set up and kept by the respective national society exclusively for its own use whereas the international part would comprise the IT STAR Professional Pool and the "International Keeper" or body designated to operate the system (as referred to in the preceding paragraph) would have free and unlimited access to it. There must be no direct input of data on individuals into the international database. On the other hand, users will be provided data on individuals only upon request to the international database and from it. The only exception is when a user requires a team composed of individuals from one country, then he may address the national data base keeper (the national society). In this case the national society has an obligation to report the case to the international data base keeper.

Figure 2: IT Professional Pool setting

It still remains to establish the criteria and requirements regarding who qualifies, and what certification is acceptable to be included in a system which is intended to facilitate the establishment of expert and professional teams. Such teams would be available to execute international and national projects and other short to medium term activities. The following has been agreed upon regarding the content, keeping, and operation of the data base (A copy of a part of a material prepared for the Bratislava meeting)

There are still some open issues about the privacy of personal data and the distribution thereof, but considering that entering into the data base is only voluntary and that the data base keeper may not use the data for purposes other than those declared and collected for, there is no real underlying legal problem. A practical matter of more concern is currently the role of IFIP in the future, since it has been involved all along and has also agreed to serve as a focal point in the process of collecting requests and relating data. It is to be hoped that the present uncertainties will be resolved before long.

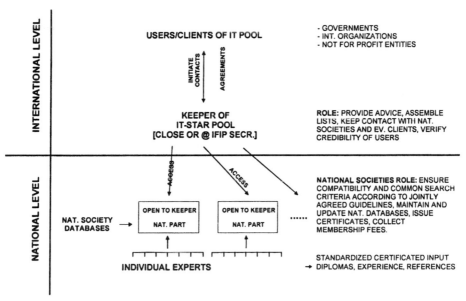

Figure 3: Operation of IT Professional Pool

It was agreed in the beginning that just the goodwill to collaborate should be considered enough, so there is no membership fee, no affiliation of any kind required, no presidency and governing bodies nor any other type of formal organization, except that the computer society of the host country has the responsibility to prepare everything needed for the meeting. It is also true that all the IT STAR member societies are IFIP members as well. For the goodwill to last, and for the interest in collaboration to persist, there must be more than just a meeting. As desired and feasible products, a newsletter, a web page, and a project were envisaged. The IT STAR newsletter can be reached via the IT STAR web page at the address http://www.ifip.org/. The project that has been proposed and accepted is a database on IT professionals qualified and certified to take part in national and international IT projects for non profit-making organizations such as: societies, governments, universities, foundations and the like. Interest in joining IT STAR has been expressed by several national computer societies from the region, but also from those not quite a part of the region. Hopefully, no one will be turned down, as the idea is also to extend the paradigm of cooperation.

THE WIDER PERSPECTIVE

It is rather obvious that within IFIP a new kind of integration has emerged that deserves attention and is worthy of being copied. The initiative was born in Middle Europe, which throughout history has been characterized by a vast diversity of all kinds (cultural, ethnic, economic, political, linguistic, geographical), but also by an intense common communication. In this region there were always connections that have overcome whatever partitions were current to the times. A recent example is the Alps-Adria Common Venture.

While we are inclined to combine information and communication technologies (ICT) with globalisation, it is also true that they open new prospects of regional integration. It would be strange if the peoples between the Alps and the Adriatic Sea - the Middle Europeans – did not take advantage of this new communication potential. There are many general reasons for connecting within the domain of information:

- the region is a historical junction of south-to-north and west-to-east directions and is actually one large node in the international traffic network;
- the peoples in this area have a considerable history in common about which they may have a lot to say to each other and which also speaks for itself with a common, private language;
- the region is a meeting point of many different cultures that are of interest to one another and benefit from one another;
- there are many excellent scientific and research centres that generate new knowledge which is of importance for the whole world.

Information science and practice has a great responsibility to provide for the efficient exchange of electronic information promptly and at a high level of quality. In Middle Europe this is a very demanding mission, as until recently the area was governed by diverse kinds of governance, and even some that were opposed to each other. This legacy is reflected in a lack of standardization which is of utmost importance for successful deployment of ICT. The countries are trying hard to make up for lagging behind in computerization, which is in part also due to a negative attitude of the former regimes towards information technology. It is important that Middle European countries assist each other in specifying visions for their development and in providing prerequisites for their information society.

Successful growth and sound maintenance of information systems may in many cases depend on the logic of the economies of scale. If global monopolies in the field of information are to be avoided, cooperation beyond country borders is of the utmost importance. Professional associations of computer specialists can prepare the ground by improving personal contacts and bringing people together. This has been the mission of IT STAR from the outset and we have strong reasons to believe that we are bound to succeed. The intention is to exchange information, experience, and documents regarding all elements of transition into an information society. This will provide the grounds for assessing the best practices as well as the convergence of particular systems, such as education and the training of computer professionals, public information services, broadband lines, the role of information technologies in making politics more democratic and more.

In history there were intrepid pioneers who made the shape of Middle Europe, construction workers, followed by printers, glassmakers, railway men... Tomorrow the place of these former-driving occupations may well be taken by information professionals. It is important to understand that none of these changes happened by themselves. Rather, an actual historical challenge was the impulse that provoked a particular reaction. Middle Europe has the potential to be on the leading edge of ICT developments, provided that it makes wise moves in good time by establishing links in the area. On the other hand it may become a white patch on the map of Europe and lag behind if it renounces the potential of synergy. The IT STAR initiative will help to formulate awareness about the importance of ICT for the development of the region, it will offer grounds and suggestions for political and business decisions and – lastly, but most important – it will mercilessly criticize anyone responsible for the missed opportunities.

CONCLUSIONS

Advantages of Scandinavian countries in implementing ICT have undoubtedly risen from cooperation of informatics professionals in the region. It is very likely that such examples are to be found elsewhere and the underlying common feature of success is a tradition of common projects. A possible success of IT STAR would demonstrate that informatics professionals are able to create a development synergy even in less favourable environments and that we are not offering just a new technique, but a new understanding of a development paradigm. Following such a course would provide a rather novel additional model for the organizing and functioning of IFIP that would be applicable in many parts of the world.

An important issue in practically any collaboration is that meetings are not enough. The same issue has been raised at the first IT STAR meeting where it was agreed that the body should meet to discuss matters of common interest, that a kind of an information bulletin and a web site should be set up to demonstrate to the world that there is a life in IT STAR, and, very important, that a product should be devised of interest to most if not all members, as only this is a guarantee of a lasting interest for our common endeavour. The latter was found to be the IT PP.

As a conclusion let us add that the above described initiative is very open. It requires no substantial funding beyond the regular cost of operation of national computer societies, although it is also clear that additional funding would help. It requires no extra resources to collaborate in common projects, beyond those already at the disposal of those societies. It requires no extra administration, neither for the body, i.e. IT STAR, nor for the projects, as their administration is part of the project itself. Projects should be of a specific kind so that they can be of real use, as well as suitable for non profit-making entities such as information societies. While it seems that projects like that are not easy to find, it is an actuality that there are suitable enterprises to be found if we only look around and observe what is needed. As an example, let us point at the domain of culture, the variety of which is a European asset that is just presently coming into focus through the enlargement of the European Union. But surely there are more. The ambition of the IT STAR initiative is therefore to enhance regional collaboration, to offer a model to IFIP, and to provide a paradigm to the rest of the world that may need it and want to use it.

REFERENCES

1, http://www.ifip.org/
2. IT STAR Newsletters.
3. Niko Schlamberger, Plamen Nedkov: IT Professional Pool (A Proposal)
   Bratislava, Slovakia, 2002 (distributed, not published).
4. IT STAR Meetings Minutes.

Controlling and Enhancing the Information Society in the United States

J.A.N. LEE
IEEE Computer Society
janlee17@verizon.net

"The advent of the computer...has changed the way we do business, the way we live, the way we educate our children, and a myriad other things we do on a regular basis. So far, US Internet governmental policies have been targeted toward economic development, not toward societal impact. Efforts to create legal approaches limiting what have been determined by a minority to be the less appropriate uses of the Internet have not been wholly successful."

Key words: USA, CDA, Communications Decency, COPA, protection of Children, COPPA, regulation.

INTRODUCTION

The Internet has been a self-developing, self-directed, self-governed entity, even though in many ways it developed from a collection of networks that had more organized origins. Crossing international boundaries, individual countries have their own approaches to the control of the usage of the Internet primarily influenced by indigenous cultural beliefs and expectations. The interrelationships between Internet users and their governments is also significant, principally relying on the understanding of the responsibilities of the government to provide an environment which is in the best interests of its citizens. This is not simply a difference between a benevolent, representative governance system and a totalitarian government system, but is instead a function of the acceptance of who knows best what is best for individuals. Is it a totally utilitarian governance system or one that has respect for minority opinions and the dignity of the individual? This paper reports on the legal aspects and potential legal approaches to the governance of the Internet but concentrates on the cultural expectations of governance within one country – the United States of America.

IMPACT

Of any country in the world, the USA has probably been impacted by computing and advanced communications technologies to a greater extent, through the intrusion of those technologies into almost every aspect of the daily lives of its citizens. The computer and the computer industry found a receptive niche in a society that has always been open to new ways of doing business. Prosperity has also been kind to the USA, thereby permitting a larger proportion of the population to indulge in adding gadgets to the home and the office, mostly in the name of time-saving capabilities but often for the mere thrill of adopting novelty. The analogy of the Information Superhighway is an appropriate metaphor when one reflects that the USA has been the host to a number of revolutions that included the integration of the automobile into the American way of life. The problems arising today, in response to the demand to control the Internet, show parallels to the problems of controlling automobiles on the early, primitive roads. The primary purpose of the "rules of the road" is to create an environment in which users can more easily get from place to place with due respect to those others who have similar goals. Over the years, as automobiles have been imbued with greater capabilities, these rules have been amended to include regulations protecting users against their own indiscretions. It is rare, for example, that the failure to use a seat belt has a deleterious impact on others involved in an accident. Speeding can be dangerous to the public, but regulations on maximum speeds also seek to limit drivers to a range within the capabilities and skills of the average driver. Automobiles can be used, as can much advanced technology, for nefarious purposes, just as the telephone can be used for purposes beyond the original intentions of Alexander Bell. Just as the Polaroid camera and the camcorder provided the means to forward the proliferation of objectionable images without the potential intervention of commercial photo-developers, so the Internet can be used in ways that are not always acceptable to everyone who uses it. Yet in what manner will we be ready to accept "rules of the road" for the Internet, and to whom will we ascribe the right to make those rules?

The advent of the computer and advanced communications has changed the way we do business, the way we live, the way we educate our children, and a myriad other things we do on a regular basis. So far, US Internet governmental policies have been targeted toward economic development, not toward societal impact. Efforts to create legal approaches limiting what have been determined by a minority to be the less appropriate uses of the Internet have not been wholly successful.

Throughout the 1990s, and primarily during the administration of President Clinton and led by Vice-President Gore, numerous attempts were made to introduce legislation to regulate the impact of the content of Internet while at the same time ensuring access to information technology for all citizens.

GUIDELINES

Recall that the name of this country is the United *STATES* of America, and that differences exist between Federal and State policies, regulations, and activities. Each state is responsible for those elements of government that impact their own citizens and for which there is no need for Federal oversight. Thus the Federal government is primarily responsible for those things that deal with Inter-State commerce, social programs, and foreign relationships. Consequently, many statutes and policies reside in the domain of the locality rather than the federal government. For example, the definition of obscenity is local, based on a 1973 Supreme Court decision on the appeal of a case involving the conviction of an appellant accused of mailing unsolicited sexually explicit material in violation of a California statute. The Supreme Court provided the following "basic guidelines for the trier of fact":

(a) whether ...the average person, applying contemporary *community* standards... would find that the work, taken as a whole, appeals to the prurient interest,

(b) whether the work depicts or describes, in a patently offensive way, sexual conduct specifically defined by the applicable *state* law, and

(c) whether the work, taken as a whole, lacks serious literary, artistic, political, or scientific value. If a *state* obscenity law is thus limited, First Amendment values are adequately protected by ultimate independent appellate review of constitutional claims when necessary. [1] [Emphasis added.]

REGULATING THE INTERNET

The Communications Decency Act was enacted by the U.S. Congress in February 1996; it basically attempted to regulate the access to "inappropriate" materials by young people. The Act stated that (slightly paraphrased):

"Whoever in interstate or foreign communications knowingly--

(1) (A) uses an interactive computer service to send to a specific person or persons under 18 years of age, or

B) uses any interactive computer service to display in a manner available to a person under 18 years of age, any comment, request, suggestion, proposal, image, or other communication that, in context, depicts or describes, in terms patently offensive as measured by contemporary community standards, sexual or excretory activities or organs, regardless of whether the user of such service placed the call or initiated the communication; or

(2) knowingly permits any telecommunications facility under such person's control to be used for an activity prohibited by paragraph (1) with the intent that it be used for such activity, shall be fined ..., or imprisoned not more than two years, or both."

Initially, a special three-judge court in Philadelphia, Pennsylvania ruled on June 12, 1996 that the Communications Decency Act was an unconstitutional abridgement of rights protected by the First and Fifth Amendments to the US Constitution. The Department of Justice immediately filed an appeal with the US Supreme Court, which heard oral arguments in the case on March 19, 1997. In a landmark decision issued on June 26,1997, the US Supreme Court held that the Communications Decency Act violated the US Constitution First Amendment guarantee of freedom of speech. The Court's opinion, written by Justice John Paul Stevens, claimed that the Act comprised a censorship of the on-line medium. Commentators lauded this decision as establishing the fundamental principles that would guide any judicial consideration of the Internet for the 21st Century. A major portion of the arguments against the Act involved the proposed use of "blockers" in schools and libraries, and by Internet Service Providers that blocked more than the prescribed offensive material. Many legitimate medical advice sites were blocked as well as sites related to sex education.

In 1998, Congress introduced the Child On-Line Protection Act (COPA), which was a "Restriction of Access by Minors to Materials Commercially Distributed by Means of World Wide Web that are Harmful to Minors":

(a) Requirement To Restrict Access.--

(1) Prohibited conduct.--Whoever knowingly and with knowledge of the character of the material, in interstate or foreign commerce by means of the World Wide Web, makes any communication for commercial purposes that is available to any minor and that includes any material that is harmful to minors shall be fined not more than $50,000, imprisoned not more than 6 months, or both.

Very quickly this new law was challenged, and a temporary restraining order was filed to prevent the US Justice Department from enforcing it. The U.S. Supreme Court reversed the earlier US appeals court ruling which found the 1998 Child Online Protection Act (COPA) too broad in scope in May 2002. In an 8-1 vote, the justices ruled that the appeals court could not bar enforcement of the law on the basis that it relied on community standards to identify harmful material.

To reinstate many of the concepts within the Computer Decency Act, the Children's Internet Protection Act (CIPA) was signed into law by President Clinton in December, 2000. This law required public libraries receiving certain federal funds to: (1) adopt Internet safety policies; and (2) use mandatory filtering software to block Internet access for children and adults to materials that are obscene, contain child pornography or were deemed to be harmful to minors. The Act required that schools and libraries that receive federal funding verify that they had both "Technology Protection Measures" and an "Internet Safety Policy" in place. The Technology Protection Measure required that blockers or filters be installed to prevent access to visual depictions on the Internet that were considered to be obscene, to child pornography, or to other sexual content that is claimed to be harmful to minors. The law required that the Internet Safety Policy similarly must address access by minors to inappropriate material, and, in common with COPA, ensure the safety and security of minors when using email or other forms of electronic communication. By linking these requirements to federal funding, the Congress attempted to circumvent previous criticisms that it was not in the purview of the Federal government to regulate private institutions. However, there are very few schools or public libraries that do not receive some form of federal funding!

The American Civil Liberties Union and the American Library Association both challenged the constitutionality of CIPA and in May 2002, a three-judge panel in Philadelphia, Pennsylvania, held that CIPA is unconstitutional because the mandated use of blocking technology on all computers will result in blocked access to substantial amounts of constitutionally protected speech. The Court found that filters both overblock (block access to protected speech) and underblock (allow access to illegal or unconstitutional speech). At the same time the Court enjoined the government from withholding funds from public libraries that chose not to install blocking technology on all their Internet-ready terminals.

In June 2002, the U.S. House of Representatives voted by an overwhelming margin to pass the Child Obscenity and Pornography Protection Act of 2002 (COPPA). The bill, sought to criminalize the production, dissemination, or possession of computer-generated, or computer images that are, or are virtually indistinguishable from, child pornography. Civil liberty groups immediately warned that this new bill contained similar flaws to the Child Pornography Prevention Act (CPPA), a bill banning obscene images that "appear" to be of minors, which was declared unconstitutional by the United States Supreme Court in April 2002. COPPA criminalized as child pornography any image as long as it is, or is indistinguishable from, child pornography. This would include images in which adults were used and made to look like minors. COPPA also prohibits selling or receiving materials that are, or are advertised as, child pornography. Furthermore, in Section 5 of HR 4623, it criminalizes anyone who knowingly produces, distributes, receives, or possesses a visual depiction that is, or is indistinguishable from, a pre-pubescent child engaging in sexually explicit conduct, including drawings, cartoons, sculptures, and paintings. Several persons have been successfully prosecuted for contravening the provisions of this bill.

PRIVACY

Not to be deterred by the striking down of the CDA, the US Congress responded with the passage of the "Children's On-Line Protection Act" to control one aspect of Internet usage – the solicitation of children for immoral purposes through persons who attempt to pass themselves off as friends of children. The Children's Online Privacy Protect Act (COPPA), passed on October 23, 1998 [2], and described as "Regulating Unfair and Deceptive Acts and Practices in Connection with the Collection and Use of Personal Information From and About Children on the Internet", prescribed that (slightly paraphrased):

(1) In General.-- It is unlawful for an operator of a website or online service directed to children, or any operator that has actual knowledge that it is collecting personal information from a child, to collect personal information from a child in a manner that violates the regulations prescribed [elsewhere].

(2) ... Notwithstanding paragraph (1), neither an operator of such a website or online service nor the operator's agent shall be held to be liable under any Federal or State law for any disclosure made in good

faith and following reasonable procedures in responding to a request for disclosure of personal information ... to the parent of a child.

The Protection of Citizens' Privacy on Federal Web Sites Act [3] was passed in December 2000, primarily requiring the reporting of the collection of personal data, not the prohibition of any collection activity:
... the Inspector General of each [Federal] department or agency shall submit to Congress a report that discloses any activity of the applicable department or agency relating to --
(1) the collection or review of singular data, or the creation of aggregate lists that include personally identifiable information, about individuals who access any Internet site of the department or agency; and
(2) entering into agreements with third parties, including other government agencies, to collect, review, or obtain aggregate lists or singular data containing personally identifiable information relating to any individual's access or viewing habits for governmental and non-governmental Internet sites.

THE DIGITAL DIVIDE

There have been concerns about the accessibility of electronic information by two major communities – the socially disadvantaged and those with disabilities. On August 7, 1998, President Clinton signed into law the Rehabilitation Act Amendments of 1998 (originally passed in 1973.), which covered access to federally funded programs and services. The law required access to electronic and information technology provided by the Federal government, and required Federal agencies to ensure that this technology was accessible to employees and members of the public with disabilities to the extent it did not pose an "undue burden." It does not apply to web pages of private industry. Interestingly enough, it was not until 2001 that the White house upgraded its own site to conform to this requirement. In September 05, 2001 the Bush Administration unveiled its accessibility-improved web site, www.whitehouse.gov. The White House had come under a barrage of criticism from the disability community for deficiencies in its web site's accessibility features. The White House's web site is now accessible to people with disabilities, especially blind, visually impaired, hearing-impaired and deaf individuals, and includes a Spanish language section, multi-media components, and an area designed specifically for children (www.whitehousekids.gov). For blind and visually impaired individuals the web site is programmed so a voice synthesizer can read aloud the contents, including online forms and photo captions. For the hearing-impaired, videos of presidential events will be captioned, and efforts are underway to encode previous video with captioning.

The Digital Divide Elimination Act of 2001 [4] was introduced into the U.S. House of Representatives in July 2001. The bill would provide tax incentives to working families wanting to purchase a computer and increase the charitable deduction for technology donations.

PRESIDENTIAL EXECUTIVE ORDERS

Since the President has direct management responsibilities for the Federal government departments, he can direct that certain procedures be followed without the need for Congressional legislative actions. Two of these involve the activities of Federal departments in use of Information Technology to improve society (December 1999) [5] and the need to protect "Critical Infrastructure" (October 16, 2001) [6], both signed by President Clinton.

In using IT to improve society, Clinton suggested that studies should be undertaken to:

1. promote expanded access to higher quality, cost-effective health care to underserved rural communities and inner city clinics;
2. make "school report cards" available on the Internet;
3. to remove legal and regulatory barriers to high-quality distance learning, to increase awareness of the availability of distance learning as an alternative means of
4. education and training, and to find ways to promote the earning of
5. credentials through distance learning;
6. determine how telecommuting might be used to help more disabled Americans get jobs and to provide jobs for Americans located in geographic regions outside traditional commuting areas;
7. encourage the private sector to make web content, software, standards consistent with the Web Accessibility Initiative;
8. develop a national strategy for promoting environmental applications of information technology (such as disseminating information about manufacturing techniques that reduce pollution, and increasing the timeliness of environmental information).
9. identify services that can be delivered electronically to rural Americans and develop the policies needed to promote;
10. encourage more effective use of information technology by nonprofit organizations.

The Executive Order regarding the protection of critical infrastructure created a national policy that stated (in part): It is the policy of the United States to protect against disruption of the operation of information systems for critical infrastructure and thereby help to protect the people, economy, essential human and government services, and national security of the United States, and to ensure that any disruptions that occur are infrequent, of minimal duration, and manageable, and cause the least damage possible. The implementation of this policy shall include a voluntary public-private partnership, involving corporate and non-governmental organizations.

FEDERALLY FUNDED RESEARCH

Throughout the history of computing, even going as far back as the work of Charles Babbage, governmental funding has had a significant impact on the computing field. While some of this work has benefited the military establishment, there has always been significant fallout in the non-governmental fields. The funding of ARPANet, and NSFNet led to the Internet, and new funding is now developing the next generation, logically named "Internet2". [7]

Internet2 is a consortium led by 200 universities, working in partnership with industry and government, to develop and deploy advanced network applications and technologies, accelerating the creation of tomorrow's Internet. Internet2 is recreating the partnership among academia, industry and government that fostered today's Internet in its infancy. The primary goals of Internet2 are to:

1. Create a leading edge network capability for the national research community
2. Enable revolutionary Internet applications
3. Ensure the rapid transfer of new network services and applications to the broader Internet community.

The Federal government is playing a critical role in both support of some key technology development projects through the National Research Foundation, as well as direct collaboration with university and industry researchers investigating next generation internet technologies and infrastructures. In parallel, the Federal government has its own advanced Internet initiative, called the Next Generation Internet (NGI) initiative. The Next Generation Internet (NGI) initiative is a multi-agency Federal research and development program that is developing advanced networking technologies, developing revolutionary applications that require advanced networking, and demonstrating these capabilities on test-beds that are 100 to 1,000 times faster, end-to-end, than today's Internet. The key distinction between the NGI initiative and Internet2, however, is that NGI is led by and focuses on the needs of the Federal mission agencies, including NASA, National Institutes for Health and others.

THE US CULTURE

Beyond these special aspects of any attempt to control the Internet, the culture of the USA promotes policies that primarily favor non-governmental development of control mechanisms and the support of self-discipline through appropriate organizations. Thus it is appropriate that The Internet Corporation for Assigned Names and Numbers (ICANN) and the Internet Society (ISOC) have taken on those responsibilities that in many other countries are under governmental control.

That is not to suggest that there are not oversight opportunities within the US government, with concerns to provide the best services to the general public. The primary goals are to provide:
- Economic development through collaborative projects
- Encourage competition
- Support standards
- Get out of the way and let private enterprise do its job
- Maintain American expectations of their "way of life"
- Self-regulation rather than governmental regulation
- Independent development rather than governmental development

Within these joint governmental/free enterprise collaborations there must be concern for the risks and dangers of abridging the Constitutional Rights of people with respect to:
- Freedom of Speech (and expression);
- Privacy;
- Censorship, while at the same time looking to concerns for the protection of Children; and
- the disadvantaged, maintaining throughout consideration for impartiality and equality.

There have been significant changes in the Executive Branch attitudes towards the control of the Internet since the change of administration in 2001. Whereas the Clinton administration had a large staff in the White House Office of Telecommunications, and the Vice-President actively promoted activities to enhance information technology, the Bush White House has minimized the staffing of the Office of Telecommunications, and there is no one who is taken over the role of Al Gore.

OVERVIEW

The Internet and the content carried therein should not be treated any differently than other communications media, just in the same way that we should not treat electronic expressions any different from printed matter. In

summary we can suggest that within the US community, the overarching concerns in general are to:
- Instigate rather than create;
- Support rather than control;
- Promote rather than patronize;
- Promote competition rather than to monopolize;
- Provide diversity rather than insist on commonality; and
- Let the market find its niche.

REFERENCES:

1. US Supreme Court, MILLER v. CALIFORNIA, 413 U.S. 15 (1973), APPEAL FROM THE APPELLATE DEPARTMENT, SUPERIOR COURT OF CALIFORNIA, COUNTY OF ORANGE , No. 70-73, Argued January 18-19, 1972, Reargued November 7, 1972, Decided June 21, 1973.
2. Children's Online Privacy Protection Act of 1998, http://www.gsa.gov/attachments/GSA_PUBLICATIONS/extpub/children105_277.doc
3. Section 646, Protection of Citizens' Privacy on Federal Web Sites, Treasury and General Government Appropriations Act, 2001 (P.L. 106-554, DECEMBER 21, 2000), http://www.gsa.gov/attachments/GSA_PUBLICATIONS/extpub/section646.doc
4. The Digital Divide Elimination Act of 2001,HR 2281, statement read on the floor of the U.S. House of Representatives by Rep. Jefferson on July 2, 2001, http://www.digitaldividenetwork.org/content/stories/index.cfm?key=155
5. Use of Information Technology to Improve Our Society, THE WHITE HOUSE, Office of the Press Secretary, December 17, 1999, http://www.gsa.gov/attachments/GSA_PUBLICATIONS/extpub/31.pdf
6. Critical Infrastructure Protection in the Information Age, Executive Order 13231, THE WHITE HOUSE, Office of the Press Secretary, October 16, 2001, http://frwebgate.access.gpo.gov/cgi-bin/getdoc.cgi?dbname=2001_register&docid=01-26509-filed
7. About Internet2®, http://www.internet2.edu/html/about.html

The Information (Society) Race

László Z. KARVALICS
Information Society and Trend Research Institute,
Technical University Budapest
<zkl@itm.bme.hu

"This is the source of a paradox in dealing with the information society: it is simultaneously a sociological adventure and a daily strategic challenge, an anthropological promise and a raw commercial reality, a chance to improve the quality of life and an economic battle which hinges on gaining competitive advantage."

Abstract: This paper sets out to analyze the information competition element. Prior to a review of the roots and of the two parts of the current intensifying information society race, we will take a look at the historic prelude, the functioning of some pre-information societies – that is to say we will glean from the patterns of the making of competitive advantage in information among nations from the early high cultures to the middle of the 20th century. As a "prehistory", we will outline the emergence of the information society and its development into a competition problem: principally the movement of the American-Japanese tandem (1961-1978) and the pursuing bunch (1978-1991). And finally, we will analyze the decade (1992-2002) of comprehensive national information strategies, demonstrating that in the measurable domain of the information society there really are winners and losers: systematic information society development programs have tangible outcomes. The gap is widening, and the developed countries are winners every time. We can observe the real information society race taking place between them.

Key words: Information society, communication technology, history, competition

INTRODUCTION

When illustrating the strategic stake of the "information society" many people refer to the 1996 report of IDRC *(International Development Research Center)*. The authors of this report claim that, in the next 25 years, nine (!) out of the leading fifteen economies of our present world will fall back to the level of developing economies due to the lack of their ability to assimilate the knowledge and know-how necessary for the new communication environment. This is a challenge, others perceive, which is similar in nature to the historical relocation of the commercial routes from the Mediterranean Sea to the Atlantic Ocean. [Paquet-Sévigny, 1997]

Even if, being in possession of other data, we doubt this twister-like, rank-smashing force, it seems certain that the transformations attributed to the information society environment today demonstrate no feature or sub-field, the analysis of which would permit us to ignore the economic/commercial facet. In the meantime, our thinking is strongly bounded by the fact that we want to measure the transforming reality of the present in the light of the idealized order of the future as it relates to timeless social philosophical axes. This is the source of a paradox in dealing with the issue (or most recently: discipline) of the information society: it is simultaneously a sociological adventure and a daily strategic challenge, an anthropological promise and a raw commercial reality, a chance to improve the quality of life and an economic battle which hinges on gaining competitive advantage. That's why the term "Information Society" could become a simple rhetoric phrase, if we confuse these two aspects, and use the neutral, future-oriented everyday meaning *instead of* the competition-based strategic meaning. (We have chosen the term "race" instead of the simple "competition" to recall this negative allusion.)

Many people tend to smile upon the United States for its politicians' and pedagogues' hysterical reactions to just a few percentage-points fall in the success of American scientific education or to a slow decrease in students' relative performance in international student competitions and comparative analyses, despite the country's tower high and undoubted leading position in the information and knowledge economy. And however loud journalists may laugh at the millions of dollars spent to reverse the trend, calling these hopeless efforts a Mission Impossible, we are currently on the front line of the information society race. Strategic sensitivity enhances a sense of danger, the awareness of danger causes a pressure to act, the recognized challenge lets the field reach priority in policymakers' heads. The Clinton administration made education a question of national security since 1998, however, with this step it only followed the course of the "information highway program" launched in 1993 (attributed to Albert Gore ever since), which was in fact a disguised support of the world market competitiveness of the American information industry.

This is not the place to give a full, systematic and detailed historical overview[1]: this is but an introductory collection of examples to show the *existence* and *abundance* of those (currently) recognized information patterns. We choose not to include the fostering of information competitiveness within one state (empire or community), the information games between opposing groups, or the historical forms of information monopolies, since the close relationship between methods, professional institutions and IT-solutions chosen for the individual tasks would require common discussion in the case of another approach. Similarly, let us omit the lessons drawn from the cultural history of military and diplomatic intelligence. Instead we will focus on the amplification of the economic-social potential through a consciously planned internal information system aimed directly or indirectly at generating competitive advantage.

HISTORICAL PRELUDE:
gleaning from patterns of information competitiveness as generated among nations from the early high cultures to the middle of the 20th century

The "extension of the communicative action" is dealt with in the sense of "objectivation", the development of systems for temporary external storage and retrieval in the literature.[2] Yet innovations in information technology can also be deduced from the relations between space (physical and communal space) interconnected by communication and the time needed to carry out the connecting operations[3], as H.A. Innis convincingly demonstrated at the beginning of the 1950s [Innis, 1950, 1951]. In early imperial structures, it is very interesting, for example, to survey the osmosis of the ephemeral sets of texts and meanings, referred to as "tradition" between generations, and their code-storage media. However, the conjunctive tissues of communication within empires and the guarantee of their stability in the face of rival empires were provided by consciously developed fundamental systems of *information infrastructure* – the *information metabolism* of these societies, including the institutional forms of information production (academia), storage (library) and dissemination (communication, education).

First of all, the professional news and postal service, which turned from heralds to carrier-pigeon networks as the fastest way to deliver written records (up to the middle of the 19th century). The news and message household of Egypt and Mesopotamia involved carefully organized, painstakingly maintained and controlled channels. *Fai sát*, the highly efficient postal service of the New Empire era delivered such a great number of letters that the Pharaoh was actually required, by law, to get up early in order to read them all. A Chinese organization based on post-houses managed by the central and local powers could make the multipoint-to-multipoint sign-stream seamless in a similar way. The Persian and Roman Empires also used legendarily effective and prioritized background news industries. The medieval rebirth of the postal service, together with the cyclic *financing failures* accompanying its development, retrospectively outline the rhythm that led from the recognition of challenges stemming from outside pressures to an *increase in the recognized demand for interior communication performance*. The distinguished role of the news service, which was supported by *investment or resource redeployment* and *transitionally handled as a priority* to address this challenge[4], lapsed at the very moment when the outer pressure was relieved and the resources were needed in other subsystems. The effectiveness of the postal service reached its peak just at the time other new (partly rival) information channels (the telegraph and the telephone) were beginning to expand at the end of the 19th century.[5]

Claude Chappe's semaphore visual telegraph, a great experiment by post-revolutionary France, and one in which the French government invested heavily, came a generation before the later wire communication systems, similar to the way Minitel preceded the Internet, and remained a truncated torso in infrastructure history, likewise due to the slow adoption of more advanced new solutions. Indeed, it was the United States that began to write the next chapter of communication history with the development of its telegraph network, running parallel to transcontinental railways this system surpassed any other similar efforts both in pace and density.[6] In the next wave, at the outset of the construction of telephone networks, the champion riders of development were the free market in the Anglo-Saxon world and private enterprise, which embarked on network-building with single concession holders in other places. Meanwhile, in Germany it was *the government that put itself at the head of the telephone program*[7] – taking economic and administrative-political considerations into account.

The pace made by government and market forces in the wake of these developments can probably be best demonstrated in action in connection with the building of radio broadcasting networks[8], that great infrastructure adventure of the third decade of the 20th century. If we examine the list giving the number of radio transmission stations for each individual country in 1929 (Table 1), we can see that out of the top twenty nations in the current Information Society rankings, only Singapore, Taiwan and Israel are missing. This is no surprise, since none of these small nations existed as independent states at that time! In other words, the *"top twenty" of the present day is practically the same as seventy years ago!*

Another prominent field of fundamental information infrastructure is the library/record office/archives complex, which has, in addition to its administrative-supporting role, ever since Assur-ban-apli's great library in Nineveh, *also* been based on programs of knowledge accumulation. The competition between Hellenistic successor states (especially Alexandria and Pergamum) for the title of 'the richest library' also resurfaces in the never-ending rivalry between Italian city-states and humanistic courts. The knowledge revolution of the Renaissance emerged in its own era as luxury production and consumption, established on deep economic foundations. Directly alongside the gunpowder of philology, translated literature and the textual traditions of antiquity, this first "information boom" placed the cartridge-fuse of printing. It was able to become a generator of competitive advantage because, with its reviving fresh new waves, it created a widening transformational starting point toward technological innovation. The 15-17th centuries are those of Cardano, Leonardo and Galilei, and thus of Italy – while in Holland and England the next power/political paradigm is impending through the revolution of, among other things, public libraries.[9]

The libraries, of course, were merely "tools" serving the experts, the real vehicles of knowledge. The actual track for racing has always been these specialists (scholars, artists, diplomats, generals) and the knowledge that could be acquired through them in the form of technology transfer. The race run for the leading position in libraries still remained a friendly game compared to the unceasing battle fought for thinking people and the rush of experts (monks, students) sent abroad to study [Dedijer, 1968]. Korean specialists for example were sought after so much that one aim of Japanese campaigns and pirate attacks was just to kidnap craftsmen. (Even during the 1592-1598 war when the Japanese army invaded Korea, thousands of craftsmen were dragged to Japan). When we recall the nearly 2500-year-old story, in which the luckier ones from among those countries that contended to give shelter to the scholars hounded out by Euergetes II from the library of Alexandria, were able to launch nothing less than a knowledge-avalanche, we cannot help but recognize the fact that the United States, the great winner of the current information society race, came into possession of an exorbitant intellectual capital in the shape of immigrant Europeans, a phenomenon it repeated in several waves: after the period of pioneers, during the great immigration waves in the last third of the 19th century and in the early 20th century, then throughout the migration of the scientific elite of the period between the two world wars. We should not either forget that the production value of "...18 million German settlers was ten times higher than that of Marshall Aid [Kopátsy, 1989]."

Among the tools for the indigenous growth of knowledge capital, those processes seem the most interesting in which a nation/state could gain advantage either by a planned competitiveness program or as a non-deliberate effect of a related development. In Italy, for example: those *contuberniums* and *sodalitas* (the ancestors of later academies) that were established as "school literary and debating societies" consisting of 4-8 humanist scholars, helped the scholars in their own professional progress, explicitly developing the idea of *lifelong learning*.[10] Scholars with academic experience then became "goods" in demand throughout Europe – emperors stood in line to "hire" a well-known mastermind. Independent states in the middle of the 17th century, on the other hand, realized that, after a lot of little private academies, it was high time to establish the single, great national academy and, while constantly keeping an eye on their "rival's" academies, they set up these institutes following each other's example.

A similar "evolutionary" logic made French engineers (especially building engineers) much in demand from the end of the 18th century. From the middle of the century, Daniel-Charles Trudaine's central "drawing bureau" in Paris, recognizing that better jobs require higher qualifications, launched a special course for the best designers, led by one of the bureau's excellent engineers. This course developed into the *École des Ponts et Chaussées,* the ancestor of all later technical universities. Since these highly qualified students of the school, who therefore became much sought after and marketable, learned far more than they actually needed for their work, their unemployed "scientific valence" made them the ideal professional audience for the emerging new natural sciences.

The deliberate use of organized public education as an internal resource may date back a long time in history.[11] It was called into life and maintained by the need to train an administrative and military elite for a prolonged period, from ancient scrivener training to the hyper-specialized Sparta. The real sign of the competition factor appears with the rivalry of the slowly secularizing universities.[12]

In Japanese history, the political revolution that brought about the fall of the Tokugawa Shogunate, inaugurating an era of major political, economic and social change known as the Meiji period (1868-1912) gave the country compulsory education, which led to practically full-scale literacy by the end of the century. Most historians agree that the spectacular economic growth that modernized Japan, a land lacking natural resources, can primarily be traced to that country's investment in human knowledge resources. Similarly, historians claim the most important factor explaining the remarkably successful transformation of the structure of Danish agriculture in the last century, was in fact the cultural "deep ploughing", based on compulsory education and people's academies, which "produced" highly qualified and creative agriculturists, who remain to date the foundation of Danish welfare. We can also mention the offensive development strategy of Hungarian public education in the last third of the 19th century, which, for a long period, enjoyed the support of increasing budgetary subsidies, fixed in law by the parliament.

Among national programs for the accumulation of knowledge, Korea deserves a prominent position. In 1443, during the reign of Sejong, scholars of the *royal academy* developed Hangul (han'gul), an easy and effective *phonetic system for writing the Korean language*, considered one of the most scientific alphabets in use in any country. Before the introduction of simple phonetic symbols Koreans used Japanese symbols. However, these could only become the treasure of a few privileged aristocrats, due to the amount of time needed to acquire them. The original name of Hangul (hunmin csong-um meaning 'appropriate voices to educate the people') also indicates that it was developed as *a tool directed from above to democratize knowledge*. The easy-to-learn-and-apply alphabetic system consisting of 24 letters, including 14 consonant and 10 vowel symbols, contributed largely to a high level of literacy among Korean people and to advanced printing later on (while today it is also easily applicable in computer systems).

The above snapshot from cultural history convincingly justifies the argument that *government-led efforts to generate competitive advantage show a wide variety of forms even in pre-information periods* – and that such solutions will find and take their place (with a subtle shade of flush on their cheeks) in a new world economic environment.

PREHISTORY:
the information society emerges and becomes an issue of competition, the American–Japanese tandem (1956-1978), and the new competitors (1978-1991)

Tadao Umesao, a professor at Kyoto University, was the first to express the coming of the *"information society"* in his 1963 forecast expressing the economic headway made in the information sector. By that time, as we now know, the number of people employed in information-related jobs in the United States had long surpassed the magic 50 percent. In addition to its leading position in perceived world rankings in wired telephony, radio and television, the United States had just begun to forge ahead in content industry (mainly in the field of motion picture, animation, and rock music), and the competition takeover in the scientific research and university-based education industries was also close to coming to an end (pushing the formerly dominant British-German continental axis off the track for good).

In addition to these, the emerging computer industry also counted as an almost exclusively American "terrain".

That was the situation in which Japan, frenzied by the success of its modernization cycles, conducted by government resources under a planned-economy-like discipline, embarked upon such strategic developments as would promise comprehensive growth along the triangle of IT penetration/media consumption/industrial expansion. And though the results of these programs appeared (and will appear) to have shifted in time, by the beginning of the 70s they had provided Japan with a prominent role, as a sort of "re-versioner", yet one who after all still does not disturb the clear American supremacy. It is therefore not by chance that when the American-Japanese invitational conference was held at the Washington University, Seattle, in 1978, aiming primarily at comparing the experience gained by the two countries' information societies, the event was imbued with a spirit of collaboration and mutual search for common opportunities.

Then, from the middle of the 70s, the countries of the pursuing bunch started to regain consciousness, particularly *Canada, Sweden* and *Australia*, who found their way to the information society through the development of telecommunications (which was highly important, due to their geographical capabilities, too) involving an increase in penetration and advancement in the world of applications.

And what about Europe? The most important thing for the European Community's predecessor organizations had always been to make use of the experience, and through its own development performance, follow the footsteps of the other two world economic centers, the United States and Japan. Yet, strategic planning for the information age only commenced at the actual beginning of a continent-wide joining of forces and, in particular, subsequent to the establishment of its substantial institutional structure in the middle of the 90s. Although OECD's economic think-tank had already raised the idea of a global information society (GIS) following scientists of the "academic sector" at the end of the 60s, it was only in 1978, that the ministerial council of the common market countries launched a five-year pilot program, consisting of three major fields including the information society, and employing more than a dozen research groups. And even then, information technology had to wait until the mid-80s to take its position among these programs.

In the meantime, however, the revolution of personal computers, office automation and consumer electronics took place, and instead of the previously predicted tourism industry, it was information and communication technology (ICT) which by the end of the 80s had become the leading sector worldwide, enabling the slices of the technology-based business cake to swell – if not in equal proportion, at least permanently.

Therefore, while the markets and profits of the business forms founded on the latest technology showed relative growth as compared to earlier levels, thanks to the absolute growth of the latter, only rival manufacturers of certain product types within the same system sectors (semi-conductor producers, PC producers, software companies, system integrators) actually came into conflict with each other.

This explains why, after a while, the market-leading United States "yielded" dominance in the manufacturing of certain basic electronic components to Japan, and also why this imaginary torch was passed on after a short period to smaller "tigers", especially South Korea, which at that time was developing its semiconductor production through government intervention, as well as to Taiwan, then making headway in the manufacturing of several computer peripherals. This is further attributable to the fact that, by that time the United States had begun focusing on securing its dominant position in "third generation" products and services, leaving some of the key positions of the "second generation" to Japan through a peculiar division of labour. This global division of labour was defamed at the beginning of the 90s when it became clear that national information and communication industries would require global markets to achieve sustainable growth, together with all the consequences.

Such expansion in size required an unprecedented concentration of capital, effective and economical entry into the market demanded a new standard of product and service integration, while flexible and unbridled expansion to external markets needed comprehensive liberalization and supranational regulation standards. This explains the overwhelming wave of mergers and buying-ups we have experienced among both traditional and new players from the information, telecommunications and media industries since the beginning of the 90s. And that is also the reason why former "top" companies are forced to leap technological system levels to survive (see, for example, Microsoft's "strategic" shift toward network content provision, or the "strategic" opening of the formerly reclusive IBM). This interprets the return of the need for the "global" feature in information infrastructure, this drives governments to be the "lobbyists" for the necessary political conditions for business expansion, and this makes the buzzword "global information society" a hollow phrase which, in the political marketing of the beneficiaries of transformation, is intended to bridge structural inequalities and the widening divide, while in fact leading to the current phase of information society strategies.

THE DECADE OF COMPREHENSIVE NATIONAL INFORMATION STRATEGIES:
sprinting into the future, winners and losers (1992-2002)

Strategists of the multicultural, yet strongly authoritarian island of Singapore were considering the following at the beginning of the 90s: what is our strongest capability that we could "enhance" with the help of up-to-date information technology? If we can be successful in this field, which other fields require further information investment to enable us to "generate" new competitive advantages in addition to "traditional" ones?

It was relatively easy to address the former challenge. Singapore is a transit country that has been one of the prominent harbors of intercontinental sea trade for at least 150 years. The foremost thing therefore was to win the competition among Asian seaports – but how? They should provide the most professional and fastest service. And they did. The optical readers of the deepwater Singapore harbor (PSA, Port of Singapore Authority) can receive the necessary information, even about approaching ships, and code their containers. Then, with the help of professional crane operators, they carry out trans-shipment precisely, and at lightning speed. The accelerated customs procedure significantly decreases the waiting period per ship, so more and more companies have found it worthwhile to choose Singapore as their logistic hub. That is to say, the fundamentals were given on which the next stage of development could be constructed: to wire the population into a seamless network, to generate information-industrial expansion focusing on niche markets, and to empower a research and development potential of international standard. That's the way the 1992 Singapore "Intelligent island" program, the "father of all information strategy programs" (or new generation information society competitiveness strategies), has come into being *(A Vision of an intelligent island. IT 2000 report)*.

Since that time, nearly fifty national-scale programs have been devised following more or less similar logic and considerations. The successful strategies either evolved or "cropped up" from within traditional information-industrialization and computerization programs (and the institutions managing them), or emerged as a result of individual government (typically ministry of finance) initiatives. The former model tends to be characteristic of Asia, while the latter, with all its advantages and shortcomings, is generally seen in Europe.

The "Asian model" is inclined to proceed organically without need of new institutions, but its synthesis, the representation of social aspects, has remained rather an off chance for a long period, due to a technology-bound form of operative planning. The European model, which relies for coordination on the market instead of government agencies with a monetary approach to information strategies, preserves traditional sector boundaries better, yet its comprehensive features are weaker [Rodrigues, 2001]. All things considered, there are a number of similar features even between information strategies of faraway countries.

"Information strategy" means the new quality, which emerged at the beginning of the 90s, of political planning on various levels: national or international-regional-federal [Evans-Wurster, 2000]. The characteristic separating information strategy from its progenitors, is that information strategy raises the development of information infrastructure, the "informatization" of certain subsystems of the society and information industry development policy (IT-industry policy), out of their functions within their own sectors and, by uniting them, makes a homogenous base for long-term planning. In contrast to the former purely "coordinative" relationship, information strategy, as a central participant, adjusts the main segments of education policy, the development of telecommunication, science policy and the economy of human resources to its own targets and tasks [See Z. Karvalics, 1998].

The elaborateness and sophistication of different information strategies is extremely various. The bulk Canadian basic document is orbited by dozens of satellite-program booklets, the comprehensive Finnish strategy is accompanied by a similarly detailed strategy devised only for the educational system, while the Polish or Philippine basic documents consist of just a couple of pages. Similarly, there is a wide variety of genres: beside the precisely elaborated Japanese plans, which break down the tasks into year-long phases, the Australian strategy is content with the mere description of four possible development scenarios. Besides recommendation-like analyses (such as Gerard Théry's "Report" in France, referred to as an information strategy) we can find some countries planning implementation with an almost military discipline (e.g. South Korea). Some countries (Vietnam, Norway) plan only for five years (about until the millennium), while others, Malaysia and Japan, target 2020 and 2015 respectively.

Essentially, national information infrastructure (NII), including government information infrastructure, is the core aspect functioning as a development initiator to facilitate ideas and expectations on the social level. In consequence of the substantial uniformity of technology, national characteristics hardly appear in such programs, which review the IT-potential of healthcare, education, research & development and other fields as routinely as though they were only homework. The "teleological aspect", which deals with all these only as a tool to achieve its comprehensive vision, rarely appears: Japan, with its "intellectually creative society" program, practically sets the objective of a cultural paradigm shift, Malaysia intends to join the most developed countries through grandiose developments, while others see their perspective in creating a new quality of "welfare".

Direct objectives are relatively simple: job creation, cost reduction, increased efficiency, better practices, greater publicity, satisfied citizens. All these mainly involve similar tasks, without priorities: standardization, integration, and implementation. In order to launch local experiments, pilot projects, governments principally rely on private capital and local resources [Z. Karvalics, 1998].

It is interesting to see if we can measure the success of information society strategies in the language of numbers, based on the readiness methodology of IDC (www.idc.com). If we examine a list based on identical standpoints (the first *Information Imperative Index,* 1996) the updated data five years later (which is called *Information Society Index* in 2000), we will be able to draw conclusions through interpreting the changes (see Table 2 and Table 3 with the 2002 rankings). All the more so since the boom of the Internet and mobile telephony coincides exactly with that frame, so the selected period is not interrupted by any technological shifts.

In five years, the world slowly closes up the ranks of top information society indicators (the four basic indicators are: computers, Internet, information, society – reflecting all the relevant aspects of the information society). While in 1996 only two countries belonged to the first category (USA and Sweden), by 2000 it was 13. Five years ago Hungary's 1500 points (27th place) was only enough for the third category, but by now we stand 28th at the end of the second category with 2130 points, like the Czech Republic (we stand last but one in group B preceding Greece). That is to say, we skipped a class so that we fell back one place. Moreover, "tiny" Estonia, the Baltic States, Slovenia, Slovakia, Malta, Cyprus, and Iceland, while possessing excellent indicators are not represented on the list at all. All these clearly suggest a more comprehensive tendency: *information society indicators slowly "permeate" societies, and the gradual increase of points, at the same time, indicates a sort of equalization or levelling.*

In case of the top thirty countries we experience an average of 6-700 points of growth in five years. The "race" is very intense, especially in the upper region. In many cases, even *better-than-average point increase proved to be insufficient to prevent "backsliding":* Israel dropped back one position despite its 915-point growth, France fell 2 places despite 836 points plus, Austria ranked one place worse notwithstanding its 757-point growth.

Meanwhile a point increase close to the average of the leading countries could even cause significant advances. Malaysia's 593 points resulted in 2 places forward, China's 580 points meant 4 positions upward, Turkey jumped 3 places by 564 points plus, while 380 points also slid the Philippines up 3 positions. "Negative performance" was presented only by the United States (minus 66 points and thus losing first place) and New-Zealand (minus 74 points and falling back 8 positions), which clearly demonstrates that, in comparison to the high levels achieved earlier, it is difficult to see the way forward. But if we scrutinize some of the considerable upward movements, we will see that *only those countries that were renowned for the determination and awareness of their information society policies were able to attain above-average growth throughout five years!*

The dynamic Singapore leaped ahead 5 places by 1498 additional points, Ireland and Holland jumped 4 places by 1222 and 1129 points respectively, while Japan and Taiwan in turn sprang 3 positions forward by 1123 and 1107 points. Sweden's 1009 points were enough to take the leading position in the ranking, pushing the United States off the top. Among the leaders it is interesting to note the 2-place advances of Belgium, Portugal and Finland by their approx. 900 points plus. It is more than interesting that out of all countries Romania has come the longest way upwards to 31st place from 42nd with its 817 point advance (only to fall 3 places later in 2001...).

The message of the 2002 rankings is the sharpening struggle among the pursuers (5-13 rankings) and the highly motivated "leap-froggers" (32-41). It seems to be obvious, that a real chance for a perceptible improvement implies a higher awareness rate, which in turn engenders an information-focused development program. This accelerates IT-diffusion, and makes the density indicators higher and higher. But does it mean that the "middle" and the "end" are hopeless cases? What about the adequate strategies of the low-ranked countries? What is the answer if the question is: "informatization, what's it for"? And the most worrying side of the problem is the possible follow-up of this competitive struggle: how do we imagine the post-information (society) race?

CONCLUSIONS

- We can detect various forms of information- and knowledge-centered competitive "games" during the "first" and "second wave" periods of our History.
- If we believe in the "readiness" measurements, the world's leading countries are making fast progress in the development of their information societies in an intensified race. During the most recent period, some North-Western European and South-East Asian states have emerged as top tier countries, while we can detect the serious advantage of the small countries.

- Although even the poorest countries can display signs of growth, nonetheless, their distance in points from the leaders still widens. The slowdown of declination is expected to occur in the second part of the next five-year period, but the narrowing tendency of the divide may only commence during the cycle after that. The only real "re-versioners" to jump are Malaysia, Turkey and South Africa.

- A consciously planned, systematic information strategy devised on the level of government programs is not a marketing effort, but an "investment in the future" capable of producing real results. Otherwise, information society building success is not "time-proof", unless there are permanent development cycles, driving the process onto the next step and steps beyond.

REFERENCES

Assmann, Jan (1992): *Das kulturelle Gedachtnis. Schrift, Erinnerung und politische Identitat in frühen.* Hochkulturen Verlag C.H. Beck, München, 1992

Chandler, Alfred D.Jr. – Cortada, James W. (eds.): *A nation transformed by information. How information has shaped the United States from Colonial times to the present,* Oxford University Press, Oxford, New York

Dedijer, Stefan (1968): Early migration In: Adams, Walter (ed.): *The Brain Drain,* London, pp. 9-28

Evans, Philip – Wurster, Thomas S. (2000): *Blown to bits. How the new economics of information transforms strategy,* Harvard Business School Press, Boston

Innis, Harold. A (1950): *Empire and Communication,* University of Toronto Press

Innis, Harold. A (1951): *The Bias of Communication,* University of Toronto Press

Klaniczay, Tibor (1993): *A magyarorszagi akademiai mozgalom elotortenete (The Pre-History of the Hungarian Academia),* Balassi Kiadó, Bp. p.8.

Kopátsy, Sándor (1989): A civilizacios orokseg megnovekedett jelentosege (*The emerging importance of the civilization heritage*) In: *Trendek magyar modra OMIKK,* pp. 94-105.

Mann, Charles C. (1995): Email by any other name... Inc. *Technology Summer 1995,* Vol.17. Issue 4, p54.

Paquet-Sévigny, Thérése 1997: Convergence of Visions: a condition of effective partnerships in a multilateral and multicultural environment In: *Info-ethics.* Conference papers Monte-Carlo UNESCO, 1997

Radioamateur, (1929): A summary of the list. (In Hungarian) *Rádióamator* Vol 4. Issue 9. Sept. p. 502.

Rodrigues, Maria Joao (2001): *The New Knowledge Economy in Europe. A Strategy for International Competitiveness and Social Cohesion.* Edgar Elgar Publishing, Cheltenham, Northampton

Vekerdi, László (1971): A "tortenelem elotti idok" muveszete (The Art of Prehistory) In: *Befejezetlen jelen Magveto,* Bp.

Z. Karvalics, László (1998): Information Society Visions: from the early utopias to the adequate government-level strategic planning methods In: *Informatization et anticipations. Information Society: Looking ahead.* Proceedings, Strasbourg, France, June 10-12 pp. 63-74.

---

[1]   For the relevance of the information history-based overview, see Chandler-Cortada (2000).

[2]   See Assmann (1992) adapted from Echlich and Lotman.

[3]   In the 30s, Robert Albion, an American economic historian, used his "space-annihilating communication revolution" concept to deduce the whole American industrial revolution from communication technology as the "single and most important factor".

[4]   The Japanese postal service, which always operated at considerable loss, only received sufficient funds at the beginning of the 20th century, during the period of Japanese imperial expansion. By the way, in Southeast Asia, the three city-states of Taiwan, Singapore and Hong Kong had already taken their places among the top three in information infrastructure (especially via their prominent positions gained along cable-laying routes) at the end of the 19th century, besides Japan and Korea. We should not disregard this issue when we attempt to reconstruct their later successful information society stories.

[5]   Charles C. Mann, astonished by the fact that in 1890 the old Verdi and his librettist, Arrigo Boito often wrote 3-4 letters daily to each other, is inclined to recognize the archetype of email, which praises the advanced postal service of North Italy (especially Milan, proud of its five delivery cycles each day). (Mann, 1995) Milan, by the way, claimed to have the most advanced postal service even in the Middle Ages: they indicated the date (day and hour) of departure and delivery on letters, and they also used "up-to-date privacy policies" (the violation of the secrecy of correspondence was punished with death). It was the Berlin dispatch-tube launched in 1876 that achieved unsurpassable speed with its 15-minute delivery speed.

[6]   US Congress first voted to allocate $30,000 in March 1843 to drive further development.

[7]   The main ambition of the German Postmaster General Stephan, the leading ideologist and director of "telephony", however, was not to establish networks in big cities, but to connect smaller townships to telegraph-stations in order to be able to deliver telegraph messages from there via the much cheaper telephone. While in 1879, America had 20 city telephone networks, Berlin only opened its first one in 1881, yet, by that time there had already been about 1200 smaller rural telephone offices operating in Germany (the prototype of Infobahn itself!).

[8]   Note that the German people's wireless set program of the 30s contained the combined elements of the broadcasting network and the industry development program, which promoted the mass production of cheap end-devices. The Russian solution based on wired broadcasting was also very similar.

9   Just to "run through" the story: by the beginning of the 20th century, the public libraries of the United States became the epicenter of development, making the fact exciting that the Universal Decimal Classification "software" appears and spreads as an American development at the end of the 19th century.

10 The life of humanists is nothing else than a constant colloquium." Eugenio Garin cited by Klaniczay (1993).

11 Organized education, however, is an older phenomenon than government itself. According to Vekerdi (1971), the "perfection of prehistoric cave pictographs in itself is enough to suggest a sort of artist education"... based on the sketch stones, the several followers appearing next to the master, and the corrections made by the master...

12 The ranking of "Italy – 15-17th century – German-speaking world 18-20th century – United States of America – from the mid-20th century" outlines the "competition axis" of advanced knowledge production. It is noteworthy that American universities took the lead only much after attaining a leading position in infrastructure indicators.

Table 1: Number of radio transmitting stations in 1929 [Radioamateur, 1929]

Ranking	Country	Radio stations
1.	United States of America	648
2.	Canada	78
3.	Sweden	30
4.	Germany	28
5-6.	England	20
	Australia	20
7.	New-Zealand	14
8.	France	13
9-10.	Belgium	12
	Uruguay	12
11.	Japan	11
12.	Norway	9
13.	Finland	7
14.	Czech Republic	6
15-19.	Austria	5
	Italy	5
	Holland	5
	Poland	5
	Switzerland	5
20-21.	India	3
	Denmark	3
22.	Ireland	2
23-32	Danzig	1
	Yugoslavia	1
	Ceylon	1
	Cuba	1
	Estonia	1
	Hong Kong	1
	Indochina	1
	Morocco	1
	Peru	1
	Hungary	1

Table 2. The information society points competition: development rankings
by World Times, 1996 and 2000

Information Imperative Index 1996			Information Society Index 2000		
Rank	Country	Points	Rank	Country	Points
1	United States	5,107	1	Sweden	5,062 ↑
2	Sweden	4,003	2	Unites States	5,041
3	Denmark	3,842	3	Finland	4,577 ↑
4	Norway	3,755	4	Norway	4,481
5	Finland	3,722	5	Denmark	4,336
6	Australia	3,704	6	Canada	4,336
7	Canada	3,494	7	Netherlands	4,230
8	Switzerland	3,459	8	Switzerland	4,174
9	New Zealand	3,363	9	Australia	4,129
10	United Kingdom	3,148	10	Japan	4,093 ↑
11	Netherlands	3,099	11	Singapore	4,014 ↑
12	Germany	2,970	12	United Kingdom	3,807
13	Japan	2,970	13	Germany	3,558
14	Hong Kong	2,893	14	Hong Kong	3,484
15	Austria	2,640	15	Belgium	3,419
16	Singapore	2,516	16	Austria	3,397
17	Belgium	2,475	17	New Zealand	3,289
18	France	2,296	18	Taiwan	3,177 ↑
19	Israel	2,225	19	Ireland	3,144 ↑
20	Italy	2,070	20	Israel	3,140
21	Taiwan	2,053	21	France	3,140
22	Korea	2,008	22	Korea	2,931
23	Ireland	1,922	23	Italy	2,703
24	Spain	1,872	24	Spain	2,533
25	UAE	1,618	25	UAE	2,301
26	Czech Rep	1,528	26	Portugal	2,199 ↑
27	Hungary	1,500	27	Czech Republic	2,130
28	Greece	1,377	28	Hungary	2,130
29	Portugal	1,301	29	Greece	2,033
30	Argentina	1,215	30	Poland	1,808
31	Chile	1,181	31	Romania	1,679 ↑
32	Poland	1,159	32	Chile	1,677
33	Bulgaria	1,069	33	Argentina	1,651
34	Venezuela	1,050	34	Costa Rica	1,635 ↑
35	South Africa	1,043	35	Malaysia	1,583 ↑
36	Russia	1,041	36	Bulgaria	1,578
37	Malaysia	990	37	Panama	1,539
38	Brazil	961	38	South Africa	1,537
39	Costa Rica	952	39	Venezuela	1,491
40	Panama	918	40	Russia	1,444
41	Mexico	871	41	Saudi Arabia	1,362
42	Romania	862	42	Brazil	1,354
43	Saudi Arabia	850	43	Ecuador	1,314
44	Colombia	755	44	Mexico	1,286
45	Thailand	725	45	Turkey	1,259 ↑
46	Ecuador	695	46	Colombia	1,136
47	Jordan	695	47	Philippines	1,012 ↑
48	Turkey	695	48	Thailand	1,010
49	Peru	651	49	Jordan	942
50	Philippines	632	50	Egypt	931
51	Egypt	586	51	China	915 ↑
52	India	435	52	Indonesia	888
53	Indonesia	387	53	Peru	877
54	Pakistan	371	54	India	871
55	China	335	55	Pakistan	719

Table 3. The 2002 IDC Information Society Index with sub-categories

Country	Rank in 2000	Computer Score		Internet Score		Information Score		Social Score		Score 2002
Sweden	1	815	6	2,622	1	2,265	8	1,385	4	7,087
Norway	2	812	7	2,312	4	2,267	7	1,542	1	6,932
Switzerland	7	849	4	2,478	3	2,215	11	1,137	12	6,679
United States	4	1,362	1	2,004	10	2,167	14	1,099	17	6,632
Denmark	5	743	13	2,170	7	2,486	3	1,213	10	6,612
Netherlands	10	770	12	1,898	12	2,490	2	1,317	7	6,474
UK	6	782	10	2,224	6	2,292	5	1,139	11	6,437
Finland	3	671	14	2,132	9	2,283	6	1,337	6	6,422
Australia	8	797	9	2,302	5	1,892	22	1,350	5	6,341
Taiwan	18	581	19	1,852	14	2,602	1	1,257	9	6,292
Hong Kong	15	868	3	1,770	16	2,229	10	1,388	3	6,255
Japan	11	819	5	1,754	17	2,176	12	1,394	2	6,143
Singapore	9	800	8	2,504	2	1,953	21	810	33	6,067
Canada	12	1,001	2	2,140	8	1,805	25	1,093	18	6,039
Germany	13	623	17	1,902	11	2,248	9	1,134	13	5,907
Austria	14	660	15	1,884	13	2,175	13	1,123	15	5,842
Poland	30	247	37	436	35	1,359	30	834	32	2,875
Argentina	31	325	31	450	33	1,160	33	841	31	2,776
Chile	33	314	33	436	36	1,038	39	844	30	2,632
Panama	37	377	27	422	37	1,067	37	765	35	2,631
Bulgaria	34	169	46	308	44	1,230	32	919	28	2,625

The ISI includes 23 indicators measuring the capacity of a nation's citizenry to exchange information internally and externally.

Computer infrastructure: PC installed per capita/ Home PC's shipped per household/ Government and commercial PC's shipped per professional workforce/ Education PC's shipped per student and faculty member/Percentage of networked PCs/ Software and hardware spending

Internet infrastructure: Amount of eCommerce/ No. of Internet home users/ No. of Internet education users

Information infrastructure: Telephone lines per household/ Telephone faults/lines /Cost of local telephone call/ Television owneship per capita/ Radio owneship per capita/ Fax ownership per capita/ Cellular phones per capita/ Cable subscribers

Social infrastructure: Secondary school enrollment/Tertiary school enrollment/Newspaper readership/ Press freedom/ Civil liberties

PART 2 – THE INFORMATION SOCIETY: ISSUES OF MAJOR CONCERN

The Relation of Computers and Work

Peter MAMBREY
Fraunhofer-FIT Institute for Applied Information Technology
Mambrey@fit.fraunhofer.de

> *"Twenty five years ago this rapid development and its dramatic changes were partially foreseen by activists starting to discuss the questions of the interference between computers, humans and work ... A quarter of a century later it is now time to ask whether the problems they discussed are settled and/or obsolete, or whether they still exist and have become even more urgent, perhaps through the addition of new ones."*

Key words: Computers and work, participatory design, computers and society, quality of working life.

THE WORKING GROUP (WG) "COMPUTERS AND WORK" - AIMS AND PURPOSES

The IFIP Technical Committee 9 Working Group "Computers and Work" was founded upon the recognition that computerisation poses significant opportunities and threats for those who work with information and communications technologies. It was in 1977. Since its inception the WG seeks to understand and advance the interests of workers throughout the design and use of computer systems. This was due to the work of Harry Braverman [1974] who stated that computerisation could establish a new relation of power within organisations. In this perspective the computerisation of work was seen as a threat for the workers. The introduction of IT could lead to dislocation, de-skilling and less influence on their own work. It aims at the exploitation of living human labour. In consequence new concepts of human work and qualification have to be developed and the democratic rights of co-determination have to be strengthened.

Neutrality of technology was considered to be a management myth: computers are not artefacts, neutral machines, but a medium which establishes a new relationship between users and the work place, and this relationship is due to design. Therefore the WG focuses on the design of new work practices: the roles designers, managers and workers play during design and the different ways to design: including the different perspectives of those who are affected by design or excluding voices.

In pursuit of these aims, the Working Group is not attempting to establish itself as a separate field of study. Rather, it aims to serve as an international, interdisciplinary communications and organising forum at the intersection of other larger and more established communities of interest - most notably and in no particular order:

- computer supported co-operative work (CSCW);
- information systems research;
- feminist research;
- computer human interaction (CHI);
- social issues in computing;
- participatory design (PD);
- sociology of work and others.

The Working Group needs to draw upon the ideas and initiatives in these other areas and at the same time bring work-oriented perspectives to them.

A short statement about the current status of our domain

An important aspect of early Working Group activities was cooperation between researchers and unions, especially on design issues. This is seen in the first WG 9.1 conference, Systems Design For, With, and By the Users, which represented an important event in the development of Participatory Design. Since then the focus of WG 9.1 has widened. Today, computer use is a common activity in everyday life. Yet, for the most part, those who design computer system hardware and software remain puzzled by, and often ignorant of the conditions of use by those on the non-technical side of the digital divide. The Participatory Design Conferences, held biannually since 1990, are committed to bringing together researchers and practitioners from the humanities, social sciences, and applied sciences to report on ideas and explore new ways of applying these ideas together. The conferences and their written record in proceedings, journal articles, books and special journal issues, have been rooted in the idea that understanding the use of technology is essential for informing design. In particular the conferences have argued that people who use technology should actively participate in the design and development of the products and services they use.

The main issues in our domain

- Developing approaches, methods and tools for inclusive system design;
- Fostering the mutual understanding between designers and users;
- Establishing a platform for the exchange of ideas and best practices of different cultural ways of system development;
- Privacy - Especially the permanent threat of privacy through networked ICT is a lasting concern and topic of discussion, particularly since the twin necessities of collaborative remote work transparency and control are increasingly seen as a Janus head;
- Monitoring the activities to promote ICT in our societies, e.g. the European Policy Framework for eWork. There needs to be an ongoing discussion if the goals of the Lisbon strategy of the EC for the next decade are to be implemented in work practice: "to become the most competitive and dynamic knowledge-based economy capable of sustained economic growth with more and better jobs and greater social cohesion." http://www.eto.org.uk.

The Working Group will continue to organise conferences, which aim at discussing and exploring solutions for better work practices in a knowledge economy. The dissemination of experiences is the core of group activities.

COMPUTERS AND WORK – A RAPIDLY EVOLVING RESEARCH AND DEVELOPMENT AREA

On May 16, 2003 the author searched the Internet for hits for "computers AND work" using the search engine Google. After less than a second the search engine found 6.650.000 hits. This impressive result shows how broad this field of interest is. The field has exploded in the last 40 years and nobody can overlook all the facets of this topic. In the Green Paper "Living and Working in the Information Society: People First" [COM-96-389] the European Commission (EC) states that we are living through a historic period of technological change. The societal changes brought about by the development and widening applications of information and communications technologies (ICT) are dramatic, especially in the last decade. This technical revolution enhances efforts in restructuring the economy and the organization of work as well as other aspects of life. It is expected that this process will be both different from and faster than anything we have seen before. Using the potentials of raising flexibility and mobility, it is a huge threat to the existing situation and a huge potential for wealth creation, higher standards of living, working, and better services. But there will be winners and losers and new stratifications between supra-national organizations, national states, and regions and within all those entities.

This development is accompanied by a process of globalization, which increases the level of interdependence and intensifies global networking. As we all experience, ICTs are an integral part of our daily life, providing us with tools and services in our homes, at our workplaces in schools and especially in our leisure time. The Information Society, as a guiding vision for future development of ICT and their application [Computerization Committee, 1972], is nowadays not a society far away in the future, but a reality in daily life. It is adding a new dimension of growing importance to society: the production of goods as well as services is becoming more and more knowledge based. Comparable to the changes to working life, work organizations and productivity caused by the division of labour it is assumed that the division of knowledge will fuel societal innovation and change for the coming decades. The European Commission is aware of the challenges caused by this development. The speed of introduction and adoption of ICTs varies between countries, regions, sectors, industries and enterprises. The benefits, in the form of prosperity, and the costs, in the form of the burden of change, are unevenly distributed between different parts of the European Union and between citizens. This is not only specific for Europe but also, and even more threatening, for less developed countries as well. People are worried and demand answers to questions about the impact of ICTs. Their concerns can be summarized [COM-96-389, 3] in two main questions:

-   The first concerns employment: Will these technologies not destroy more jobs than they create? Will people be able to adapt to the changes?
-   The second question has to do with democracy and equality: Will the complexity and the cost of the new technologies not widen the gaps between the industrialized and less developed areas, between the young and the old, between those who have the knowledge and those who have not?

The 1996 Green Paper aimed at stimulating the debate on the Information Society to focus on the key issues of the organization of work, employment and social cohesion. This leads from statistical questions about the number of new jobs / losses to questions of organizing new workplaces and the quality of work. Current activities try to summarize the implementations and shifts towards "eWork". This includes continued development of telework, with its opportunities of raising flexibility in time and place. And it includes a greater concern for the "quality of work" and anticipates the changes in work for most people as new wireless and display technology change office equipment and design, and as the nature of work itself changes in a knowledge economy where creativity and innovation became more important than simple productivity in routine tasks [eWork, 2001].

THE HISTORIC DIMENSION – DISCUSSIONS ABOUT COMPUTER AND WORK IN THE 1980's – A LOOK BACK

Twenty-five years ago this rapid development and its dramatic changes were partially foreseen by activists starting to discuss the questions of the interference between computers, humans and work. They were mostly from academia and some were working for or with trade unions. The discussions they had and topics they raised are still of great interest today. A quarter of a century later it is now time to ask:
- Are the problems they discussed settled?
- Are the problems obsolete now?
- Do they still exist?
- Are they more urgent than before?
- Which new problems have arisen?

In 1979, at the second Conference on Human Choice and Computers Heinz Zemanek mentioned the state of art dealing with the human-computer relation within IFIP: "We still have, however, to convince a couple of IFIP pessimists of the usefulness of the committee and its working groups, pessimists, who would prefer IFIP to remain restricted to purely technical work" [Zemanek, 1980]. This reluctance to integrate societal questions into the design of hardware and software remained within IFIP, as in other professional organizations at a national level. In most of the national or international science communities of computer professionals the discussion of possible negative or unknown societal impacts of computing either did not take place or played a minimal role. Negative impacts were ignored. Despite that, the political system reacted by funding research and development in Technology Assessment and Technology Forecasting e.g. in the USA, The Netherlands, Denmark, Germany etc. These are some of the countries where institutions were established to scientifically answer questions related to the societal consequences of the introduction of the new technology. In Germany, for example, these conferences on Human Choice and Computers were very well perceived and had impact on those politicians and officers who were responsible for the funding of research and development on national level. As a result research programs were established to influence the ongoing process of enculturation of ICT into society [Alemann & Schatz, 1986].

Not the professional elite as a whole but only a few scientists, societal groups and politicians were concerned about these new technologies, well aware that new or improved technology does not mean simultaneously societal or individual progress. It was the time of disillusionment with technological progress and awareness of its societal risks: nuclear risks (accidents in power plants and problems of storage of radioactive wastes), "limits to growth", resource shortages, energy crisis and environmental pollution. In particular, the anti-nuclear movements in Denmark, Sweden, or Germany at this time showed that a narrow disciplinary focus on technology was overrun by much wider perspectives aiming at the usefulness of a technology for society as a whole.

At the same conference Fred Margulies argued, that the computer, in his opinion, constitutes the most important, most powerful, most human-oriented and most revolutionary tool ever created by mankind. "It is bringing about more changes in our lives that we are usually aware of. It tends to attack taboos and to extend activities beyond the border lines." [Margulies, 1980]. He pointed out clearly the main concerns against the introduction of computing. He saw a twofold menace for the labour force through computerization, namely, it threatens to take their jobs away and leave them unemployed or it may downgrade their present qualifications, leaving them with jobs even more boring and less satisfying. He concluded that there are human choices to computerization but they should not be taken by scientists or politicians but by the people themselves: "not for the people but with the people". One should realize "that in looking for alternative work organizations we must not try to design systems for other human beings to fit in. If we want to improve the quality of working life, if we want to humanize work, our main target should be to give the people concerned the maximum amount of freedom and self-determination" [Margulies, 1989].

And by his speech he formulated the credo for the Working Group 9.1 "Computers and Work" and lots of similar activities known as Participatory Design or Scandinavian Approach still going on in this century: "My understanding is that the social consequences of technological and economic development, to a very high degree, are being decided on plant level, or sociologically speaking, at the basis. It is essentially the question of how far the workers and employees are given the possibilities to influence those decisions, to participate in all decisions concerning work organization, investments, technologies etc. Industrial democracy by that description seems to constitute one of the main prerequisites for human choice. It can only be brought about if all those really interested in technological progress and in well-functioning man-machine systems, if engineers, social scientists, workers and trade unions all in their own well-founded interest will work together. Industrial democracy and human choice, to my mind, essentially means finding new solutions not for the people but with the people" [Margulies 1980, p. 16].

COMPUTERS AND THE TRANSFORMATION OF WORK(ING LIFE)

A series of conferences, at the international and national levels, discussed in detail questions of "the human side of information processing" [Björn-Andersen, 1980]. From the beginning, the use of ICT was discussed per organizational and system level: how can this technology help to design better organizations and jobs, how can organizational change be introduced? And since the beginning there was careful discussion on the role of the system designers as agents of change and as those who decide what the remaining jobs would look like [Mambrey & Schmidt-Belz, 1983]. There is until now an ongoing discussion on the role of the designer in system design. Should the designer act as a neutral facilitator or as a missionary pursuing specific goals? Hedberg [1978] advises that designers should adjust their roles; they should be reluctant to provide organizations with goals and to assist them in problem solving because the amount of rational within organizations is often overestimated. Most organizations invent their goals after the fact in order to explain what they have been doing [Weick, 1969]. "Designers who want organizations to behave more rationally – as they do in the textbooks – can cause serious problems by providing problem-solving systems for action-taking organizations, and by overstating the directive role of organizational goals" [Hedberg, 1980]. The politically and ethically based position of Margulies who sees designers developing human-centred systems which assist industrial democracy as a common goal, is augmented by Hedberg who argues functionally. He sees a lack of rationality (Lindberg's "muddling through") and the need for self-organization for an organization to survive and succeed in a changing environment. This assumption, following biological metaphors of an organization (living, surviving, learning, developing, shrinking) totally contradicts the assumptions on the role of designers as change agents for organizations in Business Process Reengineering approaches developed later by Hammer and Champy [2001]. They follow mechanical metaphors of an organization and see organizations as mechanical rational systems that can be decomposed and recomposed and thereby rationally constructed.

Pettigrew [1980] promoted his understanding of organizations as political systems being influenced by interest groups, which form within organizations around a variety of axes and for a variety of reasons. These interest groups all have different preferences and objectives; there is not "the" organizational goal identifiable and implementable into socio-technical systems. As a key requirement for system designers, Pettigrew sees their capacity to understand and influence the political processes surrounding their attempts to create change. Here the designers act mainly as communicators – as medium making goals and perspectives explicit and open for a joint bargaining process amongst the participants. In accordance with this thought, Hedberg argues that system designers should only rarely design information systems, because the design should be turned over to the people who use and need information systems. "Computer specialists can act as translators and facilitators, and information analysts can help people in organizations to structure and grasp their information flow. But systems design should evolve from within organizations" [Hedberg 1980, 28].

This position takes the organizational level as the arena for design and redesign, where different interest groups interfere in the shaping, enculturation and further development of a technical application within an organization. Briefs [1980] stresses the more general perspective on a macroeconomic level. For him, computerization is intimately linked to the conditions of economic stagnation and crisis. It is a management strategy to react to unfavourable conditions in the environment of organizations. "In a social system which is based on the exploitation of living human labour this strategy produces overwhelming negative consequences for the working class. Trade unions will have to defend the interests of the working class by an enlargement of collective bargaining and by a policy to promote full employment. Furthermore they will have to develop new concepts of human work and qualification. A further prerequisite is a thorough democratization of production and control in the economy" [Briefs, 1980, 53]. This position insists that designers work within a societal framework, which determines, to a remarkable degree, their work and restricts their autonomy or freedom to act. The first twenty years of research on the relation of computers and work were dominated by research in specific areas (figure 1).

Figure 1: Constant research areas in the field of computer and work

Automation, unemployment and job creation
Codetermination rights
Computers and the quality of working life
Health hazards
Job satisfaction; job enlargement, job enrichment
Industrial democracy
Privacy and autonomy
Surveillance
Access
Equity: distribution of wealth and resources
Individual responsibility and ethical judgment

Often research was biased in visions of future work as an Utopia or a Dystopia (options and risks; opportunities and threats etc.). The main questions were and still are:

- Who or what regime determines the way that work is organised, with what material outcome?
- Who or what regime determines work practice, with what material outcome?
- Who or what regime determines the way people communicate, with what material outcome?
- Who or what regime coordinates people, with what material outcome?
- Who or what regime determines the skill level, with what material outcome?
- Who or what regime determines the time and location of work, with what material outcome?
- How can designers help users to shape technology and work practice according to their needs?

Actors and regimes framed the space for applications of computers and work: actors who acted within a given arena and regimes that determined and framed but did not prescribe the freedom of action for individuals and groups. A lot research activity was undertaken to answer these questions [Greenbaum & Kyng, 1991]. Especially ethnographic field methods as analytical tools for design [Suchman, 1987] and participatory approaches as action research strategies [Briefs, Ciborra, & Schneider, 1983] became new paradigms in socio-technical system design [Schuler, Namioka, 1993]. The ambivalence of technological development for employees and working life was the main concern during this time [Doherty et al., 1987].

FROM TELEWORK TO NETWORKED WORK

The visions of computer use, its problems or societal impact during the early period of discussions about computers and work, were based on the use of computers for office work, clerical work, located at a well defined place and to a fixed time. The cooperative aspect of networking people was low, the dyadic relation dominated, and one can see it in the headlines for this topic: humans and computers, computers and work, computers and society. Computers stood alone at the workplace and were visible "big as behemoths filling a room".

At the end of the 90s, in different countries, the discussion about telework started. It became very clear that a new period in the relation of computers and work had begun with new options to shape work, organisation and work practice and with new risks in decreasing the number and quality of jobs [Clement, Kolm, & Wagner, 1993].

New metaphors for the technology appeared: disappearing computers, ubiquitous computing, and ambient computing. And new metaphors for work and organisation appeared: virtual work, networked work, telework, virtual organisation etc. The computer was transformed from a technical artefact to a medium coordinating people and processes. It lost face, place and time – the network dimension of computing began. In their preface to the book about telework, Korte et al. [1988] reported on the new dimensions caused by telework for structure, routine, and the content of office work. The increased implementation of telework for these will imply extensive structural changes in companies and at the work place. By linking office automation with telecommunications, telework will allow considerable decentralisation of office work, with regard to both its location and organisational control. The new perspectives and aspects of telework were discussed in depth: economically, organisationally, legally, socially, psychologically [Korte et al., 1988]. The perspectives with regard to the relationship 'computer and work' dramatically evolved:

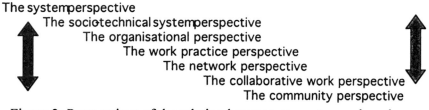

The system perspective
  The sociotechnical system perspective
    The organisational perspective
      The work practice perspective
        The network perspective
          The collaborative work perspective
            The community perspective

Figure 2: Perspectives of the relation between computers and work

Recently, new methods of work and work organisation are being discussed. Especially within the context of Electronic Commerce, the research and development of new methods of work attracts a considerable amount of research funding of the European Commission. In 2000, the Member States of the European Union adopted a strategy for accelerated development of the knowledge economy with the objective for Europe "to become the most competitive and dynamic knowledge-based economy in the world, capable of sustained economic growth, with more and better jobs, and greater social cohesion" [European Commission, 2001]. Networked computers and networked work give options to:
- New action spaces;
- New knowledge spaces;
- New types of cooperation and coordination of processes and persons.

This raises new questions, in addition to the well known areas of change, and requires new regulations and practices concerning:
- Trans-local forms of working and organisation, virtual organisations;
- Trans-local forms of codetermination and participation;
- Group growth, awareness and alienation;
- Computer based assistance and human functions in organisations;
- The role of coordinating mechanisms in virtual organisations;

- Global working (24 hours and 7 days);
- ...

In recent research, the economic dimension is more often in focus than the social dimension of work. And, furthermore, the focus on networked work, especially on assisting technologies (hardware, software, and protocols) often neglect, that "it is labour that remains the source of productivity, innovation, and competitiveness" [Castells, 2001, 90]. Martin Carnoy [2000] has documented the transformation of labour in the new networked economy: self-employment, part-time work, temporary work, subcontracting, and consulting are expanding in all advanced economies. As a general trend, following Castells, the "organization man" is out and the "flexible woman" is in. He mentions the requirements of work in the economy: labour must be able to reprogram itself into skills, knowledge, and thinking, according to changing tasks in an evolving business environment, as well as constant re-training and re-learning processes that continue throughout adult life. Castells sees a revival of work autonomy [Castells, 2001, 92] the possibility of organizing work beyond Taylor.

Actual tasks and research fields enrich the preliminary questions raised in figure 1.

Figure 3: Actual tasks and research fields (enriching fig. 1)

How can we shape:
- Virtual working environments for collaborative work;
- Knowledge division within virtual organisations;
- Keeping knowledge in an organisation;
- Augmenting glocal (= global and local) work;
- Technology and laws to avoid overall transparency and control;
- Collaborative communities, community building;

Despite these open questions we all use computers, networks and communication facilities for our work. Are we forced to use this technology? Who forces us? Are the concerns not really strong enough? Do we personally see more opportunities than threats from networked work? The main question still remains open: do computers enhance or degrade the quality of working life?

REFERENCES

Alemann, Ulrich von; Schatz, Heribert (ed.) (1986): *Mensch und Technik. Grundlagen und Perspektiven einer sozialverträglichen Technikgestaltung.* Westdeutscher Verlag Wiesbaden.

Björn-Andersen, Niels (ed.) (1980): *The Human Side of Information Processing.* Proceedings of the Copenhagen Conference on Computer Impact – 78 October 25-27, 1979 North-Holland Amsterdam, New York, Oxford 1980.

Braverman, Harry (1974): *Labor and Monopoly Capital.* Monthly Review Press, New York.

Briefs, Ulrich 1980: The Impact of Computerization on the Working Class and the Role of the Trade Unions. In: Björn-Andersen, Niels (ed.) (1980): *The Human Side of Information Processing.* op. cit., pp 53-68.

Briefs, Ulrich; Ciborra, Claudio; Schneider, Leslie (eds.): *System Design For With And By The Users.* North Holland. Amsterdam et al. 1983

Carnoy, Martin (2000): *Sustaining in the New Economy: Work, Family and Community in the Information Age.* Harvard University Press Cambridge MA.

Castells, Manuel: The Internet Galaxy. Reflections on the Internet, Business, and Society. Oxford University Press 2001.

Clement, Andrew; Kolm, Paul; Wagner, Ina (eds.) (1993): *NetWORKing: Connecting Workers In and Between Organizations.* Elsevier (North Holland) Amsterdam et al.

COM (96)389, July 1996: Green paper – Living and Working in the Information Society: People First.

Computerization Committee (1972): *The Plan for Information Society – A National Goal Toward Year 2000.* Final Report. Japan Computer Usage Development Institute May 1972.

Docherty, Peter et al.(eds.) (1987): *System Design for Human Development and Productivity: Participation and Beyond.* North Holland. Amsterdam et al.

European Commission 2001: New Methods of Work & Electronic Commerce http://www.cordis.lu/ist/ka2/welcome.html

eWork 2001: Status Report on New Ways to Work in the Knowledge Economy. September 2001

Greenbaum, Joan; Kyng, Morten (1991) (eds.): *Design At Work. Cooperative Design of Computer Systems.* Lawrence Earlbaum Ass. Hillsdale NJ.

Hammer, Michael; Champy, James (2001): *Reengineering the Corporation.* Harper Business 2001.

Hedberg, Bo (1980): Using Computerized Information Systems to Design Better Organisations and jobs. In: Björn -Andersen, Niels (ed.) (1980): *The Human Side of Information Processing,* op. cit., pp 19-33.

Korte, Werner B; Robinson, Simon; Steinle, Wolfgang J. (1988) (eds.): *Telework: Present Situation and Future Development of a new Form of Work Organisation.* North-Holland Amsterdam et al.

Mambrey, Peter & Barbara Schmidt-Belz (1983): Systems Designers And Users In A Participative Design Process - Some Fictions And Facts. In: U. Briefs, C. Ciborra & L. Schneider (eds.): *System Design For With And By The Users,* op. cit., pp. 411-416.

Margulies, Fred (1980): Why HCC Again. In: Moshowitz, Abbe (ed.): *Human Choice and Computers, 2,* (ref. hereafter), 1980, p. 12.

Mowshowitz, Abbe (ed.): *Human Choice and Computers, 2.* Proceedings of the Second IFIP Conference on Human Choice and Computers, Baden, Austria, 4-8 June 1979, North Holland Amsterdam, 1980.

Pettigrew, Andrew M. (1980): The Politics of Organisational Change. In: Björn-Andersen, Niels: *The Human Side of Information Processing*, op. cit., pp 39-47.

Schuler, Douglas; Namioka, Aki (eds.) (1993): *Participatory Design. Principles and Practices.* Lawrence Earlbaum Ass. Hillsdale NJ.

Suchman, Lucy 1987: *Plans and situated actions. The problem of human-machine communication.* Cambridge University Press New York NY.

Weick, Karl E. 1969: *The Social Psychology of Organizing.* Addison-Wesley, Reading Mass.

The Information Society and its Consequences: Lessons from the Past

Jan HOLVAST
Holvast & Partner, Privacy Consultants, NL - Landsmeer. henp.holvast@wxs.nl
Penny DUQUENOY
Middlesex University, London. p.duquenoy@mdx.ac.uk
and Diane WHITEHOUSE
European Commission, Brussels. diane.whitehouse@cec.eu.int

Key words: Consequences of ITC, control, debate, evolution, impact, information society, inventory, lessons, revolution, teaching impact of IT

INTRODUCTION

Without doubt the year 1976 was an important year for the discussion on Computers and Society. In that year Joseph Weizenbaum's *Computer Power and Human Reason* was published and IFIP's TC 9 on Computers and Society was founded. In this contribution we want to give a short overview of the history since then and answer the question "what lessons can be learned from the past twenty-five years?" Following a review of the vigorous debate on the development of computers in society that has taken place during that period, four main questions are raised:

1. Is the Information Society a new phenomenon or is it a question of emphasis?
2. Has the development led to a new revolution as never seen before, as many scientists and policy makers would have us believe?
3. What are, in a general sense, the consequences of this evolving information society?
4. Can information technology be controlled, and if so, what are the main instruments of control?

COMPUTERS AND SOCIETY

The history of the Computer and the history of Computers and Society do not run in parallel. Despite the work and the ideas of forerunners, like Schickard, Pascal, von Liebnitz, Babbage, Hollerith and many others, the history of the computer can be seen as having started in the mid 1930s, when Turing, Zuse and Aiken were producing working computers with a practical function. The real start however was shortly after the end of the Second World War.

The consequences of computers on society were first seen in the field of labour. This is not surprising when we look at the enormous amount of literature devoted to the relationship between technology in general and work. Commencing with the influence of industrialisation and work in the middle of the 19th century through to the publications in the 1960s, we see a history of incremental development. It is one continuing story, in which sociologists and political scientists play a dominant role. Predictions that computer technology would soon create revolutionary changes in the number of people employed and in the length of the working week date from the late 1950s and early 1960s. At the same time we see the effects upon the content of the work studied and discussed.

Surprisingly in the middle of the 1960s, there was one other field where the consequences of computing were seen very sharply: privacy. In 1967 the famous and influential book Privacy and Freedom by Alan Westin was published [24]. This book was the finishing touch to a project on 'The Impact of Science and Technology on Privacy' that was carried out between 1962 and 1966. Alan Westin was Director of Research of the project. Following this publication there were a number of articles and books on this subject. There was a change of emphasis from the computer as the cause of threats to privacy, to its role in data processing. An important difference with those publications dealing with labour questions is that it was not sociologists or political scientists writing about the issue this time, but lawyers. There are several other fields where the implications of computing were perceived and studied [21]. The organisational consequences are quite substantial, and one major issue has always been the extent to which the introduction of the computer leads to greater organisational centralisation. At the same time it became clear that the computer would, in any case, affect society at large: the growth in the service sector. Already by the 1950s over half of the United States labour force was employed in service industries, although it was argued that the shift would continue to progress gradually.

It was theorised that radical changes could be expected if computerised information systems were to be used as efficiently and effectively in the political decision-making process. Such amenities as education and medical care could be provided to all members of society. The relationship between computers and democracy received greater attention. Some believed that more and more decisions would be placed in the hands of experts, whereas others believed that computers could be used to establish a system of direct democracy. Ideally citizens should have a direct voice in political decision-making. Through the sheer amount of information and the number and speed of new discoveries, there could be great difficulty for people in trying to keep 'well informed'.

Therefore computers could have a great effect on education. In other words, the computer was seen as an aid in the process of using knowledge. Using computers in schools for instructional purposes was an important challenge, although computers raised the fear that they would increase dehumanisation by substituting machines for live teachers.

Computers were seen as having major consequences for the natural as well as the social sciences when computers were used for both data analysis and problem solving. One field, art, was seen as rather futuristic: "The use of computers in the arts has often been a subject of either good-natured humour or ridicule." [21, p.19] Somewhat greater progress has made towards an understanding of human cognitive processes. Cybernetic research compares the functioning of the human brain with the functioning of computers.

Many of the developments and implications outlined above are from the reader on computers and society, *The Computer Impact*, the first attempt to bring essays on implications of computer technology together in one volume. As the editor, Irene Taviss, stated, the essays are intended to present a broad sampling of the major issues raised. They were selected to give the reader a sense of the concrete developments of computer technology and their implications in specific spheres of social activity. Taviss hesitated on the choice of the title, although the most appropriate title for a discussion on the social implications of computer technology might appear to be *Computers: Curse or Blessing?* It is clear that the computer generated great fears and great hopes. "It has become a symbol for all that is good and all that is evil in modern society." [21, p.3]

Although this book was one of the first with a general overview and a vision of computers in society as a whole, it was important not necessarily for the attention it received, but for the discussion that was generated as a result.

The real start of the social discussion on Computers and Society was probably the publication of Daniel Bell's *The Post-Industrial Society* [2]. Bell's analysis posits that the advanced countries were moving from the industrial stage towards a 'post-industrial stage' of development. He claimed that the majority of economically active people would earn their living from different kinds of post-industrial service sector occupations. In a pre-publication ·he indicated his notion of a 'knowledge society', characterised by research and development and a knowledge field with a large proportion of the Gross National Product and a large share of employment [1]. Although his analysis was North American in orientation, we can assume it could be extended to a variety of other countries.

As Annti Kasvio [17] rightly observes, the term 'post-industrial' was however used for the first time by Alain Touraine in his book *La societé post-industrielle*, which was published in 1969. In this book, and following the tradition of sociologists dealing with computer technology, Touraine studied the consequences of the new society on labour and the industrial working class.

A BREAKTHROUGH IN THE DISCUSSIONS – THE WEIZENBAUM PERIOD

In 1976 a book was published that influenced the discussion on computer and society in an enormous way. It was Joseph Weizenbaum's *Computer Power and Human Reason* [22]. In this book the way in which computers can be used is criticised for the first time, specific applications are censored or perhaps even 'excommunicated'. Weizenbaum had been shocked by the way people reacted towards the computer program ELIZA, that he had designed to play the role of a psychologist or doctor. This experience led him to attach new importance to the question of the relationship between the individual and the computer.

In his analysis Weizenbaum came to the conclusion that too much power is given to technology, in particular the computer. Many problems are seen as technical problems that can be solved by a computer. The computer is seen as more powerful than human beings, and 'common sense' is replaced by science. The consequence is an over-emphasis on rationality and instrumentalism. Those who protest against this development are perceived as anti-technological, anti-scientific and, finally, as anti-intellectual. In reality, however, the price - which in Weizenbaum's view is actually paid - is servitude and impotence. Therefore human beings, in particular scientists and engineers, have responsibilities that transcend their situation. Every individual must act as if the whole future of the world, of humanity itself, depends on him or her.

Two kinds of computer applications might either not be undertaken at all, or - if they are contemplated - should be approached with the utmost caution. The first kind includes all projects that propose to substitute a computer system for a human function that involves interpersonal respect, understanding, or love. These are the human functions for which computers ought not to be substituted. The second kind of computer application that ought to be avoided is that which can easily be seen to have irreversible and not entirely foreseeable side effects. If computers cannot be shown to meet a pressing human need that cannot readily be met in any other way, then their use ought not to be pursued.

THE BEGINNING OF THE DEBATE ON THE IMPACT OF THE INFORMATION SOCIETY

The growth of interest in computers and information technology is largely due to this initial publication by Weizenbaum. Other resulting publications are two voluminous books published in 1979 and 1980. The first is *The Computer Age: A Twenty-Year View*, edited by Michael Dertouzos and Joel Moses [8], the second *The Microelectronic Revolution*, edited by Tom Forester [11]. Both books have similar content, although not necessarily treated in the same order. Dertouzos and Moses' publication contains five main chapters: Prospects for the Individual, Trends in Traditional Computer Uses, Socio-economic Effects and Expectations, Trends in the Underlying Technologies, and Critiques. Forester's book starts, as promised in the title, with the technical: The Micro-electronic Revolution, followed by Economic and Social Implications, and ends with a view of the future: The Micro-Electronic Age. Although many of the impacts of computing are mentioned, in both books the emphasis is on economic aspects, in particular, the impact for employment and labour.

It is both remarkable, and at the same time revealing, that in both volumes three articles are copied. The first is Bell's famous article on information society,[1] the second a critical reaction of Weizenbaum on Bell's ideas, and the third a reply to Weizenbaum by Bell. Since these articles are widely discussed and have each in their own way contributed to a more general discussion of the social implication of information society, we will give a short overview of them.

In the comprehensive tradition of his earlier publications Bell gives an overview of the changes on societal level [4, pp. 163-212]. What he was calling in 1968 the Knowledge Society and in 1973 the Post Industrial Society, becomes the Information Society, a term that has since been adopted to describe this society. In Bell's view, we are living in a society in which information and knowledge are the crucial variables. This information explosion can only be handled through the expansion of computerised and subsequently automated information systems. This means that the computer is only a tool for managing mass society, since it is the mechanism that orders and processes the transactions - whose huge number has been mounting almost exponentially because of the increase in social interactions. His basic premise is "that knowledge and information" are becoming the strategic resource and transforming agent of the post-industrial society. Inevitably, the onset of far-reaching social changes, especially when they proceed as these do through the medium of specific technologies, confronts a society with "major policy questions". In his view, any technology, such as the computer, is only instrumental, and its impact depends on other social and cultural factors.

In his response Weizenbaum speaks of the 'Computer' Revolution - to make clear that it is not information that causes the changes but the computer [439-463]. He agrees that society is transforming into an information society, however it is not information that is responsible for that but the computer. The central question therefore is not who is responsible for the information, but who is responsible for the actions based on these computer systems. The crucial issue is that of responsibility and control, and the consequences of the computer.

In his reply Bell does not add anything to the content of the argument. He begins with the remark that Weizenbaum is knocking down an open door. He repeats that the computer is purely instrumental. The crucial decisions are sociological, not technological. In his view Weizenbaum is a moral absolutist with tunnel vision.

Clearly stark positions are taken up. While both authors agree that we are tending to live in an information society, their analysis differs and, with that, so do their questions as to what has to be done to prevent unforeseen, and unwanted, side effects. In Bell's vision it is information and knowledge that determine the development and there is nothing that can or should be done to handle or correct this development. Weizenbaum on the other hand blames the computer and incites human beings, especially scientists, to take up their responsibility and raise questions such as: "Who is the beneficiary of our much-advertised technological progress and who are the victims? What limits ought we, the people in general, and scientists and engineers particularly, to impose on the applications of computation to human affairs? What is the impact of the computer, not only on the economies of the world or on the war potential of nations and so on, but on the self-image of human beings and on human dignity? What irreversible forces is our worship of high technology, symbolized most starkly by the computer, bringing into play? Will our children be able to live with the world we are here and now constructing? Much depends on answers to these questions" [23].

In a sense the Weizenbaum-Bell dispute is the forerunner of the debate which still dominates today. It is not only information versus computer, but it is also the discussion between the optimist and the pessimist, between people who see information technology as a societal blessing and those who only see the darker side, the side of the shadow. The discussion between information and technology was more or less decided in favour of the latter, when Tom Forester presented his next volume on *The Information*

Technology Revolution [12]. From that time on everybody talked of the new science of collecting, storing, processing, and transmitting information. Although the position seems to be a compromise between Weizenbaum and Bell, in reality the emphasis is always on technology.

SOCIAL IMPLICATIONS AND THE TEACHING CURRICULUM

Already in the beginning of the 1970s there began a search for a curriculum on Computers and Society. Among the first to raise attention to this idea was E. Horowitz and his colleagues, who cited three purposes for such a course:
- To educate computer scientists on the present and future impact of computer technology;
- To investigate some of the difficult moral questions concerning the responsibility of scientists; and,
- To gain a more humanistic perspective on the use and misuse of computers. [14]

Some years later these courses were elaborated in more detail. Two of them became more or less examples of university-level courses, because they had a broader impact and were more seriously discussed in the literature. Willy Jensen made a distinction between the broad arena where the consequences of computers were to be observed [16]:
- Economic life: trade, industry, automation, management, structural changes;
- Government: new services, bureaucracy;
- Work: employment, quality of labour;
- Culture: education, communication, informational media, quality of information, minorities;
- Leisure: quality of life, social contacts, entertainment, telework.

All of these developments were seen to have important consequences on democracy, freedom, protection of privacy, welfare and possibilities of control

A most important and useful classification was made by Friedrich, who classified the consequences of computing into the social aggregate hierarchy of international, national, business and individual levels [15]:

International level: the battle on the information market. Examples are the exploitation of databases, communication satellites, and the computer industry.

National level: national information monopolies, technology policies. Political questions are solved with computer supported planning and decision systems, networking, the gap between citizen and government, vulnerability of society due to the dependency on information.

Business level: quality of work, employment, control of the workplace, personal information systems.

Individual level: man in control. Loss of individual space of freedom, privacy, technical relations instead of human relations, technical help instead of human help.

THE POST WEIZENBAUM PERIOD

After publication of the volumes by Dertouzos and Moses, and Forester, a whole range of books were published detailing the social implications of the information society - very often as a spin-off of a conference devoted to such a theme or as a specific project such as in IFIP-WG9.2 [5]. This period culminated in *The Information Age* trilogy of Manuel Castells in which he searches for the social and economic dynamics of the information age [7]. In these books Castells sees as his main task the analysis of the informational modes of development of societies. This analysis revolves around three fundamental axes: the changes that take place in the areas of material production, human experiences, and the structures of power. Two main trends are seen as the driving force: globalisation of the economy and the digital revolution.

In the mid 1990s, when information was recognised as an important factor of economic growth, we see a political interest emerging. One of the early actors in this field was the Japanese Ministry of Industry and Trade (MITI), which made Japan the global leader in the development and production of microelectronics [17]. After the stock market crash in 1987 and the economic recession in the early 1990s many political leaders looked to the digital revolution as a form of salvation. We can cite, as an example, the United States' National Information Infrastructure Programme, launched by president Bill Clinton and vice-president Al Gore.

This kind of stance was taken up in the European Commission's report 'Europe and the Global Information Society'. The report was prepared for the European Council meeting in Corfu by the so-called High-Level Group on the Information Society, chaired by Martin Bangemann [13]. The report starts with two key messages. The first is that the advent of the information society is inevitable and will lead to an industrial revolution comparable to that of the 19th century. The second is that Europe's entry into the information society will be, as stressed also by Jacques Berleur and Jean-Marc Galand in this book, market-driven. Therefore a common regulatory framework must be set up at the level of the European Union in order to maximise the effect of the market while guaranteeing an appropriate level of protection for intellectual property, personal data, and network security.

This last statement is noteworthy insofar as, for the first time at international level, it was accepted and admitted that the development towards an information society is accompanied by risks. "The main risk lies in the creation of a two-tier society of have and have-nots, in which only a part of the population has access to the new technology, is comfortable using it and can fully enjoy its benefits." [13, 8] but this is not the only risk. A regulatory response is also needed in key areas like intellectual property, privacy and media ownership. Above all encryption becomes increasingly important, with the provision that governments need power to override encryption for the purpose of fighting against crime and protecting national security.

Whether this attention to societal risk was purely instrumental in terms of avoiding the possibility that 'individuals will reject the new information culture and its instruments', it was the first time that an internationally influential body accepted and confirmed that there are indeed risks. In light of the influence this report has had for various national programmes in their approach to the development of an information society, and that these programmes have almost always paid attention to societal and human aspects of the information society, its relevance cannot be underestimated.

INFORMATION SOCIETY

In his article on the Information Society, Bell uses four criteria to judge when this entry has been accomplished [4]
- In almost all social processes, storing, processing and use of information are the central factors (information as new energy instead of the previous human power and electricity);
- More than half of the employed population consists of people working in the information sector (information as an important economic force);
- Information technology (computer and telecommunications) form the most important infrastructure in society;
- Most social and political decisions are changed drastically by the use of information and information technology (information as an important factor of change).

Looking at these criteria we can confirm that, at the start of the 21st century, we have indeed entered the information society, but at the same time we can raise the question: What is new in that? Have we experienced the revolution that many people would have us believe?

As we have seen, Forester first speaks of the microelectronics revolution and later of the information technology revolution. Barry Sherman uses the word 'The New Revolution' and even Castells uses this heavily laden word: "A technological revolution, centred around information technology, is reshaping, at accelerated pace, the material basis of society" [7].

But is this society indeed a radical new phenomenon or has it been more an evolution than a revolution? To answer this question we will reconsider the four criteria presented by Bell, starting with the importance of information.

THE RISE OF THE INFORMATION SOCIETY: REVOLUTION OR EVOLUTION?

As a consequence of the use of terminology, it is clear that the main feature of information society and information technology is information. Recording, processing and distributing information is as old as mankind. Proof of this can be seen in the caves in France, Spain and Africa, just as in Egyptian hieroglyphics. Distributing information in a very primitive form can be seen in the smoke signals of North American Indians and the horn blowers in some other countries. The importance (and consequences!) of information can also be read about in the Bible where the history of the first census takings is told. Counting people is an early instrument in the preparation of war making.

During the Middle Age the importance of information rose, strongly related to the development of the first important type of information technology: printing. Although there is discussion whether printing was first developed by the German Johannes Gutenberg or the Dutchman Laurens Janszoon Coster, there is nevertheless agreement on the importance of this invention.

As a consequence, the production of paper was stimulated, becoming one of the main products of the Industrial Age. In 1714 a new phase in this development was the invention of the typewriter by the Englishman Henry Mill, the forefather of the electric typewriter and the modern text processor.

Information is more than text. Information is also a means to recording and distributing of sound and images. Thomas Edison's name is strongly related to the development of recording and distributing sound. Telephone, telex and telegraph are the results of his creativity, just as some time later was the gramophone. This development was later combined with the microphone, developed by Alexander Graham Bell and first demonstrated at the World Exhibition in Chicago in 1876.

Even more impressive is the development of the practice of recording and distributing images. For the first time images were automatically recorded successfully in the middle of the 18th century. This resulted in the first photographic-style images at the beginning of the 19th century, rapidly leading in the direction of the modern cameras and movies ('moving pictures'). All these inventions have come together in computer technology, which finally combines text, sound and images using the calculating principles of Pascal and numerous others.

Information is, as we have seen from this short overview, an important factor of the new form of information society, but to say that it is a new phenomenon is going too far. Information has always been important. Its importance has increased and it is perhaps more important than ever, but it cannot seen as the factor underlying society. This means at the same time that there have always been people working on the collection, processing and distribution of information. Their number has also increased. On the one side, as a consequence the number of more traditional jobs has been reduced. On the other side, new information jobs have been created (such as programmers and system analysts). All these are signs that society has changed, but it is not the first time that a new technological invention has had societal consequences. The same has been seen with telex, telephone and television. The most important difference is that we have, for the first time, a convergence of all the technical components with the result that the consequences have been more rapid and radical. However, they have not been revolutionary in the sense that the consequences are unexpected and unpredictable. One of the proofs of this is that even now, after twenty-five years, nobody can tell exactly when the information society has made its entrance, in the same way that is impossible to say when the industrial revolution came into force.

We therefore prefer to speak of gradual evolution instead of revolution. This means that we are almost never totally surprised by the consequences of the development, but in most cases can more or less predict not only what the consequences are, but also to what extent and in what areas they are likely to appear. For that reason we can even make an analytical scheme, in part based on the teaching courses presented by Jensen and Friedrich, of the fields where the consequences of the information society will become visible.

TOWARDS A MODEL FOR AN INVENTORY OF THE CONSEQUENCES OF THE INFORMATION SOCIETY

Looking at the developments of the last twenty-five years, we can see a variety of technical innovations, all of which in one way or another have influenced human life. Describing all these consequences asks for a kind of classification. The first distinction was made between consequences for the labour force and those affecting everything else. Other distinctions or classifications took the particular sector where the consequences were seen as a starting point: healthcare, education, business, transport, art and science, defence and the mass media. Although this type of classification had the advantage that each separate sector could be described in detail, the disadvantage was the resulting overlap. A lot of developments happened in each and every sector with consequences there for labour, privacy and human relations.

Although the classifications of Jensen and Friedrich have advantages and disadvantages, a combination of classifications has been shown to be the most appropriate analytical structure: that is, there is a distinction between macro-, meso- and micro- levels.

The macro level describes society as a whole: national and international. At that level we can think of the consequences for employment, the digital divide, distinctions between the information rich and information poor, the growing vulnerability, and the problem of information overload.

At a lower level we have the meso-level or the level of the organisation, institutions, and the people who work and live in that organisation. This includes organisational changes, quality of labour, and privacy of the employee. With privacy we are on the frontier of the meso- and the micro-level.

At the micro-level the consequences for the individual are the primary focus: telework, privacy, human relations, and family life. Although this classification - as with all analytical distinctions - has some overlaps, it has proved useful for describing the general consequences of computing.

CONTROLLING INFORMATION TECHNOLOGY: THE DEBATE

The conclusion we have made in this contribution - that technological development is an evolution rather than a revolution - is more than a mere statement. It is also a conviction that consequences may be predicted and that it is possible one way or another to control the development - in particular the all too negative consequences. This argument opposes the ruling attitude of technological determinism, which asserts that developments can neither be predicted nor controlled. Such determinism reduces humankind to powerless pawns who can only accept their fate and wait to see what other people will do to help them. It is our belief that more can be done by human beings themselves than is often admitted.

Over the course of time there has always been a vehement discussion between the optimists and pessimists regarding the possibility of controlling technology. It is as Abbe Mowshowitz observed: "The central question is the nature of technology's role in our society. Is it purely instrumental, as most observers believe; or has it become an autonomous, formative element in human affairs?" [18] The pessimists believe that technology is a completely autonomous power in itself that cannot be controlled. In other words, the consequences of technology, both positive as well as negative, have to be accepted as they are.[2] The optimists, like Dorothy Nelkin, believe that in one way or another technology can be influenced and directed. This view is at the same time a vision of the future, so perfectly demonstrated by the statement of James Branch Cabell: "The optimist proclaims that we live in the best of all possible worlds, and the pessimist fears that this is true".[3] Langdon Winner, who made a study of autonomous technology, agrees that that it is not a conflict between pessimists and optimists, but a question of whether technology is out of control and follows its own course. In his view therefore technology influences all aspects of human life. It is a form of technological determinism that has as its characteristics firstly, that the technical base of a society is the fundamental condition affecting all patterns of social existence, and secondly, that changes in technology are the single most important source of change in society [25].

The discussion on autonomous technology and technological determinism was in particular fuelled by publication in 1954 of a book by the French sociologist and philosopher Jacques Ellul *La Technique ou l'enjeu du siècle* [9]. This book received international attention after its American translation to *The Technological Society*. In Ellul's view "technique" [technology] as a totality of methods is always striving at absolute efficiency, with the consequence that spontaneous actions disappear and we are left in a completely artificial world. In this world the individual's role will be less and less important in technical evolution. Technique has become a power endowed with its own peculiar force and is for that reason influencing everything: the economy, the state and the essence of what it is to be a human being. In that sense it even influences human behaviour, which is now oriented to adapting humankind to the technical world. In Ellul's view, in the technological society, there is no place left for a vulnerable human being. "The state, on the contrary, has need of whole, strong human beings, in full moral, intellectual, and physical vigour, who alone can serve it best. What the state requires is the technical means for integrating completely whole beings, and these means are on the point of becoming reality" [9, 386]. It will come as no surprise that Ellul's vision on the future is gloomy. Through the developments of technique the state will become totalitarian and will absorb citizens' lives completely. Although Ellul was challenged in his opinions by numerous opponents, he never changed his mind and in later publications he repeated his forecasts of a totalitarian society.

In discussing Ellul's view of technology we should not underestimate the period in which the book was originally written (1954) – that is, the social and political context in which it was set. It was written at the time of the Cold War, when human beings seemed to be less important, and when they were intensively studied not only by sociological methods, but in particular by psychological testing. It was also the period of the lie detector. In that sense Ellul's pessimism to a greater or lesser extent was endorsed by philosophers like Helmut Schelsky, Erich Fromm, Forester, and Langdon Winner. It is the virtue of Winner, however, that he focussed attention on the problem of human beings in a technological society.

Ellul has been severely attacked for his pessimism, or as some have called it, fatalism. In particular his belief in technical determinism, the argument that technique is the prime mover controlling all developments, was fundamentally criticised. Determinism as a part of philosophy is a notion that has been in evidence since its beginning, only the name of prime mover has changed: God, Economy, Culture, Power. The difference is however that technical determinism in particular is criticised as not making a distinction between technology, technique and the use of technique. Freeman, Layton, and Winner are among Ellul's critics. As Winner states "Ellul fails to notice any difference between invention and technical implementation and apparently believes that for all intents and purposes these activities are identical" [25, 64]. In his, and others, view there is a clear distinction between what is happening in the laboratory and what happens when discoveries are put to work in the world at large.

Therefore a distinction should be made between the knowledge aspect and the application aspect. In some languages this distinction can be clarified in terminology between technology and technique[4]. Between both aspects there is a time lag, although due to technological developments this lag is becoming smaller and smaller[5]. But it is not only necessary to make a distinction between technology and technique, between knowledge and application, but also between the application and use of the technique. Numerous examples show how the use of technique is dependent on several societal aspects, money, the state of the art, and politics. Therefore it is too simple to say that technology is absolutely determined. Technique can, to a greater or lesser extent, be controlled.

THREE FORMS OF CONTROL

The question that we should therefore ask is: what can be done? To answer this question we would again go back to the past and offer up the old classification of Nelkin [19]. Nelkin presented a general model for control, which can be used for assessing control mechanisms. She uses the well-known distinction between control at three stages: afterwards, before and during and calls them respectively reactive, anticipatory and participatory control. Reactive control is oriented towards the protection of interests of human beings and is a type of control exercised by institutions and government reacting to a certain development. Well-known forms of reactive control are legal and other punitive or disciplinary measures that attempt to prevent all too negative consequences. Also included in this category are the possibilities of claims and complaints, as are expert groups that are installed once the developments are started.

Participatory control deals with the involvement of citizens in the introduction and regulation of technology. In this capacity the most well known forms are protest movements and activities aimed at raising awareness. In some sense this has also been introduced in the labour movement under the heading of participatory design. Another form that is sometimes mentioned is self-regulation, under the condition that (consumer) organisations are involved in the process.

Anticipatory control consists of procedures for predicting social, political and economic consequences of new scientific and technological developments. This is particularly important when consequences are becoming visible, usually when the development has matured and changes are almost impossible. The most well known form of anticipatory control is Technology Assessment: identifying the possibilities of applied research and technologies together with the unwanted side effects. "It is a method of analysis that systematically appraises the nature, significance, status and merit of a technological process" [p 428].

Looking at these forms of control it is significant that reactive control is the one that is most used, followed by participatory control. Despite all pressures, participatory control has had little or no influence. For an appropriate form of control of information technology all three types of control are needed in combination. The practice, however, is that the emphasis is placed on reactive control, and for a small part on participatory control. For David Flaherty such practice gives every reason to be critical. "The belief that surveillance societies are not going to emerge because of efforts in data protection is naive; in fact, the existence of Data Protection Commissioners may actually stimulate the flavouring of surveillance societies by lulling the public into a false sense of security." [10, 381] The dangers exposed by Flaherty's observation of reactive control are alarming. A greater emphasis should be placed on the two other forms of control, anticipatory and participatory.

CONCLUDING THE DISCUSSION ABOUT THE INFORMATION SOCIETY

Reviewing these last twenty-five years and more, we can see three important periods. The first period (before 1976) can be seen as the period of growing awareness in several fields. The most dominant are labour and privacy. In numerous articles and books the consequences of computing, mostly in a negative sense, are predicted as a result of the emergence of the computer. The privacy discussion during this period is concerned with computer privacy, rather than informational privacy.

The second period (1976-1993) can be seen as the period of growing scientific awareness with, as an important starting point, the critical analysis of Weizenbaum who confronts computer power with the importance of human reason. Numerous analyses are made based on inventories of the consequences of computing. The publications of Dertouzos and Moses in collaboration, and Forester, are the most significant examples. It is also the time that university courses on the theme of computers and society were started. Together with these analyses some thought is given to what can be done. Faced with a dominant trend towards technological determinism, legal solutions are sought. As Nelkin observes, it is the time of reactive control.

Starting around 1993, a third period of political awareness begins. At this time, it is not the social implications that are of concern, but the consequences of these consequences. They are seen as a potential obstacle for the use and the development of the so-called electronic highway (which we now commonly think of as simply the Internet) and thus hindering the possibilities for economic growth. In an integrated way all types of measures are promoted to tackle the various social implications. A combination of legal, technical and self-regulatory measures is suggested.

What however is missing is an holistic approach – only in this way we will be able to get a real grip on the development of the information society. Such a holistic approach can be reached when at least three conditions are met:

- First of all we have to be convinced that technique is not autonomous but can in a way be predicted and controlled;
- The three stages of development in social consequences of information communication technologies – awareness, scientific knowledge and political willingness – must be integrated;
- In controlling technique a combination of reactive, participatory and anticipatory control is necessary.

It is in this arena particularly that TC 9 'Computers and Society' has attempted to focus its activities and to show the whole sphere, breadth, depth, and complexity of discussions in relation to the introduction of computing into the social arena.

REFERENCES

1. Bell, Daniel, The Measurement of Knowledge and Technology, in: Eleanor Bernert Sheldon and Wilbert E. Moore [Eds.], *Indicators of Social Change*. New York: Russell Sage Foundation, 1968.
2. Bell, D., *The Coming of Post-Industrial Society: A Venture in Social Forecasting*. London: Heinemann, 1973.
3. Bell, Daniel, A Reply to Weizenbaum, in Dertouzos and Moses, [8], 1979, pp. 459-463.
4. Bell, Daniel, The Social Framework of the Information Society, in Dertouzos and Moses, 1989, pp. 163-212.
5. Berleur, J., A. Clement, T.R.H. Sizer and D. Whitehouse [Eds.], *The Information Society: Evolving Landscapes. Report from Namur*. New York: Springer Verlag-Captus University Publications, 1990.
6. Clarke, R. and J. Cameron [Eds.], *Managing Information Technology's Organisational Impact*. Amsterdam, New York, Oxford, Tokyo: North Holland, 1991.
7. Castells, Manuel, *The Information Age, Economy, Society and Culture*. Volume I: *The Rise of the Network Society*. Oxford, UK: Blackwell Publishers Ltd, 1996.
8. Dertouzos, Michael L. and Joel Moses [Eds.], *The Computer Age: A Twenty-Year View. Cambridge*, Massachusetts, and London, England, 1979.
9. Ellul, Jacques, *The Technological Society*. New York: Vintage Books, 1964
10. Flaherty, David, 1988. The Emergence of Surveillance Societies in the Western World: Toward the Year 2000. In *Government Information Quarterly*, 5,4, 377-387.
11. Forester, Tom [Ed.], *The Microelectronic Revolution*. Oxford: Basil Blackwell, 1980.
12. Forester, Tom [Ed.], *The Information Technology Revolution*. Oxford: Basil Blackwell, 1985.
13. High Level Group on the Information Society, Europe and the Global Information Society, in *Cordis focus*, Supplement 2, 15 July 1994.
14. Horowitz, E., J.L. Morgan, A.C. Shaw, Computers and society: A proposed course for computer scientists, in *Communications of the ACM*, 1972, volume 5, pp. 257-261.
15. Informatica en Maatschappij als thema voor de Informaticastudie, in *Informatie*, jaargang 24, nr. 4, 1982, pp. 213-224.
16. Jensen, Willy, Teaching Social and Political Consequences of Information technology, in R. Lewis & D. Tagg [Eds.], *Computers in Education*. Amsterdam: North-Holland Publishing Company, 1981, pp. 503-507.
17. Kasvia, Annti, The Emergence of 'Information Society' as a Major Social Scientific Research Programme, in Erkki Karvonen, *Informational Societies, Understanding the Third Industrial Revolution*. Tampere: Tampere University Press, 2001, pp. 19-48.
18. Mowshowitz, Abbe, *The Conquest of Will: Information Processing in Human Affairs*. Reading, Mass.: Addison-Wesley Publishing Company, 1976.

19. Nelkin, Dorothy, Technology and Public Policy, in Ina Spiegel-Rösing and Derek de Solla Price [Eds.], *Science, Technology and Society, a Cross Disciplinary Perspective.* London and Beverly Hills: Sage Publications, 1977, pp. 393-443.

20. Sherman, Berry, *The New Revolution, The Impact of Computers on Society.* Chicester, New York, Brisbane, Toronto, Singapore: John Wiley and Sons, 1985.

21. Taviss, Irene [Ed.], *The Computer Impact.* Englewood Cliffs, New Jersey: Prentice Hall, 1970.

22. Weizenbaum, Joseph, *Computer Power and Human Reason, From Judgment to Calculation.* San Francisco: W.H. Freeman and Company, 1976.

23. Weizenbaum, Joseph, Once More, the Computer Revolution, in Dertouzos and Moses, [8], 1979, pp. 439-459.

24. Westin, Alan F., *Privacy and Freedom.* London: The Bodley Head, 1967.

25. Winner, Langdon, *Autonomous Technology, Technics-out-of Control as a Theme in Political Thought.* Cambridge, Mass. And London: The MIT Press, 1977.

1   Although it is sometimes suggested that Bell was the person who introduced the term 'information society', Marien states that information society apparently was first used in Japan in the late 1960s by Kenichi Kohyama. See Michael Marien "Some Questions for the Information Society" in [12, pp. 648-660].

2   As a consequence the distinction between the optimists and pessimists is not always true - some believe that this autonomous technology will bring a better world and others are opposing this.

3   Our translation of the following German expression "Der Optimist erklärt, das wir in der besten aller möglichen Welten leben; de Pessimist fürchtet, das das wahr ist". Cited in Heinz Brandt, Nostalgie als Schwellenangst, in *Technologie und Politik, aktuell Magazin*, nr. 1, Reinbeck bei Hamburg: Rowohlt, 1975, p.33-47.

4   It is curious that Winner mentions the distinction but at the same time uses technology and technics in the same sense in the title of his book.

5   In particular Alvin Toffler gives several examples of the diminishing lag. See Alvin Toffler, *The Third Wave*, New York, Toronto, London: Bantam Books, 1980.

Historic, Contemporary, and Future Effects of Information and Communication Technologies (ICT) on People with Impairments

Geoff BUSBY
British Computer Society Disability Group
"Geoff Busby" <disability.grp@bcs.org.uk>

> *"Particularly with the invasive technologies, there are real ethical questions that we cannot ignore.... These kinds of technologies will soon be here and will be applied, and we will not have thought through the consequences. We need to do more thinking."*

THE HISTORICAL CONTEXT: WHAT HAS HAPPENED OVER THE PAST FIFTEEN YEARS

When did information and communication technologies begin to impact on people with impairments, and how? Basically, it all began with Apple. The company was very effective, working with community groups and with disability groups, particularly on the west coast of the United States. It was the first company to have a department specially set up to address accessibility and people with impairments.

In Britain in the 1980s, the lead was taken by the BBC computer. The BBC was very dominant in the educational area, and it provided a lot of specialist software. The BBC was introduced into many schools in England, whereas in Scotland it was the Apple Macintosh that had the lead. Historically, the IBM personal computer then came along (but the work that IBM did on accessibility and disability was chiefly for its own employees, and on training). Then came Microsoft, and Apple took a nosedive. Microsoft took on much of Apple's software.

IBM's achievements in the United States had more to do with providing information about where to get equipment for persons with special needs, and any special interfaces needed. This work was based in Atlanta, Georgia.

Microsoft, in contrast now has 37 people employed in its Unit in Seattle, which is a very big commitment. Microsoft does a lot of work on accessibility, tapping into the skills of people with disabilities. People with disabilities are involved in beta-testing and in focus groups.

Why is Microsoft so good? The company's software has the access features that are already in-built. That all stems from the 37 people who work in Seattle, at least one of whom used to work previously for Apple. The front end of Word, for example, looks like an Apple, but it doesn't matter what technology you have, you have to change people's mindsets!

It is important to emphasise just how important interfaces are. Laptops, palmtops, telecommunications, and WAP: this is what can turn an impairment into a disability!

Since those early technology days, there has come convergence, the Net, and many forms of new ideas and new technologies. Equally, in terms of legislation, we have seen the Americans with Disabilities Act, the United Kingdom Discrimination Disability Act, and new areas of legislation in other European member states and in OECD countries like Australia and Canada. There is currently no overall European policy, but such policy is needed.

THE CONTEMPORARY CONTEXT - SOME SOCIAL AND ETHICAL CONSIDERATIONS

There are different models of disability: the medical and the social. It is particularly important that the information and communications technologies industry follows the social model. In it lies the creation of markets and potential income.

Currently you have to talk about computer-literate people with disabilities - including the older generation. There are now senior citizens who grew up with computer technology: we see this every day of our lives. Fifteen years ago, older people would not look at technology. Now, if you go to what in the United Kingdom is called 'adult education' you see a lot of older people - people who are 60+ or 65+ - really trying to take information technology on board, in day classes and in evening classes. There are a lot of retired people who are taking computer courses in basic word processing and email use, for example. They are no longer scared - it's not taboo. It's the way the world now is!

For example, eCommerce is becoming a useful facility particularly for older people and people with impairments who, in common with the rest of society, are beginning to use it.

There is far greater attention to web accessibility. What are the criteria for web accessibility? You name it, we have it. Even the Labour Party was online during the last election in the United Kingdom. It is increasingly likely that people who design web pages will have to comply with the Americans with Disability Act and the United Kingdom Disability Discrimination Act. In 2002, all web sites have got to be accessible.

The British Computer Society Disability Group receives a lot of questions from people who are designing web pages. The United Kingdom government does not have a department which can help with web accessibility. Anyone who is in a government department and who wishes to start up a website, does not receive any help. But there are guidelines like World Wide Web Consortium and tools like Bobby which will allow you to check the accessibility.

One question to ask is: are we moving to a situation of total inclusion or to social exclusion? The idea is to get more things accessible, and to create more time for people. But we don't know whether that will work. It is sometimes easier to pop down to the shops or go to companies and to ask the personnel to help you.

There are now a lot more online security checks. You used to be known to your local bank. However, there has recently been a mass of online fraud, and levels of security are increasing. You cannot just phone up the bank, now you need to name your first school or your favourite historical date, or the second, third, and fifth letter of your password – items that are relevant only to you. If you have dyslexia, what hope have you got! There surely must be data showing that this is not ethical.

My personal fear is that technology will be used as a vehicle for compliance - and to avoid making public services and public buildings accessible. If you can provide services through technology, you can perhaps avoid the need to make buildings accessible.

Turning to education and training at all levels: will that really become the same? Institutions claim that they are open to everyone because their courses are online. There needs to be both a concept and a culture of accountability.

Older people are forced to use telephone banking: it is becoming more dominant. We are definitely seeing changes in people's use of technology. But rather than telephone banking, what about the use of digital television? You don't really need computers as such. Sky TV is already producing interactive television.

Now, we have legislation like the Disability Discrimination Act in the United Kingdom. There is also important civic and equal rights legislation for example in Australia and Canada, besides the very famous case of the United States of America and its Disability Discrimination Act. What is needed is to take a look at the Americans with Disabilities Act and also the Disability Discrimination Act, and to see how they are impacting on the lives of people with disabilities.

Where is Europe on all this? For example, the eEurope action plan 2002 focuses on inclusion and participation through web accessibility, design-for-all, centres for excellence, and standardization. People say that mainland Europe is more socially conscious. But if you look at what has happened in the United States and in the United Kingdom, it is more advanced. To my mind, Europe is like America in so far as it has lots of (member) states that make legislation. There is both European-wide, and national legislation. Just as in the United States there is both federal and state legislation. So, why can't Europe have a Europe-wide piece of legislation on accessibility and disability that cuts across all the member states?

INFORMATION AND COMMUNICATION TECHNOLOGIES IN THE FUTURE

First, there are the benefits of information and communication technologies for people with impairments. If we look into our crystal ball, we see developments in ambient intelligence and ubiquitous computing, miniaturisation, smart homes, virtual reality, neural networks, artificial intelligence, neuro-surgery, and cybernetics.

As people grow older, they are much more likely to acquire impairments like mobility difficulties or cognitive impairments. The quality of life has now changed enormously for a person with Down's syndrome, who can easily live to the age of sixty. Medical science and effective diagnoses have really helped. However, the quality of life has probably not changed a lot for a person with muscular dystrophy.

In general, it is important to tackle diseases of the nervous system using information and communication technologies. Using a chip, it would probably be possible to interrupt the nervous system of someone who has cerebral palsy or Frederick's ataxia. To give you an example, my arms move a lot on their own: there is plenty of impromptu movement. The brain sends various erratic messages to the nerves and to the limbs. If it were possible to normalise such messages over a certain frequency or intervene in such a nervous system, that would lead to a vast improvement in the quality of life of an individual.

There will also be more importance placed on focusing on skills development - training young people with disabilities to go into the information and communication technologies industry. If young people with disabilities are empowered to use information and communication technologies, they would be all the more likely to go into the computing hardware or software industries.

In 2020, what is the potential and what are the barriers of information and communication technologies? At that time, there will be instantaneous translation and there will be computers on every wall. There will be neural networks implanted in our brains to replace any damaged areas that exist (this is already being done for people who are deaf, or who need eye implants), and chips to stem people's shakes if they have cerebral palsy.

Now, some concerns. The use of closed circuit television (CCTV) is just like George Orwell's 1984, which was spot on. The television screen is watching you. There is a constant watching of individuals occurring in the United Kingdom right now. It could be said to be good - for example in terms of physical crime control or of identifying trouble-makers – and it probably is. But it is also invading people's citizenship. Everywhere in the United Kingdom, you are being watched. But you don't even need CCTV if you have strong enough satellites! The authorities must have huge dossiers based on their global positioning systems!

The recent film Charlie's Angels used GPS-based voice technology. They were reading patterns in people's voices when they were using mobile telephones, to be able to tell where they were. If you see a technology in a film then someone somewhere is surely already using it. It would be surprising if, in the early 1960s, the very first heart transplant was really Dr. Christian Barnard's first attempt.

A man who has been blind since birth who knows me quite well, still expects me to be able to do a lot more physically than I actually can because he cannot see my disability. So, currently, a lot of people who have a disability (but not a speech impediment) would be very happy to hide behind the telephone - because the person at the other end of the phone cannot see that you are a disabled person. But as you get more audio- and video-based communications, that opportunity is going to disappear. So, you have two sides to the question. At least people will come into contact with each other, and become more aware.

By hiding behind a phone, you can avoid people's pre-conceptions. This is true for a lot of activities like telework and other interactions. A lot of disabled people who work in conventional workplaces say, 'I can't do my job because of people's attitudes towards me.' But people soon get used to working with a person with a disability. They soon see the person rather than the wheelchair. People soon get to know you.

Videophones would be very helpful in the process of getting to know people rather than letting people sit behind the telephone. Some of the most magnificent brains on the planet have a disabled body beneath them. But some people with impaired bodies still choose to hide away, especially academics.

We have to change people's attitudes, and we have to change attitudes in the media!

We should not lose sight of the importance of the digital divide, and of the potential that information and communication technologies can offer. But, at the end of the day, it comes down to world governments, including European governments, applying particular policies which can change people's expectations and perceptions. Wherever they are living in the world, whatever their age, people with disabilities should be able to share accessibility, empowerment, social inclusion, and independent living.

Unless you can get out of the bed in the morning, technology is not going to help you very much! But in many countries you need a great deal of support to be able to get sophisticated technologies. The public provision of services is still pretty mediocre in many countries. Commercially, most companies are not likely to do anything until governments get involved. And I think that is the real outcome!

LASTLY, A WORD ABOUT IFIP

In my opinion, IFIP seems to be built on academics, and so it is about the impact of their work in research and technological development. I would like to see more commercial involvement, but I do not think it will happen for three reasons. One, because IFIP is IFIP and it has a history of having members who are academics; two, it is difficult to change such people and to encourage them to make an impact on policy; and then, three, you have the IEEE which is much more business-oriented.

Particularly with the invasive technologies I have talked about, there are real ethical questions that we cannot ignore. It would be especially important for IFIP to look at such issues. IFIP does tend to be strong on ethics. These kinds of technologies will soon be here and will be applied, and we will not have thought through the consequences. We need to do more thinking.

Ethics of Computing

Penny DUQUENOY
Middlesex University, London.
p.duquenoy@mdx.ac.uk

> *"The Introduction of words like "ethics" and "ought" into conversations about science seems almost always to engender a tension ..."* (J. Weizenbaum) [13]

Key words: Computer ethics, professional responsibility, ethical design, software applications, artificial intelligence.

INTRODUCTION

Prior to the launch of new technologies we hear of the benefits these latest developments will bring. As the latest innovations become integrated with, and form the infrastructure of, everyday living, we begin to experience some less positive aspects. Clearly, computer technology brings both benefits and disadvantages – the degree to which either has an impact on individuals and their ability to live a "good life"[1] is the degree to which ethics is relevant to computing.

A number of ethical issues have been discussed and debated over the last twenty years or so under the broad category of "computer ethics". This rather loose term has been criticised for placing ethics – a uniquely human characteristic – onto computers. Despite early predictions in Artificial Intelligence we are still far from being able to ascribe a moral viewpoint to mechanical devices. If, however, we talk about the ethics of computing we are talking about the use of computers – thus placing the moral perspective (and consequently the moral responsibility) firmly in the hands of computing professionals and the users.

It is issues of moral responsibility and moral choice that are at the heart of this paper.

Many computer professionals take the view that they are simply the providers of "tools", and what people choose to do with these tools is not their responsibility. Whilst acknowledging that it would be naïve, and grossly unfair, to put all the moral wrong-doings of society at the door of computer developers, they cannot abdicate all responsibility. They, after all, are the ones who determine through their construction of artefacts the potential and limitation of actions (see [8] for example).

This paper begins by drawing on early discussions concerning ethical aspects of computer technology [9, 13, 14] and proceeds to use them to highlight different problem areas: technical, application, and environment. We then look at some of the major issues under discussion since these early writings, to show the scope of the problems, as well as their changing nature, as different technologies are introduced. This background sets the scene for the discussions of moral responsibility, and moral choices referred to above. Looking towards the future, we then discuss some of the technologies that are on the horizon, and notice some correspondence to concerns raised more than 20 years ago. Finally, we bring together the moral points raised in this work to provide a set of questions that could provide the basis of moral consideration when designing for the future.

BACKGROUND

As early as the mid-1950's Norbert Wiener [14] warned of the dangers implicit in machines that "acted" faster than we could react, and that had a complexity beyond our understanding. He foresaw the human loss of control in situations governed by computers - i.e. the loss of any timely intervention in an adverse situation, coupled with the inability to understand the cause of the problem. The focus here is on the technical characteristics (speed and complexity) of these machines, and their practical consequences. Clearly, if we do not understand what causes a problem then we can neither resolve it, nor predict other outcomes. If we are unable to predict future behaviour or outcomes we are in effect "out of control" of any situation determined by such complex devices. Similarly, if events are happening faster than we can respond to them, then those events are also beyond our control.

Some twenty years later, and prompted by the upsurge of interest in Artificial Intelligence, Joseph Weizenbaum's concern was with the envisioned practical application of computers [13]. That is, the view that computer technology, by virtue of its logical operation could mimic the rationality of human beings. Not only that, but also because they were not prone to 'human error', they could be relied upon to perform tasks more efficiently than humans. His views on the moral limitations of computer applications are presented below.

These two pieces of work are important not only because they were the first early milestones in the area of the ethics of computing and tremendously influential to the ensuing debates. In the context of this article they are useful, in that they identify the two most fundamental aspects of computer technology in relation to ethics. In the first instance Weiner is concerned with the *technical* characteristics of computers, in the second Weizenbaum addresses the problem of their *application* in a social context.

The growing realisation that ethics was not only relevant but a vital consideration of computing gained impetus in the mid-1980's. Attention turned once more to technical characteristics, and their unique properties prompting a debate lasting 10 years on whether computers raise "special ethical issues" [9]. Central to this debate was the notion that the digital environment of computer technology does not easily map onto its analogue counterpart. In other words, the representation of material in binary form presents difficulties in a world that has traditionally operated with an analogue model. This latter observation sets a different context − the operational environment.

The above three articles identify the features of computers that, individually and in combination, provide the foundation for many of the difficulties we now face: their particular technical attributes, their application, and a digital domain that challenges previous mental models. We will return to these three categorisations later when discussing moral responsibility, and the moral assessment of computing.

THE ISSUES RAISED

To assess the impact of this technology, let us now look at the issues that have been raised by the different dimensions discussed above.

The topics covered and issues addressed between 1985 and 1995[2] are naturally indicative of the chronology of developments during that time. For instance, in 1985, liabilities in relation to defective programmes, and related issues of codes of conduct and professional ethics were major areas of concern. Also on the agenda were privacy, security, as well as power and democracy (as in [4] for example).

As personal computers became more widely available from the 1990's onwards, we see the increasing use of computers in the workplace. Consequently the topics under discussion reflect this move: quality of personal life, quality of work life, impact on employment and third world, legal issues and computer crime. Around this time we also have the introduction of floppy disks and networks – all allowing file transfers – which bring hacking and viruses, and other computer crimes onto the scene. In addition, the topics of artificial intelligence and expert systems make their first appearance.

In latter years (since 1995) the phenomenal upsurge in computer use and inter-connection that has been enabled by the Internet and, in terms of public access, the World Wide Web has broadened the field further. The issues covered reflect the hazards of "interconnectivity": junk email; email monitoring and other aspects of surveillance; intellectual property (now including publishing issues relating to web pages, trademarks and logos); issues of anonymity and pseudo-nymity (including misrepresentation); easy access to illegal and harmful material (in particular pornographic material and its availability to young children); to name but a few.
Furthermore, we see issues discussed in human rights terminology such as freedom of speech, technology and democracy, and equality of access. We also see the appearance of items that are of global concern, specifically: Internet governance and regulation, free speech and content control, encryption, etc.

The issues of privacy and security, on the agenda from the early years, - remain a major concern but gain a change of emphasis. For example, discussions on these subjects in later books (since the Internet), along with discussing personal data, also emphasise monitoring, tracking (i.e. cookies) and surveillance. Thus, whilst there has always been a concern for issues falling under the banner of human rights, the details of how such rights are threatened change as the technology changes and allows a more diverse range of human action. The focus on the impact of the Internet is particularly apparent since 2000 [1, 3, 6, 8, 10, 11].

MORAL RESPONSIBILITY

Looking at the range of issues above it would be understandable to take the view that "these things happen", and that such problems are simply the trade-off we make when we embrace new technologies. However, whilst all of them are the result of developments and decisions made by computer scientists, as noted previously not all the blame should be placed at this door. However, there are some areas where responsibilities for outcomes most obviously fall to the experts. These are the directly technical aspects, such as defective programmes and failed systems, and the problems of hacking and viruses, for example. We have seen from the survey above that the profession has been addressing these issues with professional codes of conduct, and developing technical security measures to combat unauthorised access.

It could also be argued that the privacy issues fall within the technical domain – if general-use programmes (applications) are produced that are lax in their protection of others (email for example) – then the shortfall should surely be the responsibility of the developers. However, other issues of application – such as how and where AI and expert systems are used for example – are the decisions of the users. Taking a wider perspective, how Internet applications are used - whether to exchange ideas or pornography - is also clearly the users' choice.

One of the dominating issues throughout the period is that of Intellectual Property. This is often used as a prime example of the difficulties of mapping digital to analogue [9] – in other words, a problem of understanding and adapting to the new environment as categorised above. It is difficult to ascribe responsibility in this case to either technical experts or users. The resolution of many of these problems has fallen to legislators (in the case of Intellectual Property this is a natural outcome, as it is a legal construct), but who also in their professional capacity have to understand and clearly define the difficult areas. Technical design can allow or disallow access to intellectual property (as in Digital Rights Management applications), but unless some balance is achieved regarding access and cost, users will seek ways to overcome the technical constraints.

MORAL CHOICES

Taking responsibility implies free choice. Society recognises that where individuals do not have a choice in their actions they should not be held responsible for them. Ethical action is also about choice – choosing good over bad, right over wrong, whatever we might determine such things to be. If we are asking technical experts, users and legislators to take moral responsibility for their actions or decisions, we have to assume choices are available. In the following paragraphs we return again to the three articles introduced above, and find that in each of the domains (technical, application and environment) each of the authors offer some interesting ideas for deliberation in this regard.

It is clear that, when designing and developing new technologies, choices are continually being made – how to improve performance, reduce costs, do something that has not been done before, etc. etc. These are all familiar and uncontroversial goals, but each one depends on previous work. In other words, new development does not happen in isolation. This is the gist of Weiner's warning - that even though scientists may have every good intention as to the outcome of their work, that work is part of a larger picture. Each part contributes to continuing development and, eventually, to the whole. In other words, we should be always conscious of where our developments may lead us. Naturally it is beyond our capabilities to envisage all eventualities, but Weiner advocates a "continual scanning and re-evaluation" as the development proceeds, and he presses us to always "exert the full strength of our imagination to examine where the full use of our new modalities may lead us". [3]

Moving on to the second domain, the application of computer technology, Weizenbaum is very clear about his choices. He names three areas where computer applications should not be pursued. In the first category are "ones whose very contemplation ought to give rise to feelings of disgust in every civilized person" and "all projects that propose to substitute a computer system for a human function that involves interpersonal respect, understanding and love in the same category"[13]. We must remember that these comments are set against a background of new research into Artificial Intelligence. The first quotation refers particularly to connecting animals to computers (specifically visual and brain systems) the second is a response to suggestions that a programme he created to demonstrate computer "conversation"[4] could be used to replace psychotherapists. Concerning the latter suggestion he states "...there are some human functions for which computers *ought* not to be substituted. It has nothing to do with what computers can or cannot be made to do. Respect, understanding, and love are not technical problems." [13].

Finally, Weizenbaum warns against anything which "can be seen to have irreversible and not entirely foreseeable side effects", especially when there is "no pressing human need for such a thing". He illustrates his point using the example of speech recognition, pointing out that although promoted as an efficient method for physicians to record notes and take actions more efficiently "such listening machines, could they be made, will make monitoring of voice communication very much easier than it now is." With uncanny foresight, he continues: "Perhaps the only reason that there is very little government surveillance of telephone conversations in many countries of the world is that such surveillance takes so much manpower ... speech-recognizing machines could delete all "uninteresting" conversations and present transcripts of only the remaining ones to their masters". [13].

The choices are not so explicitly laid out in James Moor's paper. As a philosopher, his mission is to identify the "revolutionary" aspects of computers rather than pursue an opinion. However, these aspects – which according to Moor are their invisibility, logical malleability, and social impact – give grounds for discussion. The invisibility factor has a similar consequence to Weiner's warnings about loss of control – when processes are out of sight we are likely to either ignore them, or be unaware of them. In both cases these are usually classed as the benefits, if not the purpose, of computers – that is, to take the cognitive load off the user. Designers can choose to enhance or reveal "invisibility" – dialogue boxes for example reveal occurrences in programmes, often warning that something is wrong. Dialogue boxes characteristically offer the user choices, but users are often unaware of their choices (for instance, in rejecting "cookies"). The charge to designers and developers is to at least be aware of the inherent dangers of "invisibility", and to incorporate choice for the user in the design where necessary – particularly where safety is an issue.

What about "logical malleability"? Moor's explanation goes as follows: "Computers are logically malleable in that they can be shaped and moulded to do any activity that can be characterized in terms of inputs, outputs, and connecting logical operations ... The logic of computers can be massaged and shaped in endless ways through changes in hardware and software" and consequently "the limits of computers are largely the limits of our own creativity."[9] The scope for choice here is clear – we can shape and mould computers to create an environment of our choosing. And so we arrive at his third revolutionary aspect – social impact. There is no doubt about the social impact of computer technology, we need look no further than the list of issues mentioned earlier to see the evidence of the range and scale of impact. However, if further evidence should be required we have only to remind ourselves of the almost global panic as we approached the year 2000, and the cost of the Y2K bug!

THE FUTURE

We have seen the way discussions in the field have been progressing and how the priorities for consideration have changed since the overwhelming rise of the Internet. It seems likely then that there will be more changes in the future. Having said that, some of the current issues - such as Internet governance, and security and privacy, are far from any resolution and will continue to confront us for a long time yet.

The security loopholes of the Internet are almost impossible to address [6], and whilst the emphasis is currently focussed on individuals as intruders into our computer systems (hackers), it is also possible that governments can use these loopholes as well. The debates on privacy are likely to increase as surveillance and monitoring become easier, and governments continue to feel threatened by secure encryption (which may be used against the interests of national security, and law and order).[5]

Regulating, or governing, the Internet is not an easy task - for any regulation to be effective a global approach will be needed. It is likely that the "Net" will fragment into sectors - one level reverting to the original government and scientific communications medium (this is already planned, and referred to as the "Grid"), another level supporting eCommerce, and yet another level providing the public communications space that we are now using. It is possible that we may see a move away from government (democratic) regulation, towards "self-regulation" - which is in reality decided by large corporations. We can see already that regulation is implemented via the technology itself - for example, access to certain web sites can be restricted; encryption protects intellectual property on video and audio content[6] - and there is no reason to suppose this approach will lessen. It is more likely that these technical means will be developed and used in the interests of government and corporate policy. In other words, developers and designers will set tomorrow's scene.

The past has shown us that developments in computer technology are a result of choices made in many areas: development, infrastructure, government policies and take-up by the population. The technological drive is not pre-determined, and there is no "inevitable" future. The future, both beneficial and otherwise, will be formed from the technology that exists at the moment, and choices that will continue to be made in the areas mentioned above. Some choices have already been made, in the sense of research initiatives promoted by governments and other bodies encouraging research in particular areas - current key words are "ambient intelligence", "ubiquitous computing", and the "semantic web"[7]. It seems that future technologies are likely to be increasingly "intelligent" and everywhere! (Even in our clothes, and in our bodies.)

It would be foolhardy in these times of extraordinarily rapid change to offer predictions for the future. Past experience shows technologies put to very different uses than those originally envisaged by the developers (the Internet is a prime example, as is text messaging and mobile phones). It is possible however to consider the consequences of emerging technologies on certain basic human values such as free will (characterised by the ability to make choices), and respect for human life and human dignity (suggested by Weizenbaum).

Work in the field of Artificial Intelligence (AI) has been steadily progressing since at least the 1950's following Alan Turing's celebrated insight relating computation with intelligence. Questions raised even now can be projected towards any future work in this area. So-called "expert" systems and intelligent agents put decision-making in the control of computer technology. Evaluative judgements are inherently human attributes and, as we have noted, provide the basis for ethical action. What ethical and philosophical questions are raised when they are put into the domain of intelligent agents? Will we simply be exchanging human fallibility for machine fallibility? If so, have we gained or lost? With judgement and decision-making comes responsibility and accountability (a basic premise of the judicial system) - how are we to accommodate these attributes into the domain of Artificial Intelligence? And finally, if any notion of ethics is dependant on free will, and the freedom to choose between actions, what is the ethical status of "intelligent agents" that exhibit free will and free choice? There are particular areas of concern where intelligent systems are used and making decisions and judgements on our behalf - for example in medical diagnosis[8]. Perhaps we should give consideration to Weizenbaum's question "is it there a pressing need for such a thing"? [13]

Computer simulations have proved immensely helpful in training - for instance aircraft pilots (and almost certainly in military defense). Simulation techniques are the backdrop for Virtual Reality (VR) - a technological representation of the physical world which includes human representation. Thought must be given to what is represented, and how it is represented. Representations in a virtual world could have an impact on personal identity (impersonation and misrepresentation), or on human dignity (violence or degrading behaviour) [12]. We will need to ask whether the interactive nature of virtual reality surpasses boundaries which might have previously been considered acceptable (e.g. in film making) when directed at a passive audience. Does it make a *moral* difference whether we watch, or we participate? Intuitively it does.

Experiments have been carried out in the area of computer implants[9] and computer chips are now used in animals. Further research is likely to investigate the potential of implanted technology in humans for medical assessments and monitoring. What are the implications of being "always connected"? If tagging is seen as acceptable (used to track offenders instead of being in prison), why not implanted tags? After all, animals are tagged for the purposes of tracking and tracing, as well as for records of medical status. Aside from any health implications, these issues will ensure that the privacy debate will remain lively and controversial.

In all of these examples we are reminded of Weizenbaum's concerns: connecting animals to computers; simulating human functions involving respect, understanding and love; and surveillance.

Finally, if we are to take information itself as a value - justified by a right to knowledge - then we must accept that everyone should be entitled to equal access. Whilst many governments are committed to promoting equal access to communication technologies - what about equal access to the information they provide? There are risks of preventing access to information through software, for example "digital rights management software" - introduced as a response to fears regarding entitlement to Intellectual Property. This software is designed to specifically restrict access, and is supported legally by United States government through their introduction of the Digital Millennium Copyright Act 1998 which criminalizes any attempt to technically side-step Digital Rights Management technologies. In this case the technology has government backing – but in other situations corporations and organisations can, through software, regulate use. [8]

CONCLUSIONS

We have seen how computer technology not only changes interaction, but also facilitates different ways of interacting, and opens up potential activities hitherto unrealisable. When taking the ethics perspective it is easy to be dismayed at the possibilities of adverse intent. We should not forget that when all is said and done, computer technology does provide real benefits in a great many areas – a prime example being global communications. We do recognise that the benefits of these technologies have been immense. However, the arguments for the benefits of new technologies are well supported by the companies who develop and supply them, and the media. There should also be a balancing point of view – and this too is gaining momentum. There are already a number of initiatives in the field of business ethics, and computer ethics is gaining ground in this respect[10]. Raising public and organisational awareness is a first step.

Just because new technology introduces ethical challenges, it is important not to forget that how we respond to them, and how we can shape the future, is in our hands. (After all, someone chooses what programming code will be devised and written.) There has always been, and will always be, those who exploit situations for their own advantage and against others. Fundamental to any discussions on ethics is the principle that human beings have free will - that is, each person can make a free choice in regard to thinking and their actions. We should perhaps follow Wiener's advice and "exert the full strength of our imagination to examine where the full use of our new modalities may lead us".

Taking some of the key values drawn out in this paper (choice, dignity and respect, equality of access) can provide a basis for "examining new modalities". We could ask of future technologies:

- To what extent do they allow or prevent individual choice?
- To what extent do they raise or diminish human dignity?
- To what extent do they respect or impoverish person-hood?
- To what extent do they provide equal opportunity, and equal access?

168

And in all cases we should ask ourselves: What is the trade-off, and how far are we prepared to go?

REFERENCES

[1] Baase, Sara (2003) *A Gift of Fire: Social, Legal, and Ethical Issues in Computing* (2nd Ed.). Prentice Hall.

[2] Duquenoy, Penny. and Harold Thimbleby (1999) "Justice and Design" in *Human-Computer Interaction*, INTERACT'99, M. Angela Sasse and Chris Johnson (Eds.) IOS Press on behalf of the International Federation for Information Processing (IFIP).

[3] Hamelink, Cees J. (2000) *The Ethics of Cyberspace*. Sage Publications.

[4] Johnson, Deborah G. and Snapper, John W. (1985) *Ethical Issues in the use of Computers*, Wadsworth Publishing Company. (Out of print).

[5] Johnson, Deborah G. (1985) *Computer Ethics* (2nd Ed.). Prentice-Hall Inc.

[6] Kizza, Joseph Migga (2002) *Computer Network Security and Cyber Ethics*. McFarland.

[7] Kling, Rob (Ed.) (1991) *Computerisation and Controversy: Value conflicts and Social Choices* (2nd Ed.), Academic Press.

[8] Lessig, Lawrence (1997) *Code and other Laws of Cyberspace*. Basic Books.

[9] Moor, James H., (1995) "What is Computer Ethics?" in *Metaphilosophy*, 16 (4)

[10] Langford, Duncan (Ed.) (2000) *Internet Ethics*. McMillan Press.

[11] Spinello, Richard (2000) *Cyberethics*. Jones and Bartlett.

[12] Whitby, Blay (1996) *Reflections on Artificial Intelligence*. Intellect Books.

[13] Weizenbaum, Joseph (1993) *Computer Power and Human Reason*. W.H. Freeman and Company, San Francisco. First published 1976.

[14] Wiener, N. (1960) "Some Moral and Technical Consequences of Automation". *Science*, 131, pp.1355-8.

---

[1] Aristotle's Eudaemonia – where well-being and morality are intrinsically linked.

[2] The initial analysis of topics covered in the computing ethics literature between 1985-1995 was carried out by Prof. Jacques Berleur, and the 1995 to current survey was a collaboration between Prof. Berleur and Penny Duquenoy.

[3] A similar approach was suggested in [2] whereby the idea of using John Rawls Theory of Justice, in particular designing from a "veil of ignorance" was used to encourage designers to imagine different possible perspectives.

[4] Called "Eliza" this programme responded to input questions with seemingly intelligent replies.

[5] There have been many discussions on this topic. For both sides of the argument see Dorothy Denning "Clipper Chip Will Reinforce Privacy" and Marc Rotenburg "Wiretapping Bill: Costly and Intrusive" in [6]. In the UK the

Regulation of Investigatory Powers Act (RIP) (2000) provoked a storm of protest from civil liberties groups.

[6] This technology is promoted as "Digital Rights Management" software (DRM).

[7] For example, the Engineering and Physical Sciences Research Council (UK) proposes to further research into ubiquitous computing, and the "semantic" web; the European research funding agencies refer to "ambient intelligence". Tim Berners-Lee: " the semantic web will raise moral questions" (speaking in Oxford, UK, 2001).

[8] For discussions on ethical aspects of Artificial Intelligence and Virtual Reality see [11]

[9] For example, the research of Kevin Warwick, Professor of Cybernetics at University of Reading. (http://www.kevinwarwick.com/)

[10] Ethics is gaining a higher public and organisational profile. To take just one example, the Royal Society of Arts in 1997 organised a Forum for Ethics in the Workplace. The discussions have instigated a number of projects addressing similar questions to the ones raised in this article. Who makes the decisions about innovation in industrial science? At what point in the R&D process are these decisions made? What are the criteria? Do ethical or social considerations play any part? *RSA Journal,* 1/6 2002 p.26.

Ethical Questions on the Governance of the Internet

Jacques BERLEUR
IFIP-TC9 and SIG9.2.2 Chair
University of Namur (Belgium)
jberleur@info.fundp.ac.be, http://www.info.fundp.ac.be/~jbl

Key words: Code of ethics, deontology, governance of the Internet, self-regulation

INTRODUCTION

The writings that initially launched the debate on the ethics of computing date back to 1985. 'Computers and Ethics' was the title of a special edition of the journal *Metaphilosophy,* published by Terrell Ward Bynum,[1] in which James Moor defined 'Computer ethics', a term which was reused in Deborah G. Johnson's book, which would become a classic in its class.[2] And here we are today invited to think about 'Cyberethics'.[3]

We should not forget, however, that Joseph Weizenbaum's 1976 *Computer Power and Human Reason* explicitly touched upon the question of ethics, specifically in chapter 10, 'Against the imperialism of instrumental reason', in which he indicated the types of research that he would not undertake, except after careful consideration and within defined limits.[4] It should also be remembered that from 1979 to 1982 the Council of Europe, under the direction of Herbert Maisl, drew up a number of reports on the deontology of computing, but which were not followed up, other than in the form of the normal Council recommendations of a more legal nature.[5]

The available literature in the English language has become abundant and, all too often, everything and anything becomes an occasion to reorder, under the heading 'Computer Ethics', subjects which would otherwise fall into the category of 'Computers and Society': privacy, the responsibility and reliability of software, intellectual property rights, computer crime, security, and so on. This hesitation is felt in the attempts at classification, such as that of Herman Tavani for example.[6] We are not fond of the term 'Computer Ethics' and prefer 'Ethics of Computing', one that better allows us to comprehend the choices that individuals, companies, and society are able to make.

Few works in the French language are to be found under the category 'Ethics of Computing' or under similar categories, but numerous subjects are reused elsewhere in the doubtless more disciplinary works. This is certainly the case for issues in which the law intervenes more explicitly.

We might like to focus our subject matter and follow the development of works that have been carried out within the International Federation for Information Processing (IFIP).[7] They will successfully illustrate, we believe, the trends that are found again in the mainly Anglo-Saxon works, whose global influence is growing.

The IFIP has mainly worked in three domains of the ethics of computing: the codes of deontology of its member Societies, the position of ethics in the governance of the Internet and more recent questions about self-regulation.

ON THE CODES OF ETHICS OR OF CONDUCT FOR IT PROFESSIONALS

From 1988 to 1992, the IFIP as an international association examined the possibility of adopting an international code of ethics that would have bound all of its members. However, apart from some members, who were individually recognised for their service to the federation, membership of the IFIP is only awarded to national Societies who are composed mostly of IT professionals. This situation in a way renders obsolete those arrangements that bind just the associations and not the individuals. Furthermore, certain unwillingness was exhibited by numerous member Societies to a way of advancing which would cause the cultural, social and legal differences to be less apparent and that would impose an approach that in effect was more characteristic of an already dominant culture.[8]

Starting almost from scratch, a Task Group carried out an analysis of all the existing codes within the IFIP and proposed recommendations, which were adopted at its General Assembly meeting in 1996.[9]

The objects of this study were the roughly thirty professional codes enacted by 20 Societies (of the fifty or so having a statute of full member, affiliate, or corresponding).

No title seems meaningful: both codes of ethics or of conduct are spoken of, as are guidelines, standards and so on. The obligations most often link individual members, but can sometimes concern the Societies themselves. It is interesting to note that the obligations refer not only to customers, but also to the society as a whole, or to 'users', thus overreaching the strict design of codes of *professional* deontology.

A pattern emerges from the analysis, which concerns the contents on which the duties are based. Five main fields of obligation are thus covered:

- *a general attitude of respect,* including respect for the interests or rights of the people involved (15/30), respect for the prestige of the profession (11), respect for the interests or rights of the public (10), and respect for the welfare, health of the public and for the quality of life (10);

- *personal (/institutional) qualities such as professional conscientiousness, honesty and positive attitude, competence and efficiency:* conscientiousness and honesty are encountered under the expressions such as acceptance of responsibility (19/30), integrity (26), respect for contractual obligations (14), conscientious work (11), professionalism (7), the credit given for work done by others (6); competence and efficiency are covered by terms such as professional development and training (19), the limitation of work to one's field of competence (18), general competence (13), efficiency and quality of work (12), etc.;

- *the promotion of the private character of information and the integrity of data:* confidentiality (22/31), privacy in general (14), respect of property rights (12), no computer crime, no information piracy or misuse (7), etc.

- *the production and the flow of information:* flow of information to concerned parties and to individuals (23/31), public information (16), and so on; and finally

- *an attitude vis-à-vis regulations:* respect for the code (13/30), laws (13), professional standards (12).

Examination was also made of the capacities of enforcement, the procedures relative to complaints and penalties. This comparison turned out less straightforward, since membership structures often affect the efficiency of penalties or sanctions in particular.

We have said: these codes are the distinctive feature of a very Anglo-Saxon tradition, that has been anchored in countries that have had regular contact with the United Kingdom, such as Australia, Canada, the USA, India, Zimbabwe, New Zealand, and so on. Of the twenty or so Societies counted, only two escape this sphere of influence, Italy and Germany.

Furthermore, to avoid falling back into 'monoculture', it has appeared wise to recommend that these elements of analysis be examined by other national Societies in the 'Spaces for discussion', which evaluate its relevance. The Task Group has suggested developing a 'procedural ethic', according to the more theoretical views of Jürgen Habermas,[10] as well as one in which beliefs and convictions may be exchanged, from which an order of principles may arise that can be developed in the various situations.[11]

The method seemed all the more important because an in-depth work should be embarked upon in the domains most directly linked to computing. Of the five domains mentioned above, two effectively deal with questions more directly linked to this discipline. The IFIP has suggested paying particular attention to questions, such as those, which are regulated today by the Council of Europe's recent convention on cybercrime: illegal access to, or illegal interception of data, data interference, system interference, misuse of devices, computer-related forgery, computer-related fraud, offences relating to child pornography, offences relating to infringements of copyright and related rights, attempt and aiding or abetting.[12] The IFIP had also underlined that the development of the Internet should focus more closely on the diversity of nations and that questions could only be addressed on the basis of respect for differences and therefore that it was urgent to put in place spaces for discussion, where problems could be examined according to different cultural, social and legal situations. In whatever form it takes, the important issue was that the ethical question remains in place in the different debates that surround the development of information and communication technologies.

ETHICS AND THE GOVERNANCE OF THE INTERNET

The questions linked to the governance of the Internet came to light, or in any case, became more lively in October 1998, at the moment of transfer of authority for the attribution of IP addresses and domain names from the IANA (Internet Assigned Numbers Authority), under contract with the US government, to the ICANN (Internet Corporation for Assigned Names and Numbers), a private non-profit association, which represents the interests of the business world, the technical world, the academic world and the wider community of Internet users.

However, by launching its campaign 'One Planet, One Net' in December 1997, an association of activists called the Computer Professionals for Social Responsibility (CSPR) made known that the debate on governance was not restricted to technical questions of the IANA and the ICANN, but also covered questions of standardisation, content development and control, as well as access to the Internet.[13]

Defenders of regulation, of non-regulation, of an unfettered and unregulated Internet,[14] of a co-regulated Internet have provoked a debate that is far from over today.

A certain number of initiatives in relation to Internet codes had preceded this process of awareness. We reflect on the 10 commandments of the Computer Ethics Institute, Washington DC (1992), on the 12 commandments of the Internet issued by the Internet Society of New

Zealand (1997), on the Wartburg Charter developed in the context of the closure of German sites of Compuserve (1997) in connection with certain illicit content found on its servers, on the French Internet Charter (1997), proposed immediately after the work of the A. Beaussant Commission, not forgetting the rules of Netiquette[15] or the numerous codes developed specifically by associations of service providers, etc.

All these documents were in the charge of groups which were larger than the professional IT societies and, one way or the other, were attempting to show certain problems linked to the Internet, either to offer some first solution principles, or to suggest procedures, or simply with the aim of 'legally' protecting the firms or organisations which were involved in the Internet. Thus, the British 'Internet Service Provider's Code' (ISPA-UK, 1996, Rev. 1999), for example, or the one from the same association in Belgium (ISPA-Be, 1998), or the French Internet Charter, (although it was never adopted), were quite representative of the questions being studied by the service providers associations. The subjects and domains towards which the 'Internet actors' made a commitment to respect certain rules and usages, dealt with manifestly illicit content and actions (mainly paedophilia, incitement to racial hatred, denial of crimes against humanity, the call to murder, mediating for prostitution, drug trafficking, attacks against national security), prejudicial, harmful and sensitive content (pornography and violence)[16], fundamental rights and freedoms (freedom of expression, right to information, safety, privacy, property rights, and so on), protections of intellectual property rights, the protection of consumers in electronic commerce.

But where was the ethical dimension in all that? Certain documents appeared normative, without any doubt, but nevertheless remained very vague in their stipulations. Others went into detail, but quickly turned out to be a way for service providers, for example, to protect themselves in relation to voluntary and involuntary abuses by their clients.

The IFIP Special Interest Group on Ethics of Computing documents (IFIP-SIG9.2.2) has drawn up a certain classification and a rearrangement of the questions in these.[17] There are, we conclude, what one might call a *pragmatic agenda* for which 'electronic commerce' will undoubtedly be one of the motors. We find again questions related to risk, to security measures, to reliability, to legal responsibility, to intellectual property rights, to all that is to be found under the category of 'computer crime', to the examination of the protection of competition, to questions of privacy and of confidentiality, to encryption and to questions linked with the key escrow, to the protection of consumers (among others vis-à-vis the power of monopolies), etc.

Some of these questions were already on the agenda of governments and international and public authorities. One could doubtless add diverse less-publicised questions to the list: at a cultural level – the study of all technological dreams, utopias, metaphors, and their power of self-legitimisation and, more fundamentally, all the questions linked to education and training; at the socio-economic level – the impact on the world of organisations and, finally, the re-examination of the roles of governments and the questions raised by the concepts of 'co-regulation' or 'multi-regulation', as discussed during the 1999 Summit of the Regulators, to which we shall return later.[18]

IFIP-SIG9.2.2 therefore proposed to concentrate the ethical debate on questions, some of which featured, perhaps, on the 'pragmatic agendas', but on the subjects where *ethical content* was even more explicit: equity in the right of access and specifically 'universal service', questions linked to the respect of the dignity of the person – protection of minors and human dignity, illegal and harmful content, paedophilia, racial hatred, denial of crimes against humanity, incitement to murder, to drug trafficking, violence and so on; questions of social justice and exclusion – the 'digital divide' not only in North-South relations, but also in the redistribution of labour. Respect for the interests and the rights of the individual, free speech and the examination of questions of censorship, quality of life, the right to information, personal qualities (honesty, competence), the refusal of the abuse of power. Respect for cultural differences, the anchoring of the virtual in the real, upholding the freedom of choice in relation to electronic services, etc.[19]

In conclusion, IFIP-SIG9.2.2 called for a clarification of questions under debate, in attempting to specify their cultural, economic, legal, social or ethical character to better measure the interests of the actors present. It noted the return of ethics in the field of daily practice (the 'lifeworld' of Habermas) and advocated, like in 1996, the development of spaces for discussion where the whole of these questions could be debated by all the actors involved in governance. It did not exclude the argument forwarded by certain people of an 'instrumentalisation of ethics' aimed at employing the probable legitimisation of moral measures to clean up the Internet, and so lead the charge against opponents of regulation itself, by imposing a system of self-regulation that would protect private interests. Who knows? It matters, we repeat, that the ethical dimension is present in debates about governance, since it is about the domination of technological development, about 'control', about regulation of a technological system integrated into our social practices.

ETHICS AND SELF-REGULATION

Since 1999 governance seems to press the question of self-regulation more forcefully. Why 1999? The debate clearly pre-dates this. Codes of deontology, which have already been mentioned in the first section, already represent a sort of self-regulation, as do too the widely distributed codes of 'Business Ethics'. In March 1998 the Business and Industry Advisory Committee (BIAC) and the OECD jointly organised a Forum on Internet Content Self-regulation.[20] We note however that the list of 'relevant sites and documents' was still not very rich. We are specifying 1999, because events appear to stand out: the Summit of the Regulators that we have already mentioned, the work of the Bertelsmann Foundation on the self-regulation of Internet content and the 'recommendations' of the Global Business Dialogue on Electronic Commerce (GBDe), created in January 1999, whose first assembly was held in Paris on 13 September of that same year,.

Starting again its research of self-regulation in a more systematic way, IFIP-SIG9.2.2 established a classified inventory of about forty texts adding to the thirty or so professional codes previously listed. Their analysis had been established following an analytic framework identical to that normally used in the analysis of legal texts: we examined, successively, *ratione personae*, the authors and individuals concerned or affected, then *ratione loci*, the geographical areas in which the agreements were applicable, then *ratione materiae*, the subjects and domains mentioned, and finally the application measures or enforcement and the sanctions and penalties.[21]

This is not the place to expand upon the results of the analysis of those documents. We have done so elsewhere.[22] We will however, go over some essential elements related to the governance of the Internet. What immediately comes to mind is that we have nowadays given up on self-regulation 'in general' to expand it in more and more specific domains of virtual communities, service providers (as already mentioned), the other service providers (less localised, such as Excite, GeoCites & Yahoo, Global One, and so on), certain services and governmental actors, industry in general, and finally a set of private sectors, - among these that of health, editing, electronic commerce, software publishers, telemarketing, and so on. However, from the most general to the most specific, the form of norms seems to be changing from norms of more or less deontological nature when it concerns the Internet *in general,* to increasingly precise clauses, but of an essentially contractual type when we tackle the most specific domains and, above all, the specific sectors. Thus, in examining, for example, the eHealth Code of Ethics by the Internet Health Care Coalition, we will not be surprised to note that when buying medical 'products and services' one engages in 'responsible business relationships' and that one is guaranteed 'best business practices'.[23] Medical treatment is dealt with in a very similar way to all 'business'. We are not really surprised when we learn that 52 million Americans look up medical and health information on the web and that the paper which gives that information in fact comes from the

Department of Trade![24] The rules of the advertising and marketing organisations on the Internet point out, from their side, that obligations exist concerning: the declaration of identity, the information to be supplied to consumers and its quality, the non-sending of unsolicited commercial messages, etc. [25] In the publishing sector, we are told how many paragraphs we may quote – without prior consent – without being prosecuted for plagiarism, as well as conditions for 'electronic reproduction' or archiving, etc.[26]

Where are ethics in all that, without reducing the rules to good conduct, very often unchecked, if not 'uncheckable', and, in any case, devoid of any complaints procedure or penalties?

Self-regulation, regulation, co-regulation? Such were the key words of the Regulators World Summit of 1999 that we already mentioned earlier, a gathering of more than 60 regulating authorities from five continents.[27] Does that mean that everyone sung in chorus? Far from it. Certainly, for some (Canada, for example), self-regulation seemed to be accepted, it should be accompanied by parental guidance. For others (Lebanon, Burkina-Faso, Italy, for example), at the extreme end, regulation should be set at many levels, where fitting: at the international level first, general rules; at the national level, following and in accordance with the first, their specification. The proponents of co-regulation (Australia) proposed the development of codes of conduct in partnership and in accordance with the Australian Broadcasting Authority. M. Vivant underlined in his summary of the debates, that without a will to make everyone agree, it seems quite evident that the Internet will experience 'multi-regulation' or a 'plural regulation' while noting that in view of the present inequalities – notably in access to the Internet – "between the strong and the weak, it is the law that liberates and freedom that oppresses." (Lacordaire) As for co-regulation, the concept in itself demands clarification, because if, for some, it means that self-regulation is not envisaged except under the charge of public authority, for others it implies the application of a strict principle of subsidiarity. M. Vivant suggested considering "the institution of dialogue and consultation structures between public and private Internet actors." It is in this sense, very certainly, that the Forum of Internet Rights was set up in France in 2001.[28]

On the subject of self-regulation, it is certain that the electronic commerce sector is getting all the attention today, if not from all partners and protagonists, at least as much as from those promoting it. To give an example, we might reflect on the Dutch initiative 'Electronic Commerce in Nederland' (ECP.NL) and on its 'Model Code of Conduct', whose simplicity has not greatly changed as one advances through successive versions: reliability, transparency, privacy, confidentiality remaining the only chapter headings. In spite of the many comments concerning the necessity of anticipating rules on enforcement, as well as a complaints and penalties process, nothing is visible in the final version, except, as was already indicated in previous versions, that it would be a good idea to plan them.[29]

Another motor of self-regulation in electronic commerce is certainly the Global Business Dialogue on Electronic Commerce (GBDe) whose president of the French Forum on Internet Rights, Mrs Is. Falque-Pierrotin, wrote at the end of 1999 that it was about "a caricature of this new Church that wants to limit state intervention as much as possible in the name of pragmatism and economic realism."[30] The 'caricature' is on the up! GBDe is an initiative of CEOs of big businesses such as AOL Time Warner, Fujitsu, Vivendi Universal, Accenture, Toshiba, Telekom Malaysia, Korea Telecom Freetel, Cisneros Group of Companies, Seagram, Eastman Kodak, Walt Disney, Hewlett Packard, IBM, MCI Worldcom, Alcatel, ABN AMRO Bank, DaimlerChrysler. With their 'sherpas', the CEOs go from summit to summit, the 'Davos' of eCommerce as they say. In Paris in 1999, 8 topics were on the agenda: authentication and security, consumer confidence, commercial communication and content, infrastructure and market access, intellectual property rights, legal jurisdictions and responsibilities, the protection of personal data, and taxes and tariffs. At the summit in Miami in 2000, the themes were much the same, but we see alternative methods of dispute resolution, digital bridges (as opposed to digital divides); cybercrime, commercial trustmarks. The Tokyo summit in 2001 brought some new modifications into the scope of the conference, thus the list became: consumer confidence (personal data privacy protection, alternative dispute resolution, trustmarks), convergence, cultural diversity, cyber-security, digital bridges, eGovernment, intellectual property rights, Internet payments, taxation, and trade/WTO.[31] The Brussels (2002) and Tokyo (2003) recommendations have added new items such as the Brodband, the Spectrum management policy, the unsolicited electronic communication (Spam), and the Radio Frequency Identification (RFID).

The reports exhibited during these summits still have not taken the form of self-regulation documents, but are full of recommendations to companies, as well as to public authorities. Two examples: in the recommendations on eGovernment (Tokyo 2001), the authors noted (within a dozen lines) that the success of IT investments will heavily depend on the digitalisation of government administrative functions. They then recommended certain specifications for eGovernment, from the point of view of the private sector, that would contribute to its effective achievement, then concluded: "the new role assignment will be a model for a new social system" (sic!) ... able to make the aforementioned investments profitable (Nda). In another field, that of 'Cyberethics', a Statement of Principles on Cyberethics in two pages, does not talk much about subjects other than prevention relating to "unethical material, such as pornography involving children, anti-Semitic, racist or xenophobic content" and the promotion of "free speech and expression as well as artistic and journalistic freedom." Nothing in this declaration concerning the other domains in which the GBDe operates intensively, it is as if no ethical questions were raised there.

Finally, we would like to briefly evoke the hard work carried out under the direction of the Bertelsmann Foundation, and in particular its political media division, on 'self-regulation of Internet content'.[32] It is useful to know that talking about 'content' regarding the Internet is the same as talking with prudery about what was brought up in the European Commission's Green Paper on the protection of minors and human dignity, the Communication on Illegal and Harmful Content on the Internet, and the Action Plan on Promoting Safe Use on the Internet, the so-called 'Internet Action Plan'.[33] The Foundation's project, carried out from 1st February 1999 to the end of March 2001, comprises several parts: support for hotlines, codes of conduct, the development of filters, education in schools, and so on. Several seminars punctuated the project's steps, aimed at developing alternative regulatory structures and at increasing the awareness of the new roles played by service providers and users; to guarantee the effective protection of minors, while not hindering the free flow of information, and to promote filer technologies. One 'Model Code' was put to discussion.[34] It concerned propositions essentially aimed at content and service providers and which dealt with illegal and illicit content, with the position to adopt when faced with unwanted messages, with the protection of data and with privacy and so on. In fact, we are faced with a library of existing codes that have the advantage of representing widespread ideas. We also appreciate the offer of public consultation and the evaluation framework that accompanied this 'Model Code'. We have been recently informed by the Bertelsmann Foundation that there was no follow up to the 'Model Code' proposal. We mention again that the Bertelsmann Foundation is one of the partners of the Internet Content Rating Association (ICRA) which today is trying to promote labelling standards within the framework of, notably, the Internet Action Plan.[35] Here again we find some large firms, AOL Inc., Bell Canada, British Telecom, Cable and Wireless, IA Japan, IBM, Microsoft, Yahoo, besides, of course, organisations whose prime function is to protect children from the dangers of the Internet: the Internet Watch Foundation, the Parents Advisory Group for the Internet, Kids Domains Inc, amongst others.

Would it not be correct to question the reasons for the presence of all these firms in the nerve centres of Internet self-regulation, in particular in a field as sensitive as the protection of children? Curiously, public authorities appear absent if not sidelined from these places, where the common good should prevail and where fundamental ethical debate begins. Would it not also be right to question the power of organisations whose convergence is precisely one of the major economic interests? Where is the leeway for the public in this game?

IFIP-SIG9.2.2 concentrates today on defining what it believes should be the minimum standards to which the self-regulation codes should conform, specifically from the ethical point of view. Similar works have been undertaken in relation to eCommerce, using the framework of the International Chamber of Commerce, for example[36]. We also reflect on the eConfidence Forum programme of the European Commission and on the principles that are being discussed regarding codes of conduct for eCommerce.[37] The Bertelsmann Foundation's 'Model Code' proposition doubtless comes down to the same preoccupation in the field of the protection of content.

CONCLUSION

To be read and known, a code should, we say, be brief. The other side of the coin is that it will be terminally vague, or, in any case, will not go into too many details. Would it be enough to guarantee a minimum of regulation? How can a code deal with questions like privacy in a few lines, whereas the European directive on the subject 95/46/CE expands on 34 articles, spread over 20 pages of the *Official Journal of the European Communities*? Reading these codes is sometimes perplexing and we have the right to ask if laisser-faire is an adequate solution. What is their place in the legal pluralism? Are they a complement or a substitute to the law or are they the anticipation of it?

Our object was not to ask ourselves questions about self-regulation as such, but rather to consider the ethical questions surrounding the governance of the Internet. It is the question of governance itself that has led us to question self-regulation. And it is from within this concern that our questioning has sprung.

The recent tendency to multiply the instruments of self-regulation compels us to ask the question as to whether, in the name of ethical requirements, there are not contents that should escape self-regulation.[38] Should we leave it up to certain private interests, even if they are enlightened, to define the norms in domains that concern relationships not only to economic, but also cultural, social and political life? We have given ourselves a criterion that, without solving everything, appears to us to be a direction for reflection, one that is linked to the Kantian type of deontology: as soon as the interests of the majority are put at risk and the individuals concerned by that risk are being made more vulnerable and fragile, an authority should intervene that keeps open the 'horizon of universalism (or universalisation)' specific to the ethical dimension.[39] It is clear that this criterion, and in particular the 'horizon of universalism (or universalisation)' leads to a concentration of the primordial questions to be put to discussion: equality of rights of access, the fights against social exclusion, the protection of minors and of human dignity, etc.

It seems to us, however, that ethical questions do not only deal with content targeted by self-regulation, but also with the procedures through which the democratic game risks being played, out-manoeuvred or threatened. Participation in the creation of instruments of self-regulation appears essential. Is there no space to go further and to define a legal framework – according to normal democratic criteria – that allows the development of instruments of self-regulation that genuinely instil trust in people, because they will have been involved in one way or another, most specifically through systems of representation?

From the perspective of the procedural ethic that we have drawn up, ethical and democratic questions tend to meet. It would seem difficult to plan for self-regulation, such as would not be framed by law, without risking an ethical deficit.

A number of arguments put forward are often nothing but false explanations. One assumes that everything is worldwide in this global village and that the law is territorial. But one forgets to see that codes – in any case everything that we have examined – do not solve this question, for they are also all 'local'. We say that the problems are new and that the law is ill-prepared. Are we thus implying that judges are more ignorant than so-called experts? We might also insist on the subjects' evolutionary rhythm. It cannot be denied. But is it a reason for adopting tools, often hastily written, whose only effect at the end of the day is to inexpensively satisfy certain insufficiently expressed demands?[40]

The governance of the Internet should more circumspectly examine the questions that it has itself raised and which commit one more than the often-repeated shallow interests. It seems urgent to us to deepen the reflection, which we believe has been accumulated by the various codes of good conduct, but which will not be effective unless these take the ethical dimension into account. According to the Kantian categorical imperative that we referred to earlier, only that which is for the good of everybody is 'ethical'.

It is fine and good that some measures have been taken for protective reasons. But it would be doubtless misguided to have stuck at that and had to have defended some of them with an apparent air of morality. *Promoting the ethics of governance means at least two things:* increasing the participation of everyone in the procedures of drawing up self-regulatory documents and developing content of the sort that also protects interests other than the strictly economic.

May we be forgiven our insistence, our repetitions and our final revision, made without much care for literary norms? In our opinion we must, without delay:

- Pay special and particular attention to questions such as equality of rights of access and especially 'universal service', questions linked to respect for the dignity of the individual – protection of minors and human dignity, struggle against illegal and harmful content, paedophilia, racial hatred, the denial of crimes against humanity, incitement to murder, drug trafficking, violence, and so on; questions of social justice and exclusion, the 'digital divide', - not just North-South, but also in the redistribution of labour; the respect for the interests and rights of individuals, freedom of speech and the examination of questions of censorship, quality of life, freedom of information, personal qualities (honesty, competence), the refusal of the abuse of power, respect for cultural differences, the anchoring of the virtual in the real, the upholding of freedom of choice relating to electronic services, etc;
- Have everyone concerned participating, especially in the drawing up of codes of self-regulation;
- Ask ourselves if the current self-regulation documents are not, primarily, documents about self-protection;
- Agree to stop putting arguments which we know are pertinently false: the necessity to overcome legal jurisdictions, the urgency of filling legal voids, etc;
- Watch that no-one wrongfully grants themselves roles that belong to society as a whole;
- Enforce codes and let nothing into a statute that risks making it a mere pious wish. Set up penalties and procedures for complaints;
- Articulate self-regulation in law;
- Etc.

---

[1] Moor, James H., What is computer ethics?, in: Bynum, W. T., Ed., Computers and Ethics, *Metaphilosophy*, Volume 16, No. 4, October 1985, Basil Blackwell, Oxford and New York, pp. 263-353.

[2] Johnson, D. G., *Computer Ethics*, Englewood Cliffs, N. J.: Prentice-Hall, Inc., 1985, [2]1994, [3]2001.

[3] Spinello, R., *Cyberethics: Morality and Law in Cyberspace*, Jones and Bartlett, 2000.

[4] Weizenbaum, J., *Computer Power and Human Reason – From Judgment to Calculation,* W.H. Freeman and Cy, San Francisco, 1976.

5   Maisl, H., Les problèmes juridiques posés par la déontologie de l'informatique, Study for the Council of Europe (CJ-PD[79]8), Strasbourg, August 6 1979. The following works: Ethics of Data Processing, Categories and Roles in the field of Data Processing (CJ-PD-GT3[81]2 revised), Secretariat Memorandum (CJ-PD[81]8), and the last report (CJ-PD[82]19) with the minutes of the meeting (CJ-PD[82]31), Strasbourg, 1981-82.

6   Tavani, H., The Tavani Bibliography of Computing, Ethics, and Social Responsibility, http://cyberethics.cbi.msstate.edu/biblio/

7   International Federation for Information Processing, http://www.ifip.or.at/

8   We reported this story in : Berleur, J. and d'Udekem-Gevers, M., Codes of Ethics/Conduct for Computer Societies : The Experience of IFIP, in: GOUJON Ph., Heriard-Dubreuil, B., Eds. *Technology and Ethics, A European Quest for Responsible Engineering*, European Ethics Network, Peeters, Leuven, 2001.

9   See Berleur, J. & Brunnstein, Kl. , Eds., *Ethics of Computing: Codes, Spaces for Discussion and Law,* A Handbook prepared by the IFIP Ethics Task Group, London: Chapman & Hall, 1996, 336 p., ISBN 0-412-72620-3 (now available from Kluwer Academic Publishers, Boston). See especially the analysis of Berleur, J. and d'Udekem-Gevers, M., pp. 3-41.

10   Habermas, J., *De l'éthique de la discussion*, Paris, Cerf, 1992. [Orig.: Erlauterungen zur Diskursethik, Engl. Transl.: Justification and Application: Remarks on Discourse Ethics, Cambridge Mass.: The MIT Press, 1993].

11   Maesschalck, M., *Pour une éthique des convictions. Religion et rationalisation du monde vécu*, Publications des Facultés universitaires Saint-Louis, Coll. Philosophie, Bruxelles, 1994, p.376 From the same author: *Normes et contextes. Les fondements d'une pragmatique contextuelle*, Georg Olms Verslag, 2001.

12   Council of Europe - Convention on Cybercrime, STE n° 185, Opening for signature on 23 November 2001. (http://conventions.coe.int/)

13   Computer Professionals for Social Responsibility, http://www.cpsr.org/onenet/

14   Cerf, V., The Internet is for Everyone, in : *On the Internet*, July/August 1999, pp. 8 ff.

15   Rinaldi, A. H., The Net: User Guidelines and Netiquette, http://www.fau.edu/netiquette/net/

16   We refer to the consultation launched by the European Commission (DGX) in its 'Green Paper on the Protection of Minors and Human Dignity in Audiovisual and Information Services', COM(96)483, October 16, 1996, and to 'Decision No 276/1999/EC of the European Parliament and of the Council of 25 January 1999 adopting a multiannual Community action plan on promoting safer use of the Internet by combating illegal and harmful content on global networks.' *Official Journal of the European Communities*, 6.2.1999, L 33/1-11.

17   Berleur, J., Duquenoy, P., and Whitehouse, D., Eds., *Ethics and the Governance of the Internet*, IFIP-SIG9.2.2, September 1999, IFIP Press, Laxenburg - Austria, ISBN 3-901882-03-0, 56 p. This monograph can be downloaded at the URL http://www.info.fundp.ac.be/~jbl/IFIP/cadresIFIP.html by clicking on 'Ethics and Internet Governance'.

18   Conseil supérieur de l'audiovisuel, World summit of regulators on the Internet and new services: a first review. Paris, November 30– December 1 1999. If the

concept of co-regulation was promoted during that Summit, Michel Vivant, in the summary of the debates, preferred the term 'multi-regulation' or 'plural regulation'.

[19] Berleur, J., Duquenoy, P., and Whitehouse, D., Eds., *Ethics and the Governance of the Internet*, doc. cit.

[20] BIAC/OECD Forum: Internet Content Self-regulation, http://www1.oecd.org/dsti/sti/it/secur/act/self-reg.htm

[21] The net result of this analysis can be found in: Berleur, J., Duquenoy, P., d'Udekem-Gevers, M., Ewbank de Wespin, T., Jones M. et Whitehouse D., Documents d'auto-réglementation - Classification - Un premier inventaire, Namur 2001 (http://www.info.fundp.ac.be/~jbl/IFIP/sig922/selfreg.html). We would also note with interest: Internet Resources on Self-Regulation and the Internet, The ABCs of Internet Self-Regulation: An Issues Primer. November 13, 2000. Centre for Law, Commerce and Technology, University of Washington School of Law, http://www.law.washington.edu/lct/publications.html

[22] Jacques Berleur and Tanguy Ewbank de Wespin, Self-regulation: Content, Legitimacy and Efficiency - Governance and Ethics, in *Human Choice and Computers, Issues of Choice and Quality of Life in the Information Society*, Klaus Brunnstein & Jacques Berleur, Eds., Proceedings of the IFIP-HCC6 Conference, 17th World Computer Congress, Montreal, August 2002, Kluwer Academic Publ., 2002.

[23] Internet Health Care Coalition, eHealth Ethics Intitiative, http://www.ihealthcoalition.org/ethics/ethics.html

[24] US Department of Commerce, *Leaders for the New Millenium – Delivering on Digital Progress and Prosperity*, The US Government Working Group on Electronic Commerce, 3rd Annual Report, 2000, p. 20. http://www.ecommerce.gov/ecomnews/ecommerce2000annual.pdf

[25] International Chamber of Commerce, ICC Guidelines on Advertising and Marketing on the Internet, 2 April 1998, http://www.iccwbo.org/home/statements_rules/rules/1998/internet_guidelines.asp

[26] Charte d'édition électronique, (Le Monde, La Tribune, L'Agefi, Les Echos, Investir, ZDNet), http://www.liberation.com/licence/charte.html

[27] Conseil supérieur de l'audiovisuel, World summit of regulators on the Internet and new services: a first review. Paris, November 30– December 1 1999. The summary of foreign contributions in view of the Summit appeared in *La Lettre du CSA*, No. 121, October 1999. Also see *La Lettre du CSA*, No. 129, June 2000, on the activities of the CSA in 1999 and the summary of M. Vivant formerly available at http://www.csa.fr/csaflash.htm (and today *ad instar manuscr.*). This summit was placed under the aegis of UNESCO: several echoes are to be found at http://www.unesco.org/webworld/news/csa_summit.shtml

[28] Forum des Droits sur l'Internet, http://www.foruminternet.org/

[29] Electronic Commerce Platform Nederland (ECP-NL), *Model Code of Conduct for Electronic Business*, Draft 4.0, October 2001, http://www.ecp.nl/ENGLISH/publication/cocdraft4.0ENG.pdf

[30] Falque-Pierrotin, Is., Quelle régulation pour Internet et les réseaux ? in : *Le Monde*, November 1999, p. 17.

[31] Global Business Dialogue on Electronic Commerce (GBDe), http://www.gbde.org

[32] Waltermann, J. and Machill, M., Eds., *Protecting our Children on the Internet, Towards a New Culture of Responsibility*, Bertelsmann Foundation Publishers, Gütersloh, 2000. See in particular the chapter 1 'Memorandum on Self-regulation of Internet Content', p. 25-57 and, in that chapter, §3 'Self-regulation as a Foundation', p. 35-40.

[33] The full sequence of the documents and actions that can be considered as a follow up of the Green paper on the protection of minors and human dignity is given at: http://europa.eu.int/comm/avpolicy/regul/new_srv/pmhd_en.htm

[34] Bertelsmann Foundation, Toward a Model Code of Conduct on the Internet, prepared by Price, M,. E. and Verhulst, St. G., Hanover, June 30, 2000, http://www.bertelsmann-stiftung.de/internetcontent/english/content/c4000.htm

[35] Internet Content Rating Association (ICRA): http://icra.org

[36] International Chamber of Commerce, GUIDEC II, General Usage for International Digitally Ensured Commerce (version II), October 2001 http://www.iccwbo.org/home/guidec/guidec_two/contents.asp

[37] eConfidence forum, A European Commission initiative promoting information exchange and discussions about eConfidence, http://econfidence.jrc.it See : Principles for eCommerce codes of conduct.

[38] Berleur, J., Self-Regulation and Democracy: Choice and Limits?, in: *User Identification & Privacy Protection, Applications in Public Administration & Electronic Commerce*, Fischer-Hübner, S., Quirchmayr, G. S., & Yngström, L., Eds., Dept of Computer and Systems Sciences, Stockholm University/Royal Institute of Technology, Report Series 99-007, 1999, ISBN 91-7153-909-3, p. 1-19.

[39] There are several formulations of the Kantian categorical imperative, one of them being: "We must be able to will that a maxim of our action should become a universal law - this is the general canon for all moral judgement of action." See: Immanuel Kant, *Groundwork of the Metaphysic of Morals*, translated and analysed by H. J. Paton, New York: Harper & Row, 1964, p. 91.

[40] We would read with interest the dossier 'La ruée des entreprises vers l'éthique', which appeared in *Le Monde Initiatives,* December 2001.

The Home in the Information Society

Andy SLOANE
CONTACT Research Group, School of Computing and IT,
University of Wolverhampton, WOLVERHAMPTON, U.K.
A.Sloane@wlv.ac.uk

Abstract: This chapter looks at the position occupied by the home as the central focus of the information society. A working definition of the home is used and various interactions and activities that take place in the home are discussed with relation to the home, and its changing place in the move to an information society. The chapter also discusses various information activities that impinge upon the function of everyday life in the home including the use of information and information systems. Finally some of the consequences of the move to an information-based model of the home are outlined.

Key words   Home, cyberspace, inter-personal communication, interaction, design, information system.

BACKGROUND

This chapter is a review of research carried out by members of IFIP working group 9.3 (Home-Oriented Informatics and Telematics, HOIT) and others. It is not a comprehensive statement of the state of global research in HOIT but a snapshot of various areas of work and does not attempt to cover this wide-ranging and disparate field of work. It concentrates on areas that are, or should be, of current concern to designers and users of home systems. The conference proceedings of the working group have formed the basis of the sources used for the chapter and these are supplemented by significant sources from outside the working group.

INTRODUCTION

There are many functions which can be said to epitomise the "Information Society". What is common in many cases is the focus of these functions being the home environment and the interactions that take place within the home and between home dwellers, others in society and the systems and facilities of everyday life.

Much of current industrial society is based around the concept of work and in particular the "workplace". This model of the industrial society grew up around the separation of the home and the workplace. The movement towards an information-based society has far-reaching consequences for the home and the relative positions of home and work. A good deal of research has covered work and the home – but the focus of this chapter is the "home" function not the "work" function even though the boundary is becoming increasingly blurred. The work aspects of home life are largely omitted from this review. The chapter, therefore, attempts to outline various positions and opinions that have been expressed on the nature of home in the information society and the changes that are likely in this "home" function when movement towards a more information-based society takes place.

The chapter firstly outlines what is meant by the home, which, although a familiar concept, has many different interpretations in the world. Also, the changes that are taking place in the organisation and use of homes is covered. The next section then looks at the problems of studying the home environment and the attendant problems of obtaining data and meaningful results. The chapter then goes on to look at the way homes and society interact and the place that is occupied by the home, in its widest sense, in society. Finally the chapter concludes with a study of the effect of the information society on the home and its occupants, including the social effects of the increasing reliance on information in everyday life. One of the themes that will become clear through this chapter and others in the book is that the information society involves a blurring of boundaries. This is a central part of the argument of how the information society will affect the home and the evolution in the definition of home is a manifestation of these changes. What is also evident from work in this area is that the fabric of the home itself is not the sole area that should concern the designers but also the interactions of the people who live there with the various other objects and actors that influence their daily lives.

THE HOME

What is a home?

The home would appear to be a simple concept. However, the usual frame of reference of the individual is too narrow to encompass a full definition of the multitude of different possible interpretations of the home concept. What one individual may consider to be a home may by others fall short of their definition by virtue of there being some serious deficiency in the make-up of either the physical structure, the occupancy, the services provided, an emotional attachment or some other area that has a bearing on their own definition.

Therefore, where one definition may seem reasonable within one cultural setting, another may be more appropriate in a different culture. A generic definition of "home" may be possible (see [1]) but it is unlikely to bear fruit in all but the simplest of scenarios. As a working definition it is possible to consider the home as being:

> "the area which has the life focus for a range of individuals and their associated service needs including the structure, the occupants and activities that take place there, and their inter-relationships".

This may encompass many culturally unique definitions of the home but not all. Many researchers have used this type of definition [see, typically, 18] both implicitly and explicitly to frame their discussions. What is important to remember is that there are some shortcomings for this as an all-encompassing definition but it serves well as a working definition for many different cultural environments. In the framework of Western countries it fulfils the requirements for study of the Information society and the effects that it will have upon the home in the future. However, it may be that the definition itself will need to be reviewed in the future if some of the more far-reaching consequences are realised.

There are many different definitions in the literature that may also prove useful. These include one that is based on "domestic space ...appropriated psychologically and physically" [10] and also "a collection of milieus: a territory, an expression, a collection of objects..."[19]. Whilst the former is rooted in the real-life aspects of home it incorporates some hint of the virtual in the aspects of psyche that are incorporated in it. The latter definition also uses a general approach that can include these aspects as required. Both these definitions can be used alongside the more functional one chosen here.

Organisation of the home

The home is generally a private space which is occupied by a group of people - often a "family" with the various definitions that this involves. In some cases the home may be a set of unrelated individuals who live in the same physical space. The relationship between the individuals will have an effect on the organisation of the home and the activities that are carried out in it. For example, a family group may consist of an adult pair who work and some children who attend school giving rise to numerous activities that are likely to take place - paid and unpaid work, education, leisure and social activities among others. The occupants and their relationships to each other along with their positions in society will determine their range of activities - some of which will be conducted from home.

The organisation of the home is also a factor in its place in the wider social setting of society and extended family groupings. Some homes become the focus of attention for groups while others are less likely to be used for these activities. Many factors determine the range of activities that will be conducted in the home. The move to an information-based society may change the relative weight of the factors involved or remove some of them altogether.

There are many aspects of home and the interactions that occur with them that require discussion. These include the architecture of the building, the people living in it, the technology used there, the other people involved in the lives of those that live there and wider society. These aspects of the wider definition of the home are discussed later in the chapter.

The place of "home" in society

Homes in traditional societies confer a certain "status" upon the occupiers. In some cultures this is more apparent than in others but largely true to some extent. This status is often a desirable feature of the physical structure, its location, the layout of the structure or its proximity to other homes. It is rarely a consequence of the occupants of the home but this can be a factor. The information society model will have some mitigating effect upon this status factor.

The use of communication networks and information and communication technology will remove the direct link to physical space that has traditionally been the defining statement for the home and replace this with a more information-based definition that will create a new status that will have new dependencies and new factors that will be desirable. This is not to say that all the traditional values will be replaced: mostly the new factors of the information society will add value to the existing status of homes but it is possible that for some users the "connections" will be more important than the structure.

Changes in usage patterns

The move to a more information-based society will also have effects on the usage patterns in the home. A typical example given is the ability to work from home more but this is only one of the many different possibilities that are available in an information society. The use of the physical space of the home is one of the factors often discussed but the ability to mould the logical, social space is found less often but is possibly as significant as the movement of work to the home.

What is evident from the study of information and communication technologies (ICT) over recent years is that people adapt technology to their interests and requirements. The growth in text messaging on mobile phones is a good case of this. The facility is fairly limited in its scope but has become very well used in certain sections of the population, particularly the young. The other technologies that are available to users have also been used and adapted to personal requirements with some being more popular than others. What seems to be evident is that users will use a technology if they see a personal benefit and not use one if there is no advantage.

The changes in use of the home will result, in part, from the take-up of different technologies by home users and the patterns of home activities will change accordingly, based on what users want to do with their environment and how they relate to the other occupants and with other homes that they are connected with. There is also the view that ICTs fundamentally affect what is meant by "home". and have "liberated our domesticity from its dependence on physical location" [5, see also 17, 16].

STUDYING THE HOME

The place of the definitions and the discussion around the changes to them has been necessary to help decide where the boundaries are for any study that takes place. It is clear from the previous section that the boundaries are blurring to an extent that the study of the home needs to encompass more than in the past. Many previous studies have focussed on the use of technology and have been based in the physical environment, even those that look at the virtual aspects of everyday life.

One of the areas that has seen activity in recent years has been the study of the interface between users in the home and the technology involved in the Information Society. This has been an extension to the studies that have been carried out over many years, which have focussed on the use of computers in the work environment. There are, however, significant differences in the approach needed and the structure of the information gathering exercise that make it difficult to obtain valid results from experiments and surveys. Much of the difficulty is caused by the nature of the home and the way in which the occupants use the home to access the services they require. There is also the problem of the presence of the observer being a factor in the behaviour of the subjects.

For example, a study of the use of television (TV) in the home has a number of choices. The experimenters can situate observers in the rooms with the subjects but this will alter their behaviour. They could use technological devices to monitor usage but will lose information as to the dynamics of choice, or they could monitor via closed-circuit television (CCTV) but still have the problem of altered behaviour. Finally the subjects could record their activity. In this case they may not be accurate in their recording! Generally researchers have used all these techniques, and sometimes a combination of them, to gather evidence. (see [9], [11])

Studying home activities

Other difficulties are caused by the difference in the type of activity that takes place in homes. A workplace study is generally directed at making the use of ICT more effective and/or efficient and achieving a designated result. The home is less goal-oriented in some respects, as the only requirement of some activities is to be "entertained", or to spend some leisure time on a pleasurable activity. It is much less easy to measure success in this type of environment than on a workplace activity. There may also be less need to finish at a certain time. For example, a person may be making an object at home to exercise a skill - the completion of the object may be a goal, but the repeated application of the skill may be just as important and the finishing time-scale may be very vague. This can apply equally well to the information society of the present day, but the activities may change. In the past the use of tools to shape objects may have been home activity and in the Information Society the use of software to develop interactive web sites may be just as common.

There are, therefore, two major problems with the study of the home. The activities that take place in the home are difficult to assess since they are not as directed as the activities that have traditionally been studied. Also, observation and recording of data is very difficult since most techniques rely on the co-operation of the subjects and tend to interfere with the very experiment that is being conducted.

HOME-BASED INTERACTIONS

In addition to the problems that have been highlighted in the previous sections there are many different interactions that take place in the home that have an effect on the function and activities that are carried out. These range from the interaction of the home's occupants with the rest of society to the interaction with the physical environment. This section will look at five different interactional areas that are important to the study of the home in the information society.

People-architecture

The architecture of the home is often neglected. It is a factor in the move to the information society that the majority of homes have not been built with a view to being an information society home. There are many factors that could be considered in the design of structures that will be used in an information society. Amongst these are: adequate and useable space for ICT, infrastructure for ICT, the use of private domestic space for public roles in the information society and the design of the living space. Some of these issues are dealt with in the work of Junestrand and Keijer[7, 8]. The shifting boundaries between public and private spaces is also covered by Haddon and Silverstone [15].

People-home

One of the most important interactions is that between the inhabitants and the structure of the home. This has been seen in the past as the interaction between people and the building used as the home, but with the new concepts of virtual and distributed extensions to the home environment [16, 17] this interaction needs to take on an extended definition.

The concept of incorporating virtual and distributed aspects into the home is one that will be a defining characteristic of the information society. The distributed nature of home life is more a factor of modern life than of the increasing use of ICT. Family groups are more dispersed than previously, and communication technology is used to provide aspects of closeness that in the past were only possible when in proximity. It is possible to use ICT to remove the difficulties of communication caused by distribution. This will also increase as technology improves and users become more familiar with its use and possibilities. The incorporation of the virtual is a different aspect of home life. The creation of virtual existence is new, in that the participants of cyberspace do not necessarily meet in real life. These virtual aspects can become important to individuals both within

193

intellectual pursuits and in the provision of affective and emotional support mechanisms. Both the distributed and the virtual tend to change the definition of home that is relevant to this discussion.

In the past, interaction between the home and its occupants was mainly in terms of shelter, security and personal space. In future, with the extension of homes into the digital arena, the interaction will include much of what is now seen as the area of human-computer interaction (HCI) in the sense that the interaction will be embedded in the structure of the home. For example, a home that is shared between different members of a family group, in two or more different physical locations, with a digital shared link between their information sources will need a sophisticated interface to make the virtual, distributed link as transparent as possible and mimic the physical proximity of the more traditional shared environment. This transparency will bring the home and the Internet more closely into the lives of the home occupants and remove the division between cyberspace and real homes.

Home-society

The interface between the home, its occupants and the rest of society has long been of interest to researchers. The changes brought about by a move to an information-based society will allow homes to integrate more fully into local, national and international groupings. This will, however, also have the opposite effect in some areas with the information society outsiders - the "un-informationed" being at a disadvantage should the information society become the main societal model in use. There are a number of areas where the information society is being developed on this interface. Three of these areas are outlined here.

eShopping is a common activity in households where the use of the Internet has become more than a novelty. There are now many companies who specifically design eShopping web sites so that home users can order goods and services online and reduce the necessity for travel and searching through shops. There is much said about the benefits of eShopping and its usefulness but less said about the opposite problems. Positive aspects are the reduction in time spent in stores, travel to and from shops, etc the negative aspects are the increase in isolation, the necessity to pay extra for the service which can deter those that may really need it and often the lack of choice in goods offered for purchase. Research on the comparative shopping experience needs to be done to focus on the future needs of the home users in this important information society activity.

eGovernment is now a common topic of discussions, conferences and projects. The move to more open forms of government is often given as a major factor in the development of more online forms of government.

Whilst it may be true that the use of ICT may lead to more direct involvement by people in their government, it is also prone to the same problems of unrepresented minorities as the more traditional system. Solving the lack of participation will require more than a move to eGovernment and is not adequately addressed. Taking part in the eSociety will be a major area where the home and its ICT can play a part in the future.

eHealth is also an area that has received much attention. Many of the educational messages on health have been difficult to implement because of the lack of an adequate channel for them to reach the required audience. With the home embedded in the information society, the health concerns of individuals can be addressed by direct use of ICT in order to access health information and use it to interact with daily life. For example, health requirements can be programmed into home systems, which could then monitor food ordering information, so that suggested menus could take account of dietary requirements. Many of the systems in use today could do these simple tasks. With ubiquitous computing within the home, they will form a more reliable interface with the information coming from outside the home.

There are many other areas where society and the home meet and this is one of the main arenas of the information society that will shape its final form. The home is a central pivot of society and the way in which it is embedded in society is crucial to the shape that society will take in any future model; be it an information society or some other model not yet envisaged.

Interpersonal communication

A fundamental activity of human society is communication between people. Current levels of civilisation have been built on communication, since without effective means of exchanging ideas, human thoughts and concepts would remain individual. This is true in a home setting also. The structure and organisation of the home relies on communication between the individuals who live in the home space. This interaction is also critical to the everyday function of the home entity. The occupants need to communicate to keep the home environment running smoothly and to co-ordinate their individual activities.

Inter-personal communication can take many forms and many of these are used in the home at present. Voice, text and non-verbal communication are common and typical situations are easy to find. In an information society with the shape of the home changing the use of ICT to mediate this communication is seen as being an adjunct to the more familiar forms of everyday transmissions. A number of research projects are investigating these aspects of home life. Some of these are concentrating on a direct analogy to current forms of communication whilst others are looking at the use of technology to provide new avenues of contact between people in the home. Examples of the former are the work of Harris, Huang and Sloane [6] who are using the concept of the home information system to validate the use of web-mediated communication in a virtual, distributed home setting. Of the latter, there are a number of projects that are using technology to support communication in new ways. Communicating photo-frames[12], where images are enclosed by a frame that can use emotional parameters to exchange low-level information between users; and family-ware[4] where devices are used to link related individuals, thus giving them a sense of contact without direct voice or text exchange. More research in these areas is being conducted showing how technology can assume a role that serves the needs of people in the home environment. What is now clear from other projects is that the use of technology will find a way into everyday life if it is useful to people. Examples of this are the increasing use of email and mobile text messaging to keep in contact.

People-technology

The final interaction of interest is that between people and technology. This has been an area of study for a long time with many different perspectives being found to analyse the interface and the interaction between the objects of interest. There are a number of perspectives that have been developed to study the use of computers, most of which are used in the work environment. However, the home presents a different problem, as discussed earlier.

The social setting of the home requires a different rule base for the design of equipment. The assumptions that are relevant in the workplace no longer hold true. It is unlikely that the home's occupants will have access to extensive training, will want to invest time in learning difficult operating procedures, will use specifically designed ancillary equipment, such as workstations or have room to devote to equipment outside of multi-purpose living areas (or even want to do so). All these factors tend to create a situation that renders traditional analysis redundant and creates a situation that requires specific attention.

THE INFORMATION SOCIETY

The move to an information-based model of society will, therefore, present problems for home dwellers and the designers of homes and the technology that is associated with them. With this in mind it is useful to broaden the discussion to cover those aspects of the information society that are relevant to homes and to see what are the factors that are particularly important to the study of the home in this new model of society. This section will look at the general effect on homes and people, the telematic systems that will be available and discuss some of the issues that arise from their use and the models of organisation that are envisaged.

The effect on homes

The move from a mainly industrial society to one where the majority of individuals process information allows, but does not ensure or enforce, a move away from the centralised workplace to a distributed model that can be based on the home. The home can then be seen as the main unit of organisation in the information society. This leads to the home needing to employ an infrastructure that will allow it to function effectively in this setting, not only as a place of leisure and entertainment as at present , but also as a place of work and production. The infrastructure requirements of homes have also been the subject of some study with the ideas of residential gateways [13] and home network architectures [3] being common topics. What is also required is an integration of the technical and social aspects of the study of these systems, so that the user's requirements can feed into the technical specification and thereby produce systems that are flexible, adaptable and useable in the home environment. The split between the technical and social has not been of benefit to users in the workplace setting and is even less likely to benefit home-based users. The effect on people being more dramatic when their home is the scene of the interaction.

The effect on people

The move from an industrial society to an information society and its attendant re-organisation will create greater focus on the home as it becomes more of a work environment than it is at present. This will have a number of effects on the people who inhabit the home, some of which are evident in current society where home dwellers attempt to mix the functions of home.

Disparity of function. There is a difficulty when a structure has a dual purpose of not having clear delineation between the various functions it is designed to accommodate. In the case of a home it is even more problematic since most homes, at present, are not designed for work in addition to normal living. This creates a disparity between the home and the function that is trying to co-exist with it. This is likely to be less of a problem when homes are designed with the information society in mind but there is a large legacy of current building stock that is unsuitable for the move to the information society.

Peer/Family group expectations. Another area of disparity is between the requirements of work and home life. This is currently a problem in many areas but the stricter delineation between the place of work and home allows for easier management of the problem. For example, when at the workplace people can concentrate on the work task without reference to the home, and the same can be done in the home with the different locations being a useful dividing line. When the home is also the workplace, the worker/home dweller needs to have a better sense of the balance between the tasks of each and be able to function in both environments concurrently, as well as being able to switch modes between home and work.

Work place pressures/politics. The other problem of a move to using the home as a workplace is the divide between those that work at home and those that use a traditional workplace. There are problems of contact with colleagues and not being seen to be part of workplace groupings. This can affect the individual in a number of ways that can be detrimental to career development. This may be a transitional problem, a complete move to a fuller implementation of an information society renders it probable that less workers will be centrally located and the business will be more virtual. The problems will not then be those of the individual, but those of the whole group and their communication between each other. This is likely to be much fairer for individuals than the current transitional problems of those few workers using the home as a workplace. However, the move will need to be well-managed to make it as effective and fair as possible.

Security/Sharing of information

One of the aspects of the information society is the possibility of new modes of living in the home. A move to more virtual presence and contact with the home is already taking place with some virtual parts being added on to existing home modes of life. For example the use of the Internet to form alliances and exchange information between people who are widely separated is a common phenomenon of the late 20th and early 21st centuries. The models of home organisation in an information society may include more virtual presence still with people sharing their information between trusted individuals such as family members who are dispersed and living in other places.

This then leads to the concept of the distributed home where a number of physical spaces are connected together via their information resources and share their data and systems to the extent of forming a single entity of a distributed home. There are obvious limitations of systems such as these but the advantage of using information in this way is to remove the barriers that the distance between people has created

However, when models such as these are used, there is more necessity to ensure that the information being exchanged is secure and confidential as it is likely to be personal. Current systems designed for secure transmission of information in a commercial environment are adequate but often unwieldy in a domestic situation. Secure systems need to be used automatically to ensure that such a scenario is feasible.

Home information systems

To facilitate the scenarios envisaged in the previous section, the home computer needs to evolve towards a more comprehensive system that can be used to host the many functions of the home that can be performed electronically. There are many functions that can be automated and connected in the home and these have seen many different applications over the years and a number of systems are available to perform these automated functions. However, the home is a considerable user of information in its many forms and this is an area where more automated responses and storage are needed.

Some devices are now being marketed with limited functionality in this area but they are directed at single functions rather than being a comprehensive solution to the problem of organising information in the home. The systems are, however, being studied in research labs and projects around the world and a number of systems are likely to be available in the near future. How they will be used, and how people interact with them will be another area of study that will be of interest once they are more widely available.

Mobility

One final aspect of the home in the information society that will become more relevant as people learn to live with the new paradigm, is the increase in mobility that is afforded by the move. Already, people embrace mobile technology even though it is still fairly limited compared with the promise of third generation systems. The type of systems available at present will seem very under-powered and limited when the new networks finally appear and the devices that are promised actually materialise.

The move to the next generation will allow more computing power to be used along with higher speed connections and consequently there will be fewer differences between mobile and stationary systems in terms of functionality and connectivity.

The effect of this on people in an information society is likely to be the removal of barriers to mobility. The requirement to be situated in one place is often forced on the individual by the necessity to perform the work function at a specific location. With this need diminished or removed the possibility of a mobile lifestyle is more practical. It is likely to be a number of years from the introduction of the necessary systems before the effects are widely noticeable. In the meantime, the link between function and location is increasingly becoming redundant as more virtual means of communication are used between people, with telephones and email increasingly replacing face-to-face and paper communications,

SOCIAL EFFECTS OF THE INFORMATION SOCIETY

There a number of effects that the information model will have on society itself. Most of these have been documented widely in the literature and are worth considering although there is often little evidence of them being widely applicable as yet. The effects on groups and individuals in society is often stated and the opposite sides of the various arguments are worth considering. For example, the relative move towards inclusion or exclusion, wider integration or isolation, more or less mobility and wider or restricted choice.

Exclusion - Inclusion. The debate over the inclusive or exclusive nature of the information society is sure to be held widely for many years with examples of both effects being evident. The argument for exclusion usually centres around the cost of the technology to access the features that determine the information society with computers and telephone charges being the main determinants of the cost involved. On the other hand the cost has been steadily falling over the 20 years since the introduction of the personal computer, both in the actual cost and, consequently, in terms of the inflation-adjusted figures. However, the cost of access is still above the threshold of acceptability for many homes, especially when compared to more traditional forms of access to information such as television and radio.

The inclusive nature of the technology is often stated as being related to its ability to level out the differences of access to information with different types of equipment being able to access the same information. Access to information and inclusion in the online world is also less determined by the need for monetary resources as it is by the requirement to have the time available to contribute or browse.

These opposite effects of exclusion and inclusion are more symptomatic of a transition in society than a finalised change. There have always been disadvantaged groups in society and the information society is not likely to be different, but the question of whether it is the technology or society itself that is the cause of the disadvantages cannot yet be determined.

Integration - Isolation. Similar to the previous argument there are two opposing views on the nature of the integrative function of the information society. The effect that the technology has in the direction of integration is that the differences between people are not apparent in the anonymous world of cyberspace, where race, gender, age and other personal characteristics can be forgotten, removed or replaced. This can lead to a more integrative experience but tends to apply only for those that are taking part in the particular area of interest. It also tends to isolate the individual with differing views or characteristics. Some interesting studies have been published with this embryonic virtual space and they show the different attitudes that are prevalent in society being translated into cyberspace [2], [14].

Mobility. The actions that militate for increased mobility are typified by the move to third generation systems with higher bandwidth, the increasing take-up of mobile services and devices and the general move by society to be available online at anytime. The opposite of this is the need to remain private and to be able to be detached from the everyday world when necessary. Increasingly, the use of mobile devices removes personal choice by requiring full availability, yet there are many times when it is necessary to be apart from the workplace or the home without interruption. This is increasingly important when it is becoming more necessary to manage the use of personal time in a coherent manner. For example, a person may be employed by two or more different employers, be learning from home and have family commitments to manage - it makes it much more difficult to do this effectively if demands from one of the employers exceed the time available, remunerated or allotted by the worker.

Choice. Finally the move to more or less choice is an area of interest to those that study the information society. The indicator for greater choice is that the wider spread of the Internet has given individuals access to more sources of information, services and goods than was possible before it became as widespread as it has. The opposite factor of less choice is evident in some systems where standards for software and hardware do not provide the user with a viable choice of alternative system.

There are many factors that could be used in this discussion and the theme is along similar lines to the above discussions. There are often positive and negative effects from the information society that are not yet fully developed and may change with time so that they are, as yet, unclear.

DISCUSSION AND CONCLUSION

This chapter has outlined the place that is envisaged for the home in the information society and the various effects that will be in evidence when the move to an information-based model is more complete. However, this analysis has also highlighted the need for restraint in reading too much into the current outlines that have been put forward as there are still many different paths that could result in many different styles of society. The central area that is occupied by the home in society is seen as being a continuing part of any model of society, even where the definition of the home is subject to change, as is possible with the technological changes that can affect it.

Therefore, answering the question of what will determine the path of the information society is difficult, since there are so many factors, influences and possible options that all play a part in the movement from the current model to a new one. What has happened in the past may determine the way this change occurs, but it may be that a new consensus emerges that does not depend on previous changes and transitions. However, the people and homes that make up society will all play a part in its structure and development and the central role that the home now plays in society is likely to be increasingly important with the move towards a more home-based model of work. As was indicated at the beginning it is also clear that the home itself should not be the prime area of concern for designers, but rather the interactions of its occupants with the various other objects and actors that influence their daily lives.

What has also become clear from this and other chapters in this book is that the information society has led to a blurring of boundaries. In the case of the home, this is seen as the extension of the definition of home to incorporate the virtual and distributed nature of cyberspace, with home being the area where the real and virtual can co-exist. The boundaries between real-life home and cyber home are becoming less important, with people happily co-existing between of the two. This incorporation of "virtual life" into the real home is likely to be one of the defining aspects of the information society.

REFERENCES

1. Benjamin (1995) (Ed.), *The Home: Words, interpretation, meanings and environments, Ashgate,* Aldershot, UK.
2. Dibbell J. (1999), *My tiny life,* 4th Estate, London, ISBN 1-84115-058-4
3. Edens G. T. (2001), Home networking and the CableHome project at Cablelabs, *IEEE Communications magazine,* June 2001, 112-121
4. Go K., Carroll J. and Imamiya A. (2000), Familyware, in Sloane A. and van Rijn F. (Eds.), *Home Informatics and Telematics: Information, Technology and Society,* Kluwer Academic publishers, Boston MA., ISBN 0-7923-7867-9
5. Haddon L. and Silverstone R. (2000). Information and communication technologies and everyday life: Individual and social dimensions, in Ducatel K., Webster J. and Hermann W., (2000) *The Information Society in Europe: Work and life in an Age of Globalisation,* Rowman and Littlefield, Lanham MA ISBN 0-8476-9590-5
6. Harris A., Huang W. and Sloane A. (2000), Web-based family noticeboard in: Sloane A. and van Rijn F. (Eds.), *Home Informatics and Telematics: Information, Technology and Society,* op. cit. [4].
7. Junestrand S. and Keijer U. (2000), Measuring and evaluation of ICT-supported services in the domestic environment, in: Sloane A. and van Rijn F. (Eds.), *Home Informatics and Telematics: Information, Technology and Society,* Volume 2, IFIP, ISBN 3-901882-12-X
8. Junestrand S., Keijer U. and Tollmar K. (2001), Private and public digital domestic spaces, *Int. J. Human-Computer Studies,* 54, 753-778
9. Kjaer A., Madsen K. H., and Petersen M. G., (2000), Methodological Challenges in the study of technology use at home, in Sloane A. and van Rijn F. (Eds.) *Home Informatics and Telematics: Information, Technology and Society,* op. cit. [4].
10. Lawrence R. J. (1995), Deciphering home: An integrative historical perspective, in Benjamin (ed.), op. cit. [1].
11. Monk A. (2000) User-centred design: The home use challenge, in: Sloane A. and van Rijn F. (Eds.) *Home Informatics and Telematics: Information, Technology and Society,* op. cit. [4].
12. Mynatt E. and Rowan J. (2000) Cross-generation communication via digital picture frames, in: Sloane A. and van Rijn F. (Eds.), *Home Informatics and Telematics: Information, Technology and Society,* op. cit. [7].
13. Nguyen T.-A. and Bouwen J. (2001), The next-generation residential gateway, *J. Inst Brit. Telecom Eng,* 2, 3, 134-138.
14. Rheingold H. (1994), *The virtual community,* Secker and Warburg, London ISBN 0-436-20208-5

15. Silverstone R. (1993), Domesticating the revolution: Information and communication technologies and everyday life, *ASLIB Proceedings,* 45(9), 227-233.
16. Sloane A. (1994), Homelink: An international collaboration for HOIT, in: *IFIP Transactions A*, Volume 53, North Holland, 142-147, ISSN 0926-5473.
17. Sloane A. (1995), The distributed home environment and the new OIKOS, in: A. Dix & R. Beale (Eds), *Remote Co-operation: CSCW issues for mobile and teleworkers, Springer*, London. ISBN 3-540-76035-0.
18. van Rijn F., Bjerg K. and Frerk G. (1992), Perspectives on Home-oriented Informatics and telematics, in: Aiken R. M. (Ed.), *Information processing '92*, IFIP Transactions A-13, Education and Society, North Holland, ISBN 0-444-89748-8, 494-507.
19. Wise J. M. (2000), Home: Territory and identity, *Cultural studies*, 14(2), 295-310.

Information society and the Digital Divide Problem in Developing Countries

Chrisanthi AVGEROU and Shirin MADON
London School of Economics,
c.avgerou@lse.ac.uk, s.madon@lse.ac.uk

> *"... the root of counter-development obstacles to ICT, might be the extent to which the information society conveys aspirations, and privileges technologies, information and knowledge that are irrelevant to the way the majority of people in many communities in developing countries live their lives."*

Key words: Digital divide, developing countries, social exclusion, marginalisation.

INTRODUCTION

Soon after its emergence in the USA and in Europe in the early 1990s, the information society discourse became linked with the discourse of development for the poorer countries of the world. In political rhetoric, policy documents, and international aid agency analyses the diffusion of information technology, the construction of modern telecommunications infrastructure, and the concomitant increase of communication and access to information resources were designated as *sine qua non* prerequisites for development. With few exceptions, developing countries, often assisted by international institutions, drafted strategies for their race towards becoming information societies and launched suitable initiatives. Nevertheless, and for many not entirely unexpectedly, by the end of the 1990s, the 'information societies' of the developing countries were a cause of apprehension within the international development fora. With rapidly increasing trends of globalisation spearheaded by the political and economic institutions of the advanced industrialised nations, the grossly uneven spread of ICTs around the world came to be seen as a digital divide at a global scale.

In this chapter, we examine the developmental significance of the information society vision and its accompanying threat, the digital divide. In the first section we review briefly the arguments that fuel plans and actions under the information society banner. We point out that the discourse on information society is based on the notion of development as 'catching up' with the advanced industrialised world, which involves aiming at the achievement of economic indicators of advanced industrialised countries by following their footsteps of technology and socio-organizational innovation. Catching up pressures and efforts are accompanied by the threat of marginalisation in the global free market economy. Another significant aspect of the information society discourse is the way it privileges knowledge, and information, seen as a-contextual resources with universal developmental value.

In the second section we examine current understanding of the digital divide problem and its link to the chronic socio-economic problems in many developing countries. We argue that the root of counter-development obstacles to ICT, that find their expression in terms of the digital divide problem, might be the extent to which the information society conveys aspirations, and privileges technologies, information and knowledge that are irrelevant to the way the majority of people in many communities in developing countries live their lives.

In the third section we suggest alternative ways of analysis to overcome the narrow techno-economic vision of information society and its accompanying concept of the digital divide. We propose to build on research approaches that avoid the universalistic discourse of ICT and development and are capable of shedding light on the particular, historically formed, circumstances within which ICTs and information resources acquire meaning. Specifically, we suggest three streams of theoretical work as promising approaches to that end: the conceptual perspective that challenges the a-contextual cognitive view of the information society, the analysis on hybridisation of culture in the context of globalisation highlighting the important role of intermediaries, and the work on social exclusion.

THE INFORMATION SOCIETY DISCOURSE IN DEVELOPING COUNTRIES

IT and telecommunications have always been perceived as opening unprecedented opportunities for developing countries. Early computers were seen as tools to assist their public bureaucracies to overcome endemic gross inefficiencies. It was suggested that microcomputers and educational software could stretch the limited capabilities of poorly trained teachers to introduce their pupils to the vital fields of science, technology, and train them with skills for modern business. Similarly, expert systems were considered capable of empowering their limited medical and nursing human resources. Such potential appeared to increase vastly with advances in telecommunications in the 1980s and 1990s. It is not difficult to perceive the possibilities of eGovernment, of enhancing education in even the most advanced topics and in the most remote communities, of practicing telemedicine, of accessing worldwide markets from any place of agricultural production, of gaining lucrative contracts on the basis of lower labour costs in a range of service industries.

Against this background of interest in ICT for development, the discourse on information society that emerged in industrialised countries in the 1990s was quickly transferred into political circles, the international development agencies, the academic literature, and the popular debate arenas of most developing countries. Many high profile initiatives have been undertaken, typically aiming to create awareness on the benefits of ICT, raise investment, and promote policy measures for the deployment of telecommunications infrastructures and the diffusion of ICT applications in all societal sectors. Notable examples of such projects include the Digital Opportunity Task Force of the eight major industrial nations, G-8 (Dot force initiative, http://www.dotforce.org), the World Summit for the Information Society of the United Nations and the International Telecommunications Union (WSIS initiative, http://www.itu.int/wsis) and the World IT Forum of the International Federation of Information Processing (WITFOR programme, http://www.witfor.lt).

This wave of interest on ICT for development has two salient features: emphasis on information and knowledge, and the assumption of a global free market socio-economic context. Knowledge, learning and 'social capabilities' to innovate are highlighted as the most significant factor for development. For example, Mansell & Wehn [1998] argue for the significance of knowledge-based economic growth and development, for which crucial determinants are infrastructure, experience of production and consumption, and skills. Along similar lines, the 1999 World Bank World Development Report entitled 'Knowledge for Development' [World Bank, 1999] saw IT as a powerful tool to fight poverty and underdevelopment. The report argued that the developmental significance of ICTs lies in its capacity to provide access to information sources and communication media necessary for building such social capabilities, in other words as tools for learning and innovation.

The learning that is suggested in the literature and policy manifestos of international agencies as crucial in supporting ICTs refers to acquiring capabilities to produce and use ICTs and to work out organisational changes that are conducive to continuous technology innovation. The battle of developing countries for their inclusion in the global information society involves the acceptance of a uni-directional flow of information and knowledge from the advanced industrialised world. There is recognition that tacit knowledge is significant in complementing formal and codified knowledge in the learning process, but even with regard to tacit knowledge it is often suggested that developing countries need to rely on the tacit knowledge existing in industrialised countries rather than their own: 'An optimistic scenario for developing countries in the face of the diffusion of ICTs envisages a massive transfer of tacit knowledge into information systems giving these countries access to new process technologies and products developed in the industrialised countries both rapidly and at low cost. In theory this would lead to an acceleration of the catching up process and a reduction in global inequalities' [Mansell & Wehn, 1998].

Such a developmental role of ICT is understood to require specific socio-economic and organisational interventions, namely liberalisation, particularly of the telecommunications sector, and the reform of both business and government organisations towards a management-driven governance regime. This logic is presented clearly in influential publications by various development agencies such as the 2002 World Development Report, *Building Institutions for Markets*, of the World Bank [2002] and UNDP's 2001 Human Development Report, *Making New Technologies Work for Human Development* [2001]; and the two publications by the Center for International Development at Harvard University, *The Global Information Technology Report: Readiness for the Networked World* [Kirkman et al., 2002a,b], and *The Global Competitiveness Report 2001-2002* [Porter et al., 2002].

All these publications propose ICT as an instrument for economic and social gains within a market regime, and they elaborate on the conditions under which ICT plays this kind of developmental role. The central issue in the discourse in these texts concerns the socio-economic conditions that are favourable for the mutual re-enforcement of ICT innovation and an effective market [Avgerou, 2003].

In this discourse ICT is seen to contribute to improvements of life conditions in developing countries through enabling market mechanisms. Interventions to develop community ICT services in poor regions bear implicit promises for economic benefits through participation in the global market. For example, there is a tendency to see ICT centres in poor communities as sustainable businesses in their own right [Best & Maclay, 2002]. Moreover, the introduction of business management practices is seen as a necessary reform across the range of organizations and in particular for the rationalization of citizens/government interaction. Policy advice on eGovernment, for example, the DfID policy brief 'Making EGovernment work for poor people' and the G8 Action Plan 2002 'EGovernment for Development' emphasise the importance of introducing modern management practices and computerisation within government to enhance the delivery of public services.

But despite acknowledging the importance of socio-economic and institutional change to support ICT for development, the information society in developing countries is perceived mainly in technical terms as the construction of telecommunications infrastructures. The whole ICT for development literature gives scant attention to the demand side in terms of questioning the very purpose for which communities need knowledge, and what knowledge is appropriate for particular groups. For example, at a recent IFIP WG9.4 conference on ICTs and Development held in Bangalore [Krishna & Madon, 2002], the majority of papers submitted were descriptions of pilot projects that aimed to establish the necessary infrastructure to facilitate communication and the processing and transmission of information by electronic means. Very few papers addressed the more fundamental question of how communication, information and knowledge can be effectively used as critical elements for poverty reduction and overall development.

THE DIGITAL DIVIDE

The Digital Divide has become something of a buzzword in policy circles, the popular press and academia. Norris [2001] categorises this divide into its three constituent elements: the global divide between advanced industrialised countries and developing countries, the social divide between information rich and information poor within advanced industrialised countries, and the democratic divide between those within the online community who do and do not use digital resources to engage, mobilise and participate in public life. Within each category, Norris and other writers [Wresch, 1996; Castells, 2001] discuss the divide primarily in terms of access to ICTs, rather than in terms of the information and knowledge which is of value in the context of the information society and in terms of the social capabilities for such learning as we discussed in the previous section.

In economic terms, there are vast differences among developing countries' ability to produce or to effectively use ICTs and participate in the global economy. Indeed, the literature contains exemplary cases of countries with impressive progress in ICT innovation according to the information society characteristics outlined above − mainly some of the small economies of South East Asia, such as South Korea [Lee *et al.*, 2003] − and a plethora of examples of promising initiatives and opening up of opportunities. Nevertheless, the overall picture is one of concern about the growing digital divide [Norris, 2001; Castells, 2001]. This is reflected in the literature from the World Bank, the OECD and individual agencies – 'The Digital Divide is one of the greatest impediments to development .... and it is growing exponentially' [Wolfensohn, 2000]. Leaders in Internet penetration are Scandinavia and North America followed by Western Europe with about one in five online. Central and Eastern Europe, Asia, the Middle East and South America fall below the world average with less than one in ten online, with minimal diffusion in Sub-Saharan Africa [Kirkman *et al.*, 2002b].

Inequality in the deployment of the Internet is similar to inequalities of earlier forms of communication technologies like telephones and television. Taking figures from several different sources, Norris [2001] presents evidence to suggest that the global pattern of inequality in Internet use mirrors the broader pattern of access to earlier ICTs. The disparity of Internet access between developed and developing countries is therefore not particular to the nature of Internet technology, but due to deep-rooted and endemic contextual factors within those societies.

These results are not particularly surprising – it would be naïve to expect a lesser contrast in Internet diffusion given the substantial disparities in every other dimension of life including access to earlier forms of ICTs like telephones and television. Several influential and comprehensive studies of the global digital divide point to a significant positive relationship between levels of economic development and the global digital divide. For example, a study by Hargittai [1999] and another by Rodriguez and Wilson in a World Bank sponsored study [2000] found that the economic wealth of a country measured by per capita GNP was the most important predictor of Internet access. Yet, the discourse on the digital divide is keen to present the reverse causal association between ICT and economic conditions. Economic analyses portray ICT as a significant factor of growth in the context of modern competitive economies; consequently the lack of ICT is an inhibiting factor for economic development.

This discourse surrounding the need to bridge the global digital divide for development resonates with the bias of development as economic growth in earlier modernisation literature and the need for developing countries to 'catch up' with the economic growth indices of the developed world [Sen, 1999]. This catching up goes beyond disclosing indigenous economic development disparities between regions of the world. Symbolically, the global divide is another stigma for developing countries because it prevents them from being part of the modern world.

Relatively less attention has been given to non-economic indicators of the digital divide, although they can potentially reveal important facets of the link between ICT and development. We have little knowledge of the relationship between human development indicators and ICT indicators although such information is essential for making investment decisions about ICTs in the context of other possibilities. The 2001 UNDP report [2001] attempts to take a broader perspective of the significance of ICT by associating it with Sen's notion of development in terms of human capabilities [Sen, 1999], but its analysis fails to avoid the unfounded technocratic assumptions on ICT as means for improvements in critical social domains such as education or health. Norris' [2001] analysis is more thought provoking, showing that many countries that are relatively affluent display lower than average internet penetration rates like certain oil-rich countries in the Middle East as well as SE Asian countries. Cultural restrictions on the use of the Internet become important in this analysis. In another category, some societies with higher than average Internet access show low levels of economic development but significant use of human capital and R & D potential such as Slovakia, Slovenia, Poland and Estonia. Some new democracies such as Slovenia and South Africa have achieved more advanced access to digital technologies than earlier media, suggesting that digital diffusion acquires greater significance in conditions of democratic development.

An important issue that tends to be hidden in the tables listing international digital divide indicators is the existence of in-country disparities with regard to the availability and significance of ICT and in particular internet connectivity. Kirkman et al's report on the *Readiness for the Networked World* recognizes that some countries, with India the most obvious example, have both highly networked ready communities and communities that are completely cut-off from the networked world that the report attempts to assess: '...India is renowned for its pre-eminence in software programming and for providing the world with highly skilled IT workers. India is effectively penalized in our Index for its size, the scope and scale of its many social and economic development challenges, and the smaller degree of IT penetration throughout the country as a whole' [Kirkman *et al.*, 2002b, p.13]. From a development perspective, of course, the problem with an index that is insensitive to in-country variation is not that India is penalized by its ranking, but that the index brushes aside the most important development characteristic of the country, namely that the vast majority of the country's population live in poverty. The Network Readiness Indicator framework on which Kirkman et al's report is based does not provide a way of distinguishing what network connectedness means for the rural poor, the urban entrepreneur, the district authority bureaucrat, or the central government.

In all countries, there are social groups whose members both aspire to a way of living that has been developed in the modern societies of industrialised countries and have the capabilities to learn, innovate and follow relevant changes of life conditions. But for vast numbers in very many developing countries, the information, knowledge and technologies favoured by the initiatives of the information society have little relevance for the way they live their lives. For such populations, the push of the information society vision may be merely distractive, without the possibility to create local value out of the distraction. Most of the ICT for development is based on an a priori assumption that bridging the digital divide is a top development priority without much debate as to whether ICTs are necessary or sufficient for solving developmental problems. A small group of dissidents are cautious about the developmental promise of ICTs and argue that clean water and food should come before ICTs [Panos, 1999]. This small voice, which bears the marks of earlier Basic Needs approach to development [Green, 2002], is sidelined in the dominant discourse of ICTs for development which automatically displays intolerance to alternative investment despite little evidence of benefits and little cost-benefit analysis.

ALTERNATIVE APPROACHES TO THE DIGITAL DIVIDE PROBLEM

Our critique of the current discourse on the digital divide should not be taken to imply that ICTs do not have a position in the traditional communities of developing countries that have not developed the rationalities and the organisational and economic conditions of western industrialised societies. But it implies that alternative approaches for the mobilisation of ICTs for local needs may be more appropriate and that the resulting socio-technical conditions will not necessarily be emulating those of the advanced industrialised world and the homogeneous global information society vision. An alternative approach questions the transfer of uniform information society socio-economic practice in all communities of the world and is sensitive to the historically developed variation of socio-economic and cultural conditions. In this chapter we can only hint at such alternative approaches emerging in the current debate on globalisation, knowledge, and social development.

The dominant view of development as following the footsteps of the advanced industrialised countries, as global socio-economic homogenisation, that is adopted in most of the information society and digital divide discourse, has been widely criticised as a mis-representation of the social transformation taking place in the contemporary world, see for example [Avgerou, 2002; Beck, 2000; Robertson, 1995]. The transformation processes are much more complex than the diffusion of uniform competent practices, the spreading of universal truths, and the acquisition of technologies pertaining to the same capabilities across social context. For example, Appadurai [1990, 1996] presents a complex picture of the link between local communities and the broader global context in terms of cultural flows across five dimensions of people, technology, capital, media and ideologies. To describe this process he uses the notion of 'hybridisation' as the meeting of global and local practices and ideologies. Homogenizing processes, such as trans-national business, worldwide spread of consumer products – and, we could add, ICTs and their inscriptions of best practice in a variety of tasks – are entangled with two other processes: indigenisation, and export of particular local cultural features (often indigenised global cultural features) through immigration, travel or neighbouring hegemonies. According to Appadurai, 'At least as rapidly as forces from various metropolises are brought into new media, they tend to become indigenised in one way or another' [1996, p. 32]. Recent work by development anthropologists describes the negotiations and complex processes which take place [Nelson, 1996; Schech, 2002]. Nelson provided an ethnographic account of how indigenous communities in Guatemala negotiated their position within the global information society by coming up with alternative ways of interacting with technology.

The important role of human intermediaries in any discussion of the hybridisation process between the growing digital infrastructure prevalent in developing countries and its citizens has been acknowledged [Madon, 2000; Heeks, 2002]. In developing countries, the majority of citizens are neither owners nor direct users of ICTs. Hence, ICT applications whether initiated by international or by local players rely on human intermediaries such as public servants, NGOs, community-based organisations or private sector organisations to act as a missing link between the citizen and the growing digital infrastructure such as the various e-governance projects. These local intermediaries are critical players in the delivery of relevant local content as projects are diffused from cities and towns to villages. In recent years, there has been a proliferation of such intermediaries that have sprung up in many parts of the developing world to prevent the exclusion of large sections of the population [Madon & Sahay, 2002; Lewis & Madon, 2003].

A promising route for understanding the capabilities disparity for benefiting from the various initiatives comprising the information society in developing countries, is offered by the concept of social exclusion that has gained popularity in European policy and academic circles in the field of social policy. The idea of social exclusion originated with the French government's concern in the mid-1970s to introduce programmes of 'insertion' for the long-term unemployed and the growing recognition that government cannot address unemployment without addressing income inequality, education, gender issues, ethnicity and other aspects of French society. Since then, many European countries have established a social exclusion unit spanning across several government departments and agencies to deal with a combination of linked social problems. The debate on social exclusion has mostly taken place in developed countries, but closely mirrors the debate on poverty in developing countries [O'Brien *et al.*, 1997; Clert, 1999]. The 'value added' in the concept of social exclusion is to put institutional processes at the heart of the poverty debate through an analysis of institutions and social relations at the levels of households, communities, market and state [O'Brien *et al.*, 1998].

While much has been written about social exclusion as a structural phenomenon produced by processes of globalisation, there is little understanding of how the dynamics of marginalisation unfold at the micro level. Beck, Madon & Sahay [2004] seek to understand these processes through which conditions are created, sustained and refined over time. Rather than being fully included or excluded, the authors describe how marginalized groups may occupy an in-between position with the potential of movement in either direction. The direction of movement is seen as dependent on the actions of multiple parties: those that are marginalized, those who willingly or unwillingly erect or strengthen the boundaries surrounding the dominant culture, and those who seek to open those boundaries and facilitate transitions such as mediating institutions. In this way, the authors explore the degree to which human agency and socio-political processes shape how the information society is developed and applied to bridge the digital divide.

CONCLUSION

In short, our analysis suggests that the current push of information society reforms entails a number of risks. It makes little effort to cater for local socio-economic need, as the information society vision is geared primarily towards inclusion within the global economy, carries notions of spatially un-rooted societies, and is led by imported visions of modernity. This may exacerbate existing inequalities in local social structures – as has been highlighted in industrialised countries. Moreover, the privileging of decontextualised formal knowledge, which is often drastically different from historically constructed local formal and tacit knowledge, introduces new forms of dependency. Local communities in developing countries can make no sense of such knowledge and find themselves dependent on the services of various intermediaries in order to maintain the fundamental facilities of their local communities.

At present, most international institutions involved in the initiatives of ICT diffusion in developing countries are ill-equipped conceptually to assist the development of locally meaningful ICT mediated information societies. The dominant discourse that deceptively links ICT deployment with economic growth in a global free market is incapable of addressing local efforts for the appropriation of ICTs in the diverse power/knowledge conditions of local communities and their interactions with numerous intermediaries. Thus, the impact of the information society vision that drives policy initiatives in most developing countries is limited to the minorities who find its global symbolic and material value meaningful within their way of living and therefore are willing and able to acquire the skills and attitudes required to exploit its potential. In the near future, the different speed at which the processes of appropriation of ICT unfolds in different social groups is likely to prolong and intensify existing social conflicts such as between urban and rural populations, westernised educated elites and traditional communities. To overcome such risks in this chapter we suggested the need for analytical approaches and policy initiatives fostering locally meaningful forms of the information society. But such approaches amount to a fundamentally different vision of the global information society, a vision which acknowledges and celebrates the emergence of hybrid forms of socio-economic activity and makes a society of diversity rather than uniformity.

REFERENCES

Appadurai, A. (1990) "Disjuncture and Difference in the Global Cultural Economy", *Theory, Culture and Society,* 7 pp. 295-310.

Appadurai, A. (1996) *Modernity at Large: Cultural Dimensions of Globalization,* University of Minnesota Press, Minneapolis.

Avgerou, C. (2002) *Information Systems and Global Diversity,* Oxford University Press, Oxford.

Avgerou, C. (2003) "The Link between ICT and Economic Growth in the Discourse of Development". in *Information Systems Perspectives and Challenges in the Context of Globalization,* Athens, Klower.

Beck, U. (2000) *What Is Globalization,* Polity Press, Cambridge.

Beck, E., Madon, S. and Sahay, S. (2004) "On the Margins of the Information Society: A comparative study of mediation", *The Information Society,* 20 pp. 279-290.

Best, M. L. and C. M. Maclay (2002) "Community Internet Access in Rural Areas: Solving the Economic Sustainability Puzzle" in *The Global Information Technology Report: Readiness for the Networked World,* (Kirkman, G. S., P. K. Cornelius, J. D. Sachs and K. Schwab eds) Oxford University Press, Oxford, pp. 76-89.

Castells, M. (2001) *The Internet Galaxy,* Oxford University Press, Oxford.

Clert, C. (1999) Evaluating the concept of social exclusion in development discourse, *The European Journal of Development Research,* 11, 2, pp. 176-199.

Green, M. (2002) Social Development: Issues and Approaches. In *Development Theory and Practice: Critical perspectives,* edited by Uma Kothari and Martin Minogue, Palgrave, Basingstoke, UK.

Hargittai, E. (1999) Weaving the Western web: Explaining differences in Internet connectivity among OECD countries, *Telecommunications Policy,* Vol. 23 (10-11), pp. 701-18.

Heeks, R. (2001) Understanding E-governance for Development, IDPM Working Paper Series, No. 11, University of Manchester.
Available electronically at http://www.man.ac.uk/idpm/idpm_dp.htm#ig

Kirkman, G. S., P. K. Cornelius, J. D. Sachs and K. Schwab (2002a) "The Global Information Technology Report 2001-2002: Readiness for the Networked World" *Oxford University Press* New York.

Kirkman, G. S., C. Osorio, A. and J. D. Sachs (2002b) "The Networked Readiness Index: Measuring the Preparedness of Nations for the Networked World" in *The Global Information Technology Report: Readiness for the Networked World,* (Kirkman, G. S., P. K. Cornelius, J. D. Sachs and K. Schwab eds) Oxford University Press, New York.

Krishna, S. and S. Madon (2002) "Information & Communication Technologies and Development: New Opportunities, Perspectives & Challenges". in *Seventh International Working Conference of IFIP WG 9.4,* Bangalore, May 29-31, Indian Institute of Management Bangalore.

Lee, H., R. M. O'Keefe and K. Yun (2003) "The Growth of Broadband and Electronic Commerce in South Korea: Contributing Factors", *The Information Society,* 19 (1), pp. 81-95.

Lewis, D. & Madon, S. (2003) Information systems and Non-Governmental Development Organisations: Connecting global, national and local priorities. Working Paper, Department of Information Systems.

Madon, S. (2000) "The Internet and Socio-economic Development: Exploring the Interaction", *Information Technology & People,* 13, 2.

Madon, S. and Sahay, S. (2002), An information-based model of NGO-mediation for the empowerment of slum dwellers in Bangalore, *The Information Society,* 18, 1.

Mansell, R. and Wehn, U. (1998) *Knowledge societies: Information technology for sustainable development,* Oxford University Press.

Nelson, D. (1996) Maya hackers and the cyberspatialised nation state: Modernity, ethnostalgia, and a lizard queen in Guatemala, *Cultural Anthropology,* 11, 3, pp. 287-308.

Norris, P. (2001) *Digital Divide: Civic Engagement, Information Poverty, and the Internet Worldwide,* Cambridge University Press, Cambridge.

O'Brien, D., Wilkes, J., de Haan, A., Maxwell, S. (1998) *Poverty and Social Exclusion in North and South.* Institute of Development Studies and Poverty Research Unit, IDS Working Paper 55, University of Sussex.

PANOS (1998) The Internet and Poverty: Real help or real hype? The Panos Institute Information Technology Media Briefing No. 28, London. (http://www.Panos.org.uk)

Porter, M. E., *et al.* (2002) "The Global Competitiveness Report 2001-2002" *Oxford University Press* New York.

Robertson, R. (1995) "Glocalization: Time-Space and Homogeneity-Heterogeneity" in *Global Modernities*, (Featherstone, M., S. Lash and R. Robertson eds) Sage, London, pp. 25-44.

Rodriguez, F. and Wilson, E. (2000) Are poor countries losing the information revolution? World Bank InfoDev Report.

Sen, A. (1999) *Development as Freedom,* Oxford University Press, Oxford.

Schech, S. (2002) "Wired for Change: The links between ICTs and Development Discourses", *Journal of International Development,* 14, pp. 13-23.

United Nations Development Programme (2001) "Making New Technologies Work for Human Development" *UNDP* New York.

World Bank. (1999) World Development Report 1998/99. Knowledge for Development, Oxford University Press, Oxford.

World Bank (2002) "Building Institutions for Markets" New York.

Wolfensohn, J.D. (2000) Speech made by the President of the World Bank, February 2000.

Wresch, W. (1996) Information Rich, Information Poor. In *Disconnected: Haves and Have-nots in the Information Age,* Rutgers University Press, New Jersey.

Symbolic and Structuring Effects of the Internet on Privacy

Albin ZUCCATO, Simone FISCHER-HÜBNER
Department for Computer Science,
Karlstad University, Sweden
Albin.Zuccato@kau.se, Simone.Fischer-Huebner@kau.se

Abstract: Technology has influenced human lives since the beginning of mankind. Sociologists have described the effects that technology has on society as structuring or symbolic. We will use the same concepts to investigate the capability of the Internet to influence privacy. We analyse the structuring and symbolic effects of technology on privacy and thereby demonstrate some potentials of Internet technology and their effect on our life in society

Key words: Techno-sociology, structuring effect, symbolic effect, privacy, Internet, Privacy Enhancing Technologies

INTRODUCTION

Technology has influenced human life throughout our history. Today the progress of civilization is measured by means of technology. In this paper, we will discuss the structuring and symbolic effects of technology.

One of the most broadly discussed media in modern society is the Internet. The goal of this paper is to treat the effects of the Internet on life in society. We will focus our examination on privacy and look at how sociology describes the effects of technology on society. Our sociological approach will be a description of the effects as symbolic of structuring. Using comparisons with other techno-sociological approaches we will argue why we believe that this method is appropriate. In general, symbolic effects reflect how technology influences collective practice and the (sub)cultural meaning system, as well as the social behaviour of individuals. From a social viewpoint, structural effects describe the consequences of technology on the sensory perception and the practical actions of the subject.

Before examining effects on privacy, we will define privacy and Privacy Enhancing Technologies (PET). We must also look at social phenomena related to privacy and the Internet, in order to demonstrate that the Internet has comprehensive structuring and symbolic effects on the perception of privacy in modern society.

The first step is an investigation of structuring effects and a discussion of current legislative tendencies in the area of privacy and the extent of the Internet's influence on that legislation. We further discuss what we call extensive profiling - the automatic generation of extensive personal profiles describing different aspects of the individual's customs and behaviour - and describe the increasing demand for Privacy Enhancing Technology as another structuring effect.

Secondly, we deal with the question of how far symbolic effects can be observed. As an example, we analyse how greatly the Internet has influenced the perception of privacy as this relates to legislation in Europe and the US. We will also investigate the role of the Internet in the prevention of cyber-crime, cyber-war and cyber-terrorism in relation to privacy. We discuss tendencies concerning socially and politically motivated privacy organizations founded to act in response to the Internet's privacy threats.

This article, written by members of the IFIP Working Group 9.6/11.7 (IT Misuse and the Law), should contribute to the aim of their Working Group to develop an understanding of the impacts of IT systems on current IT law and potential problems and threats associated with IT systems and related legal concerns.

STRUCTURING AND SYMBOLIC EFFECTS OF TECHNOLOGY

This article describes effects of technology on society. To do so in a methodical way we must follow an approach that supports the investigation of the problem at hand. We have chosen to describe the effects we observe as structuring or symbolic as proposed by [Steinhardt, Ste99a].

We therefore start with the definition of symbolic and structuring effects and then will look at historic examples to clarify the application of the approach. Finally we investigate other techno-sociological theories and argue why we have chosen the approach in question.

Definition

In sociology the impacts of technology are described by its structuring and symbolic[1] effects. While all technologies that find a place in our daily life develop these effects, they are sometimes neglected and a particular technology disappears, only slightly influencing social life. There are also technologies - like the railway or the car - that have had such dramatic effects that they have been adopted into social life.

In the following section, we will use the railway as an example to explain what we mean by symbolic and structural effects. The railway is chosen for its familiarity, which makes it a good example of how drastic the effects of technology can be.

First we present a definition [Steinhardt, Ste99a] of symbolic effect: *"As a symbolic form technology has a double character: On one side it is an expression of collective practice and (sub)cultural meaning systems; on the other side it affects the subjects and their social behaviour"*[2]. This means that technology not only has a socio-cultural semantic effect (influence on social life) but also an effect on the subject's world experience (it influences the perception of the world and what the individual understands this to be). Consequently, the symbolic effect characterizes how the social individual sees his/her world on the basis of the existence or use of technology.

According to Steinhardt, technology not only influences our perception but also our activities. He says that *"(...)technology structures our sensory perception as well as our factual practical actions by suggesting specific ways of action and perception, preventing others, or presenting new ones (...)"*[3] [Steinhardt, Ste99a]. The structuring effect thus influences individual behaviour in proportion to technology. The difference is that the symbolic effect gives rise to a different worldview which generates a subsequent action whereas the structural effect causes a direct reaction.

Thus the focus of this method, and this article, is to describe effects of technology on society. As we are well aware, however, technology is also influenced by society and, as [Steinhardt, Ste99a] argues, there is reverse causality for every symbolic and structuring effect.

Historic examples

The steam engine and the railway are often considered a driving factor in the industrial revolution. The railway is used as an example to illustrate how effects can be classified as structuring or symbolic.

The following description is based on [Steinhardt, Ste99b]. Of course none of the descriptions present purely symbolic or structural effects, but one effect can be considered more distinct than the other.

Structuring – Unification of time

Before the introduction of the railway, every town had its own time based on the position of the sun that differed slightly from time in other places.

This was not important: the speed of travel was so slow that a few minutes earlier or later made no difference.

In the beginning of the railway history (in Britain), each station had a timetable written in local time. This affected people from other cities such that they became confused as they tried to fit their times to the local time. It is easy to imagine that this system proved very impractical. For this reason every railway company decided to create a timetable that gave the company's home city time as the reference time. This system was not successful either, as people had difficulty adjusting the different company times to the local time. Finally the pressing need for a harmonization of a country- wide time led to the creation of the Greenwich Mean Time system.

Unified time stems from the railway - and today we see unified time as perfectly natural.

Symbolic – Change of perception behaviour

In his description of his Italian travels, Goethe writes about his departure from Frankfurt[4] with the post coach. He gives details about the different smells and portrays a farm close to his route. This is called direct perception.

In travel descriptions from the earliest history of the railway you find a very negative attitude: it is mentioned that the smell was awful and that the landscape passed at such speed that nothing was recognizable. People obviously still used direct perception. The same view is described some years later, but is portrayed then as a beautiful train trip through the passing landscape and a wonderful overall picture of the mountain area. A third author saw the same situation from another point of view: it was very refreshing to feel the pure rush of air, caused by the rapid speed of the train, on his face.

Here the perception has changed into what we call "panoramatic perception". The coming of the railway led to a different world perception mechanism, which represents a symbolic effect.

Theories of Techno-Sociology

In this section, Steinhardt's approach toward analysing technological effects on society by their symbolic or structural nature is briefly compared with other prominent techno-sociological approaches to explain why we have chosen Steinhardt's approach. We would like the reader to note however that this comparison should not be seen as a ranking or judgment of the theories described. Our only goal is to argue why the approach that we have chosen is the most suitable and appropriate one for our purposes.

We start with social constructivism as a prominent theory and will go on to investigate technological evolution, determinism and technological imperative as approaches to describing the interaction between technology and society.

Social constructivism

According to [Pinch and Bijker, PB87], social constructivism describes the *"development process of a technical artefact (...) as an alternation of variation and selection"* driven by social groups. This means that the development of a technology is driven by the selection of technological solutions to problems that social groups, interacting with the artefact, have.

This approach focuses apparently on the development of the technical artefact, whereas our goal in this article is to describe the effects of technology on society[5].

Technological Evolution

The technical evolution theory sees the development of technology in a way similar to that of Darwin's theory of evolution. [Winner, Win77] argues that humans are merely a selection mechanism that decides which technology will survive and which will perish.

As this approach assumes that humans only determine the success of technology, it seems unsuitable to use it for a description of the effects of technology on mankind.

Technological Determinism

According to [Winner, Win77] technological determinism means *"(1) that the technical base of a society is the fundamental condition affecting all patterns of social existence and (2) that changes in technology are the single most important source of change in society"*.

From a general point of view, technological determinism would be applicable to our problem. However, we do not agree with the ultimate shaping role of technology. As Mesthene[6] puts it: *"patterns of technology are themselves largely influenced by conditions of the societies in which they exist"*. We believe that technology is also influenced by social phenomena.

Technological Imperative

The concept could, according to [Winner, Win77], be put as *"technologies are structures whose conditions of operation demand the restructuring of their environment"*.

The focus on structures of operation seems too great a limitation for us, as it focuses more on physically existing technology than on a more abstract technology, which the Internet[7] is. We also assume that society itself is capable of choosing the way in which it can restructure. Thus the demanding character of technology does not fit our convictions.

After looking at different approaches, our conclusion is that the most promising way to describe the effects of the Internet on society is by symbolic and structuring means. The approach chosen is capable of structuring the effects of technology by including ideas of a backward coupling of effects on technology made by society to shape it[8].

PRIVACY AND PRIVACY ENHANCING TECHNOLOGIES

Privacy is recognized as a fundamental human right. In general the concept of privacy has three aspects [Rosenberg, Ros92], [Holvast, Hol93]:

- Personal privacy - protection of a person against undue interference, such as physical searches or information violating his/her moral sense;
- Territorial privacy - protection of a person's close physical area;
- Informational privacy - control of whether and how personal data can be gathered, stored, processed and selectively disseminated.

The first definition of privacy was given by the American lawyers Samuel D. Warren and Louis D. Brandeis, who in their article "The Right to Privacy" published in 1890, defined privacy as "the right to be let alone" [Warren and Brandeis, WB90]. The most common definition of informational privacy in current use is given by Alan Westin: "Privacy is the claim of individuals, groups and institutions to determine for themselves, when, how and to what extent information about them is communicated to others" [Westin, Wes67].

With increasing personal data traffic over the Internet and expanding Internet applications (such as eHealth-, eGovernment, and e-/m-Commerce), it is mainly the informational privacy of individuals that is at risk which, according to Westin's and other common definitions can be defined as the right of informational self-determination. Nonetheless, in the mobile and traditional Internet, the problem of unsolicited commercial emails (spam) is increasingly affecting privacy in the sense of the right to be let alone. It can also be seen as an intrusion of territorial privacy and of privacy of the person (if indecent or offensive information is distributed). Hence, with the expanding mobile and traditional Internet, all three aspects of privacy are at risk.

To protect the right of informational self-determination, data protection laws of primarily Western states, as well as international privacy guidelines or directives (such as EU Directive 95/46/EC on Data Protection [European Union, Eur95]) and the OECD privacy guidelines [OECD, OEC80], require basic privacy principles to be guaranteed when personal data are collected or processed. These include:

- Legitimacy: personal data collection and processing are admissible only if permitted by legal provisions or if the data subject has consented (Art. 7 EU Directive);
- Purpose specification and purpose binding: personal data must be obtained for specified and legitimate purposes and should not be used for other purposes (see Art. 6 EU Directive);
- Necessity of data collection and processing: the collection and processing of personal data shall only be allowed if it is necessary for the tasks falling within the responsibility of the data processing agency (see Art. 7 EU Directive);
- Transparency and basic rights: the data subject's right to information, notification and objection and the right to correction, erasure or blocking of incorrect or illegally stored data (see Art. 10 - 14 EU Directive);
- Requirement of adequate technical and organizational security mechanisms to guarantee the confidentiality, integrity, and availability of personal data (see Art. 6, 17 EU Directive).

An international harmonization of data protection legislation, besides the EU Directive on data protection is needed, but hardly achievable due to cultural, historical and political differences (see also [Fischer-Hübner, FH00]). The recent transatlantic debate about the adequacy of the Safe Harbour privacy principles in comparison with the EU data protection directive has demonstrated the difficulty of harmonizing data protection legislation. For this reason and because law is not an ultimate protection, it is required that privacy should also be protected and enforced by technology and should be a design criterion for information and communication systems.

There are two major ways of enhancing privacy in the Internet by means of technology. Privacy can be protected most effectively by technologies that avoid or at least minimize personal data and that thus provide anonymity, pseudonymity, unlinkability or freedom from observation for the users. The requirement of personal data avoidance or minimization can be derived from the legal privacy principle of the necessity of data collection and processing, which requires that personal data should not be collected or used for identification purposes when not truly necessary. However, such technologies cannot be applied in applications where personal data must be processed. Other privacy technologies can technically allow a control that personal data are used only according to legal provisions. For instance, the Platform for Privacy Preferences Protocol (P3P) by W3C [W3C, W3C02] can be used to enhance transparency and control for users over the use of personal information on Web sites they visit.. Further examples are privacy access control models that can technically enforce legal privacy requirements, such as the necessity of data processing and purpose binding (see [Fischer-Hübner, FH01], [Karjoth and Schunter, KS02]).

STRUCTURING EFFECTS ON PRIVACY

Today we face a communication era in which the Internet is structuring our privacy related behaviour and perception. An influence on our ordinary behaviour can be recognized already, and this tendency will influence us even more in the future when phenomena like eCommerce and global information society become daily realities.

Legal aspects

Provisions of the OECD Privacy Guidelines, EU Directive 95/46/EC on Data Protection and national data protection laws also apply to the collection and processing of personal data in mobile and traditional Internet environments. Nevertheless, more specific privacy requirements for the Internet were recently formulated in Directive 2002/58/EC of the European Parliament and of the Council concerning the processing of personal data and the protection of privacy in the electronic communication sector [European Union, Eur02]. This new directive, 2002/58/EC, has replaced the directive 97/66/EC concerning the processing of personal data and the protection of privacy in the telecommunications sector [European Union, Eur97] and, in contrast to directive 97/66/EC, has an extended scope to apply to both the classic telecommunication sector as well as the Internet sector. Whereas in Directive 97/66/EC traffic data refer only to "calls" in so-called circuit switched connections (traditional voice telephony), the new directive, COM (2000) 385, covers all traffic data in a technology neutral way, including Internet traffic data.

In addition to the protection of traffic data, directive 2002/58/EC also addresses location data giving the geographic location of mobile users or, more precisely, of their devices. It thereby acknowledges that, particularly in the mobile Internet, mobile location based services that allow the tracking of a user's location require appropriate privacy safeguards for ensuring location privacy. According to its Art.9 I, location data may only be processed when they are anonymous or, with the consent of the users or subscribers, to the extent and for the duration necessary for the provision of a value added service. Exceptions are formulated for emergency services (Art.10) and for necessary measures to safeguard security, defence and criminal investigations (Art. 15).

Further Internet-related privacy problems that are regulated are unsolicited communication (spam) and cookies. Art. 13 introduces an opt-in system for unsolicited electronic mail and thus restricts spam. According to Art.5 III, Member States must ensure that the use of electronic communications networks to store information or to gain access to information stored in the terminal equipment of a subscriber or user is only allowed if the subscriber or user concerned is provided with clear and comprehensive information and is offered the right to refuse such processing by the data controller. This provision should protect users and subscribers against cookies, spyware, web-bugs and other hidden privacy-intrusive data collection techniques.

We have discussed above two different kinds of structuring effects for privacy legislation. The first kind of effect is that existing legal rules are enhanced in order to cope with Internet-related privacy risks. The second type, a generating effect, is that new legislation is introduced to cope especially with problems such as spamming, cookies or location privacy which have especially emerged with the use of mobile Internet technology.

To protect privacy rights on the Internet, a more Internet-specific privacy legislation must be enacted, in addition to general data protection legislation.

Extensive profiling

Introduced in 1930, "Gläserner Mensch" - "Visible Man" [Deutsches Hygiene Museum, Deu02] made the physiology of a human visible. The term has taken on a second meaning since then, away from the natural sciences to a more sociologically oriented meaning where it is seen as a representation of a person about whom various pieces of information (private as well as public) are gathered and compiled into profiles. Profiling sufficiently extensive to generate a "Visible Man" was unfeasible without the funds of a governmental organization in the pre-Internet world, for reasons of processing and storage restrictions. However, with emerging Internet technology, where users leave traces of their communication and consumer behaviour and in which there are cheap processing and storage capabilities, profiling also becomes possible for less powerful organizations.

With the help of two examples, we will try to demonstrate the special role of data networks (especially the Internet) in their relation to extensive profiling.

Customer Profiles

A classic goal in marketing is to determine and exactly analyse the preferences of a potential customer in order to be capable of determining his/her special needs. With this knowledge, it is possible to create a demand by the customer and to then fulfil it at the present as well as in the future. In regular business, it is almost impossible to collect all data about a person's behaviour due to the limited processing capabilities of conventional tracking methods. It is of no doubt that an exact recording of every step of the customer's actions would violate privacy. The result would probably be that he or she would immediately stop the business relation.

The situation is different in the case of electronic purchases (eCommerce). Here all data about a customer's choices and purchases are available via an electronic data processing system, which makes it easy to create a profile of the demands and wishes of a customer. This information can accordingly be used as part of targeted marketing.

At the moment, Amazon.com[9] is one of the most popular eCommerce sites. The business concept of Amazon is to create a platform for the purchase of books for the customer. The customer has no contact with the delivering book dealer. Amazon plays the middleman, who passes the order to the local partner in the customer's neighbourhood. The local partner conducts the effective commerce activity and Amazon receives a part of the commission. This kind of activity is often defined as virtual business.

A model of this kind is dependent on the volume of books that is sold via the company. To reach sales goals it has been necessary to choose an active marketing policy by means of exact user profiles and, with help of this information, to offer potentially interesting books to the customer. These user profiles are based on a very precise recording of every book chosen and purchased. Such a structure of course has a very great effect on the privacy of a customer.

In some Internet sites the customer is required to register and supply a great deal of personal information about his/her preferences to be entitled to reductions or allowed to use the service. This means that the customer is asked to sell his or her privacy in exchange for certain advantages. Sites such as GMX^{TM}[10] and other free-mail providers are good examples of this. Here the customer is offered a free email account if he/she provides a multi-page preferences set. This information is then used for direct marketing. GMX^{TM} explains that it is financed by advertising and therefore needs a detailed profile. A look at their service supply page shows that they do direct marketing, based on the user profiles collected previously, to everyone.

It can be argued that privacy is deliberately given up in exchange for certain benefits. However, customers are often unaware of such privacy intrusions. We believe that if they knew they would probably not use the service or would reconsider their actions.

Thus, the structural effect of the Internet is that it enables the creation and use of extensive customer profiles, and several organizations will use these options. As such, the Internet enables privacy intrusions and related behaviour that has not possible to that extent before this time. Another structuring effect on privacy that arises from profiling is the orientation toward financial profit that often threatens privacy.

Aggregated Profiles

We described in the section above how companies can use customer profiles to their benefit. If we imagine that someone collects profiles from different sources and combines them, even more information can be gained about individuals.

In Austria and other countries, legal authorities are entitled by law ("Sicherheitspolizeigesetz" - security police law) to collect data on individuals without their knowledge. This legislation was introduced in Austria to enable law enforcement to prevent criminal activities.

In the "Briefbomber" (mail bomber) case some years ago, Austrian police used the permission granted by the "Sicherheitspolizeigesetz" to generate a profile about a potential suspect and then processed large amounts of data to look for people fitting the profile. To the police's disappointment, they did not succeed in finding any true suspects but instead severely affected the privacy of a large number of innocent citizens who had been identified as suspects. That the terrorist was found in the end was pure luck and not due to the profiling investigations. For us it is more interesting however that the whole investigation was only possible by means of interconnected computers, where a single controlled machine collected and aggregated data from different sources.

The structuring effect of the Internet here was not the release of a law - as this already existed. Internet technology in fact made it possible for the police to use the legal basis in a new way. Thus the structuring effect was that the Internet produced a new method of investigation that strongly affected privacy. It could be argued that it is acceptable to restrict the privacy of criminals. However, a large number of unrelated innocent people also had to face an intrusion into their privacy.

Looking at the potential of aggregated profiles we can imagine that, in the future, non-governmental organizations will also increasingly become engaged in generating aggregated profiles - especially if we consider large multi-national organizations or groups of direct marketing oriented companies. Here again, the Internet's structuring effect is a constructing one.

Examples of companies that engage in extensive user profiling are service providers such as DoubleClick. These companies use advertisement banners or web bugs to collect information on websites visited by a user by means of cookies and then accumulate the information on visits to all the different sites on which they put advertisements or web bugs. Hence, an aggregated profile of the Internet users' preferences can be compiled (and later be used for customizing web pages) with the data on these users, who are usually uninformed and thus unaware of this kind of profiling.

Increasing demand for privacy-enhancing technologies

Privacy enhancing technologies (PET) are important security technologies for protecting the privacy of users and data subjects. Basic technologies for protecting the user's privacy, such as Mix nets, DC nets, Anonymous Re-mailers and blind signatures, were introduced in the 1980s by David Chaum and other researchers. On the way to a networked society, where all user communication and actions on the Internet can be easily traced and compiled into extensive user profiles, privacy technologies are becoming increasingly relevant.

Thus another structuring effect of the Internet has been an increasing awareness of the need of PET and the expansion of PET research and of a commercial market for privacy technologies. PETs have also become an issue for standardization activities.

In 1995, the Dutch Data Protection Authority (the Registratiekamer), in cooperation with the Information and Privacy Commissioner for the province of Ontario, Canada [van Rossumn et al, vRGB+95], created the term PET in their reports on "Privacy-Enhancing Technologies - The path to anonymity". Since then, further PET studies and research by data protection commissioners and research labs have been initiated, and PET research is becoming an important part of security conferences and publicly funded research programs.

The IT market has also responded to the user's privacy needs. Some companies, such as Anonymizer.com and ZeroKnowledge Inc., have started to offer privacy-enhancing security products, although so far with only limited economic success. In November 2001, IBM established its Privacy Institute, which is an organization in IBM Research to promote and advance research in privacy and data protection technology. The Institute's goal is *"to develop the necessary technologies for enterprises that enable the transition from today's privacy-unaware or even privacy-intrusive ways of doing eBusiness to privacy-enabling ways*". It has created a global research program to develop new privacy-enhancing services and technologies, among others for eBusiness solutions and pervasive and mobile computing and knowledge management [IBM, IBM02].

Standardization bodies have recently given attention to privacy-enhancing technologies. An important standardization document acknowledging privacy as a significant technical security aspect is the harmonized Common Criteria [ISO, ISO99] for security evaluation, which became an International Standard (IS) 15408 in December 1999. The Common Criteria define a Privacy Class that can be used to describe and evaluate the security functionality of PET, mainly for protecting the privacy of users while communicating over the networks. One of the main privacy initiatives of the World Wide Web Consortium (W3C), which promotes interoperability for the World Wide Web, has been the Platform for Privacy Preferences P3P, which became an official W3C recommendation in April 2002. Microsoft has already incorporated P3P functionality in its Internet Explorer to allow users to be well informed about and to better be able to control the use of cookies.

In contrast to the other PET effects presented, where technology influences society, we see the phenomenon that expectations driven by society form the technology. This means that the existence and shape of technology are determined by its social application. [Steinhardt, Ste99a] argues that these influences of technology and society in both directions are true for all effects. We agree with this but would like to argue that, as concerns privacy, this effect is most notable for PET and is therefore mentioned only here.

SYMBOLIC EFFECTS ON PRIVACY

For the most part, the symbolic effects have a much deeper impact on society than the structuring effects. It is easy to see from a historic viewpoint what kinds of symbolic effects a technology has had. It is difficult to predict how present and future tendencies will develop, and it is a vague field to move in, as it is impossible to predict the potential changes that will occur in society. It is also important to keep in mind that we use our own cultural meaning system, even though we have tried to minimize its influence.

We therefore wish to clarify that our perspective is based on the central European culture and may be seen quite differently by others. Nevertheless, we hope to show some of the symbolic effects in ongoing developments and to point out the tremendous potential of the Internet in relation to the influence on our culture and subcultures.

Tendency – Privacy Regulations – Difference between the USA and Europe

Owing to different cultural backgrounds, the development of the concept of privacy has taken different directions in the USA and Europe.

Negative historic experiences, where dictator regimes violated the privacy of individuals, have led European development to foster strong data protection that covers both the public and the private sector. These regulations have raised awareness about privacy (among individuals as well as organizations).

The situation is different in the USA, however. The public sector is covered by the US Privacy Act on the federal level and, on a local level, the states have their own data protection legislation. In the private sector, statutory privacy regulations cover only a few specific areas (e.g. video rental) while most areas are unregulated by law and a self-regulation approach is supported in order to protect privacy. Furthermore, in contrast to Europe, the US has no data protection authorities to regularly monitor data processing and act upon complaints made by data subjects that believe that their privacy rights have been violated.

As demonstrated above, the Internet has developed structuring effects concerning privacy behaviour via adjusted legislation. Here we would like to present two symbolic effects related to that area.

The first symbolic effect is that a cultural awareness related to privacy has developed in both cultures, although to different extents. People are caring more about their privacy in the Internet society. The effect is that the industry has been motivated to introduce privacy extensions and privacy-enhancing technology into their products, as discussed above. An example is that more and more privacy statements can be found on companies' web pages. This has led to the interpretation that privacy is becoming a sub-cultural (here meaning the Internet subculture) topic and is receiving greater and greater attention. A further result is that the subculture starts to span over multiple cultures as a subset of them.

Another symbolic effect is expressed with the "Safe Harbour initiative" - an initiative for harmonizing privacy protection in the global world of the Internet. A cultural need can be discerned (driven only partly by legislation) to harmonize the two cultural approaches to privacy. European cultures were forced to accept the US' method for (self-)regulated privacy protection by means other than legislative ones. The US, on the other hand, must consider a more formal and stricter regulation to satisfy European needs. And even after the formal enactment of safe harbour, both parties criticized[11] and even questioned[12] the agreement and its enforcement. All the problems with its introduction underline even further the symbolic effect. If we recall the first description of the railway - which was not at all positive - we can conclude that a cultural change rarely meets with any resistance[13].

Tendency - Cyber-War, Cyber-Crime and Cyber-Terrorism

The September 11th catastrophe started very broad discussions about terrorism. Suddenly this has again become a major issue of public interest. Information scientists and the military had long spoken of the potential of using the Internet for cyber-war, cyber-crime and cyber-terrorist activities.

From a crime perspective, fraud, copyright infringement and illegal pornography have become problems impossible to ignore. The economic and social damage caused has taken dramatic dimensions.

Extrapolating a crime scenario to a terrorism scenario doubtless generates fear. There is namely a critical difference between these two forms of attacks: the crime scenario has (personal) financial profit as its motive, whiles the terrorism scenario, on the other hand, has fanaticism at its roots. It is consequently very unpleasant to imagine the potential of the Internet. Used in an organized way it could easily lead to a cyber-war.

Speculative media reports about September 11th state that the terrorists used steganography to hide their communication over the Internet. As a consequence, control measures such as crypto controls that had already been ruled out as being more privacy-intrusive than effective for fighting cyber attacks, were suddenly again proposed. In addition, new privacy-intrusive controls, such as "antiterror biometrics", are being discussed. The USA Patriot Act, signed by President Bush in October 2001, is expanding surveillance of Internet users, e.g. through wiretapping or spying on web browsing, with reduced checks and balances. In other Western countries, similar acts have been passed or are under discussion. The effects of these control measures on privacy have been broadly accepted out of fear.

Given the threat of terrorism via the Internet, the effects on privacy are that people are forced to accept restrictions to their privacy. The cultural need for privacy has been overruled by the technical possibilities of cyber attacks. Thus, a symbolic effect on society can be seen - not directly implied by the technology itself, but by means of its effects. Furthermore, the technology is the vehicle and therefore also the symbolic reason.

Looking at cyber-crime threats we can see that the (structuring) effect of the Internet is that more crime preventing legislation is starting to address this kind of crime - such as the cyber crime treaty of the Council of Europe [Council of Europe, Cou01]. This legislation entitles authorities to restrict the privacy rights of people during investigations. The symbolic effect is that, with the emerging threats of child pornography and other forms of cyber-crime, people are shocked and call for preventive actions by authorities, while at the same time accepting drastic privacy restrictions.

Tendency – Private persons organizations

With the widespread use of the Internet, several privacy organizations have received public attention (such as the Electronic Privacy Information Center (EPIC), Privacy International,...) or have been founded (Internet Privacy Coalition ...). These organizations - here called private person organizations (PPO), as their major goal is to protect private persons - try to exert symbolic and practical opposition to the existing tendency to undermine privacy through the use of insufficiently regulated technology, technology that lacks any regulation at all or out of total ignorance.

PPOs such as EPIC try for example to create court cases in the United States to make privacy violations obvious. They are active mainly against the US government but have also generated some court cases against private corporations. Here the Internet plays a double role. The symbolic effect of the Internet here is that it has caused/initiated privacy activities or campaigns organized by PPOs.

Another symbolic effect of the Internet seems to be that it enables the generation and prosperity of organizations. The "Internet Privacy Coalition (IPC)" uses the technology as a part of its name. Their motto is: *"The Mission of the Internet Privacy Coalition is to promote privacy and security on the Internet through widespread public availability of strong encryption and the relaxation of export controls on cryptography."* [IPC Homepage, 1999].

CONCLUSION

We have described a wide spectrum of privacy-related effects of the Internet. Even if we think that none of these should be seen in isolation, or as being caused solely by the Internet, they show an influence on privacy that is caused mainly by this technology.

From a structuring perspective we have seen effects that grant us more specific privacy rights. Unfortunately, there are also major structuring effects caused by the Internet that are threatening our privacy. As a secondary cause of privacy threats we have found a group of structuring effects that seems to neutralize negative effects. Recalling parts of the definition of structuring effects – *(...) suggesting specific ways of action and perception, preventing others, or presenting new ones (...)* – we see that the Internet gives rise to all three possible action modifications.

In the introduction to the symbolic effect section we wrote that symbolic effects are more difficult to analyse because of the problem of being part of the system under observation. We have nevertheless attempted to point out some symbolic effects. All the effects indicate that the Internet influences both our social behaviour with respect to privacy as well as the perception of privacy and privacy needs. Recalling again the definition – *(...) an expression of collective practice (...) affects the subjects and their social behaviour (...) – (...)*, we see the exactness of this fit. The symbolic effects provide evidence of the importance of the Internet – only a technology of this kind could have produced these effects in such a short time.

While we hesitate to predict future effects based on current trends we believe that the Internet will exert even greater influence on our daily life and on our privacy-related behaviour. We would like to go further and say that we believe that the Internet - not only with respect to privacy - will shape our society as much as the railway or the car has done earlier.

REFERENCES

[Cas56]   Ernst Cassirer. *Wesen und Wirken des Symbolbegriffes.* Wissenschaftliche Buchgesellschaft Darmstad, 1956.

[Cou01]   Council of Europe. Convention on Cybercrime - European Treaty Series - No. 185. Technical report, Council of Europe, 11 2001.

[Deu02]   Deutsches Hygiene Museum. *Kurze Geschichte der Gläsernen Figuren,* June 2002.

[Eur95]   European Union. Directive 95/46/EC of the European Parliament and of the Council of 24 October 1995 on the protection of individuals with regard to the processing of personal data and on the free movement of such data, 1995.

[Eur97]   European Union. Directive 97/66/EC of the European Parliament and of the Council of 15 December 1997 concerning the processing of personal data and the protection of privacy in the telecommunications sector, 1997.

[Eur02]   European Union. Directive of the European Parliament and of the Council concerning the processing of personal data and the protection of privacy in the electronic communications sector 2002/58/EC, 2002.

[FH00]   Simone Fischer-Hübner. Privacy and Security at Risk in the Global Information Society. In D. Thomas and B. Loader, editors, *Cybercrime.* Routledge. London and New York, 2000.

[FH01]   Simone Fischer-Hübner. *IT-Security and Privacy: Design and Use of Privacy-Enhancing Security Mechanims.* Lecture Notes in Computer Science. Springer, 2001.

[Hol93]   J. Holvast. Vulnerability and Privacy: Are we on the way to a risk-free society? In *Facing the Challenge of Risk and Vulnerability in an Information Society,* J. Berleur, C. Beardon & R. Laufer editors, Proceedings of the IFIP-WG9.2 Conference, Namur May 20-22, 1993, IFIP Transactions A-33, Elsevier Science Publishers B.V. (North-Holland), 1993.

[IBM02]   IBM Privacy Institute, http: //www.research.ibm.com/privacy/, 2002.

[ISO99] The Common Criteria for Information Technology Security Evaluation (CC) version 2.1 (aligned with IS 15408), 1999.

[KS02] Günther Karjoth and Matthias Schunter. A Privacy Policy Model for Enterprises. *15th IEEE Computer Security Foundations Workshop*, June 24 - 26 2002.

[OEC80] OECD. *Guidelines on the Protection of Privacy and Transborder Flows of Personal Data*, September 1980.

[PB87] Trevor Pinch and Wiebe Bijker. *The Social Construction of Technological Systems*, chapter 1 - The social Construction of Facts and Artifacts: Or How the Sociology of Science and the Sociology of Technology Might Benefit Each Other, pages 17 – 50. MIT Press, 1987.

[Ros92] R. Rosenberg. *The Social Impact of Computers*. Academic Press, 1992.

[Ste99a] Gerald Steinhardt. Auf dem Weg zur kaleidoskopischen Wahrnehmung. Überlegungen zur Subjekt-Konstitution und Welt-Erfahrung im Zeitalter der neuen Informations- und Kommunikationstechnologien. *Psychosozial*, 22(1): 81–98, 1999.

[Ste99b] Gerald Steinhardt. Technische Universität Wien: *Techniksoziologie und - psychologie*. Lectures notes, 1999.

[vRGB+95] Hanke van Rossumn, Huib Gardeniers, John Borking, Ann Cavoukian, John Brans, Noel Muttupulle, and Nick Magistrale. Privacy-enhancing technologies. Technical report, Registratiekamer/The Netherlands & Information and Privacy Commissioner/Ontario, Canada, August 1995.

[W3C02] W3C, www.w3c.org/P3P/. *The Platform for Privacy Preferences 1.0 (P3P1.0) Specification*, April 2002.

[WB90] D. Warren and D. Brandeis. The Right to Privacy. *Harvard Law Review*, (5): 193–220, 1890.

[Wes67] Alan Westin. *Privacy and Freedom*. Atheneum, New York, 1967.

[Win77] Langdon Winner. *Autonomous Technology*. Lighthouse Press, 1977.

---

1 For a discussion of the term symbolic see [Cas56].

2 Als symbolische Form kommt Technik ein Doppelcharakter zu: Zum einen ist sie Ausdruck kollektiver Praxis und (sub)kultureller Bedeutungssysteme; zum anderen wirkt sie auf die Subjekte und ihr soziales Handeln ein."

3 (...) strukturiert Technik sowohl die sinnliche Wahrnehmung als auch das praktische Handeln der Subjekte , indem sie bestimme Handlungs- und Wahrnehmungsweisen nahelegt, andere verunmöglicht, neue eröffnet (...)

4 His home town at this time

5 We are well aware that this is bidirectional and, as is later argued, the approach chosen also supports this understanding.

6 Technological Change: Its Impact on Man and society, p. 20, 1970, cited in [Win77]

7 We consider the Internet as all information which is interlinked and not as the physical routers, gateways and computers.

8 See arguments given in section

9 Amazon.com, Inc. – www.amazon.com

10 GMX Aktiengesellschaft – www.gmx.net

[11] A report of the European Commission in February 2002 on practical operation of the safe harbor agreement was criticized insufficient transparency among the organizations that have signed up to safe harbor.

[12] The Bush administration has pressed the EU Commission in March 2002 to weaken the proposed privacy standards for consumers, claiming that they would make it difficult for US financial institutions to conduct business abroad.

[13] Tom DeMarco and Timothy Lister discuss in their book "Peopleware" that changes almost always face resistance.

Integrating Historical and Societal Contexts in the Computing Curricula

John IMPAGLIAZZO
Department of Computer Science, Hofstra University; John.Impagliazzo@Hofstra.edu
John A.N. LEE
Virginia Tech and Radford University; janlee17@verizon.net
David C. CASSIDY,
Division of Natural Science, Hofstra University; chmdcc@optonline.net

Abstract : This paper provides instructors of computing a method to integrate computing history in the computing curriculum and to elevate the awareness of the social context of the subject. It provides suggestions by which instructors can enrich the curriculum by including history in the subjects they teach, even though they may not have had formal education in computing history or the history of science. Using history in computing very often stimulates discussion and dialogue among students and makes them aware of the social consequences of the computer systems they will use, help design, or create. Instructors can enrich the courses they now teach by integrating social and historical interludes within them.

Key words: Computing history, societal issues, computing curricula, computing in society

INTRODUCTION

The computing community has witnessed a resurgent interest in computing history. This is only natural, as time diminishes the ability of early pioneers to record the achievements and contributions they have made to the computing field. In an effort to preserve historical achievements, different institutions around the world (see Appendix A) and many history zealots have championed and preserved a new interest in computing history. Recognized historians have also promoted this interest through their publications and historical websites.

Despite this recent fervor in computing history, little has filtered into the educational arena. While pocket interests appear in specialized courses in schools, colleges, and universities, little historical content has reached the mainstream areas of education. Very few computing programs formally integrate computing history within their curricula and even fewer offer courses related to the history of computing. In contrast, one can easily demonstrate mathematical curricula that have courses or course content in the history of mathematics. Since the 1960s, organizations such as the ACM [ACM68, ACM78, Tucker91, ACM93], the IEEE Computer Society [IEEECS83], the Association of Information Technology Professionals [Longenecker97], and committees of UNESCO [Mulder00] have produced curriculum recommendations in computing. Only recently, in Computing Curricula 2001 [IEEECS01], has the history of computing received acknowledgment and credence by including it as knowledge components within the curriculum recommendation.

Furthermore, the history of computing has affected the information society in which we live. Many documented cases such as the Therac instance [Leveson93] exist where historical reflection would have saved human lives or economic loss. In this case, several people had died because of the faulty functioning of software that operated an x-ray machine. Have we as computing professionals learned lessons from such past failures? Have we learned lessons from past successes? When the educational computing culture does not encourage history to be part of a computing curriculum, we cannot expect the professionals of tomorrow–whether in the academic, industrial, or governmental spheres–to make informed decisions when they have not experienced the lessons from the past. This is another reason why computing history is important for all computing professionals and why it should be part of the computing curriculum.

In summary, we can learn much from history. From a cultural standpoint, history broadens one's perspective on the field. It allows students and scholars to explore the thinking and decisions of people as well as the socio-technical dynamics in the development, use, and re-appropriation of technological resources. From a practical standpoint, history enables individuals and enterprises to learn from the events of the past and to improve on those experiences. Both views are necessary to create an informed computing professional. Computing history should be a part of human understanding. It should also demonstrate how the development of computing has affected people and their social environment. In more advanced settings, students should be able to do a critical analysis of significant moments in the history of computing, including the social, biographical, and economic contexts of development. In this spirit, this work provides a rationale by which educators at all levels can use history to enhance and enrich their current courses by integrating computing history within them.

SUMMARY OF THE IFIP REPORT

In 1998, the International Federation for Information Processing (IFIP) adopted the report entitled "History in the Computing Curriculum," referred herein as the "IFIP Report." An IFIP joint task group (TC3 and WG 9.7) developed the IFIP Report and the technical committees TC3 and TC9 endorsed it in the summer of 1998. The journal *IEEE Annals of the History of Computing* published the report in 1999 January [Impagliazzo99]. A pre-publication electronic version of the report is also available [http://www.CompHist.org]. The IFIP Report has created much interest as educators have used it as a basis for presentations at different conferences. Appendices B and C illustrate some resources that are similar to those appearing in the IFIP Report. Appendix B provides some literary works; Appendix C illustrates some useful websites. We include them here as a convenience to the reader.

The IFIP Report provided a framework for a curriculum by proposing a knowledge base of suggested topics. It also included resources applicable to undergraduate degree programs offered at institutions of higher learning. It was international in scope and was applicable to all computing disciplines. It sought to raise the awareness of history and showed how people could use the report to improve their study and practice of the computing profession. The increased awareness of computing history has highlighted the importance of history as a tool for learning for students and practitioners, and underscored the rationale that history should be part of the computing curriculum at all levels of study.

The objectives of the IFIP Report suggested that computing history should be a part of the formal education of students, particularly those studying computing. The report fostered that concept of learning through one or a combination of the following forms:
- An integrated approach where history becomes a part of existing courses,
- A single course for computing specialists who have completed at least one year of study in their specialty,
- A single course with no prerequisite open to all students.

The report also provided hints on how educators in the computing field could make history exciting within the context of the computing curriculum. It did this by providing suggestions for course outlines, texts, resources from different media, and sample curricula so educators could have access to tools and resources needed to implement a successful inclusion of the study of computing history in the computing curriculum.

OVERVIEW OF THIS PAPER

This chapter is an extension of the IFIP report. It shows how the establishment of a history component in the computing curriculum can have a two-fold effect on students by (1) enriching their course of study through an appreciation of the origins of accepted concepts and techniques, and (2) demonstrating how events from the past affect contemporary computer science and ultimately the society in which we live. It focuses on the integration of societal and historical contexts throughout the computing curriculum not only to highlight how people have shaped the field, but also to emphasize the importance of the broader consequences and contexts of historical events. Through examples, it will show how historical events affected the socio-technical dimensions of a global society. This paper will also suggest ways in which society can benefit from the lessons of the past so that computing professionals can make decisions not only from economic considerations, but also from societal and cultural perspectives.

The approach taken here is to suggest how instructors can establish their own knowledge base of possible topics from computing history and incorporate these topics within the curriculum. The manner and depth of inclusion of these topics will vary according to the needs of the presenters and the context in which they present the material. Teachers of computing can incorporate the topics from the knowledge base into their existing courses. In courses for non-computing specialists, teachers would temper the inclusion of their knowledge base according to the level of the student and the intent of the course.

SOCIETAL PERSPECTIVES ON COMPUTING HISTORY AND CURRICULA

For the student of computing, there is a need to understand how this field has developed and matured. How many computing students know of the challenges that faced early computing pioneers and how they overcame those challenges at that time? How many students understand the social and ethical implications of the design of computer systems? Students should be aware of the principal people and the broader contexts and events that have shaped their profession. They should also understand how computational ideas and products have influenced our society. Students can learn from experiences: the successes and the failures. In doing so, students will become better global citizens and professionals. The history of computing can make that happen.

Computing professionals of all types can benefit from history. In academia, computing history can add new dimensions to courses by allowing students to reflect on past events and to conceptualize a background of their studies. In industry and government, past mistakes, misconceptions, and successes can form a basis for developing new ideas and implementing and promoting new frontiers in computing. For global citizens, computing history adds perspective to the establishment of their pursuits in a technological society.

As mentioned, the growing interest in computing history and student learning has yet to receive priority for curriculum inclusion. Part of the reluctance is the ongoing augmentation of technical topics in an already seemingly crowded curriculum. A special course on the history of computing would be ideal, but would most likely compete with a course of technical interest. To complicate the issue, teachers of computing courses have little formal study in computing history and, consequently, are hesitant to discuss computing history within their technical courses or as a special course on the subject. Although computer history institutes and museums have been diligently collecting artefacts, interviews, and archival sources (e.g. see Appendix A), these materials are not yet fully catalogued or easily accessible–either on-line or in hard copy–for use by teachers and students.

KNOWLEDGE CLUSTERS FROM HISTORICAL PERSPECTIVES

In an effort to assist instructors integrating historical and societal contexts in their computer curricula, the IFIP report provided some examples of how they can develop a topic by developing "clusters" of information to help form a knowledge base. To encapsulate structure, we had partitioned a cluster into four sections identified as Subject, Description, Topics, and Activities.

Instructors should start by developing these and/or their own clusters on topics of their choosing and caching them for eventual use in the curriculum. Several clusters per course would be a good starting point. at the appropriate time, instructors can introduce a cluster in a course. This would provide a handy set of topics and assignments to help them in the instruction process. Pre-developed clusters will help ensure that some appropriate historical/social topics will complement technical content and that assignments are available, if needed. Clusters also help avoid the "ad hoc" manner of introducing material on history, especially if students are aware that they will receive a grade on the material.

Our own experience has shown that the use of several cluster-topics per semester gives the students a welcome change of pace in the content of the course and provides a contextual perspective on the technical material of the course, enabling a deeper sense of the meaning and significance of the technical aspects. In Appendix D, we present some representative examples of historically oriented social clusters that follow this model. We encourage instructors to experiment with clusters either through their own design or by modifying those presented to reflect their own styles and needs.

COMPUTING ISSUES AFFECTING SOCIETY

Computing issues affecting society involve broader societal issues that have affected the development of the computer itself. The immediate commercial, scientific, and military applications have driven the initial development of the computer and its uses, and they are still significant today. The nearly unlimited flexibility of computer applications has enabled such applications to extend far beyond their initial purposes, touching upon nearly every facet of contemporary life, as well as upon many other unrelated technologies. Because of this, the computer's effect upon society is becoming equally diverse and nearly universal. While these effects involve new social consequences or hardly recognized social issues unique to the technology itself, in most cases the effects have magnified or resolved previously existing problems. They have also added new dimensions to already existing situations. Such issues as privacy, freedom of information, economic stratification, work environments, and copyright protection were hotly debated long before the advent of computers. Other social issues, such as access of physically challenged people to computers, computer access by economically or educationally disadvantaged, uses of computers in education, and "cyber crime" embody qualities unique to computer technology.

Because of the tremendous impact of computers upon society, it is important that future computer professionals are aware of the past, present, and possible future influence of their work and its consequences, both in positive and in negative terms. Through the inclusion of historical examples bearing on contemporary and emerging issues, we can effectively accomplish building such awareness into the computer science curriculum.

KNOWLEDGE CLUSTERS FROM SOCIETAL PERSPECTIVES

Following the model presented in the IFIP Report, Appendix D shows eight representative examples of schematic knowledge clusters on a wide range of computer-related social issues. Where appropriate, each knowledge cluster encourages students to examine the broader issues involved, both past and present, the impact of the introduction of computer technology, and the viability of possible ways to resolve or improve the situation in the future.

The clusters of Appendix D differ from those appearing in the IFIP Report. In addition to Subject, Description, Topics, and Activities, the societal clusters include an additional section called Discussion. Under Discussion, we pose some questions to stimulate class participation and interaction. Clearly, these questions act as guidelines with the hope of stimulating further questions either from the students or from the instructor. Ideally, discussion should occur after students have performed the activities related to the topics of the subject. Appendix E contains suggested resources that may be useful in developing new clusters for some courses.

ESTABLISHING AN HISTORICAL CONTEXT OF KNOWLEDGE

It is difficult to state which topics or events from history should appear in the background of a student. Many events mark different milestones in the historical evolution of computing. Identifying them is not easy. This becomes especially true when viewed in the context of courses for specialists (majors) versus courses for non-specialists (non-majors). The IFIP Report suggested a possible knowledge base. In reality, there are many possibilities. What is important is to identify courses and to include within them historical interludes to spark greater (human) interest in the technical topic and to show the broader effects of the topic.

One way to spark interest is to have students review historical chronologies and search out broader events over time that have influenced the course of a particular topic. The online version of the IFIP Report shows one such chronology; there are many others (see Appendix F). For example, we have found that exploring the historical forces and the people behind the invention of the transistor and its uses, or the story of Bill Gates and the rise and continuing saga of Microsoft, or the history of operating systems have caused a burst of student excitement and class discussions. Human, social, and economic factors start playing a role. Some students may be reticent to discuss openly a technical aspect of operating systems. However, the historical evolution of operating systems, for example, suddenly motivates them by an understanding and appreciation of early challenges and struggles leading to a better understanding and appreciation of the status of the subject. In addition, lively discussions have occurred on how operating systems affect society and why some systems have succeeded while others have failed. Overall, computing instructors should formulate their own contexts of knowledge and apply them in their own manner within their courses.

As a curriculum example, suppose one were teaching an overview of computing course for non-specialists. The context of knowledge in this case might consist of a collection of events that highlight the evolution of computing. These might include some of the so-called "firsts" that have achieved recognition by historians such as the first computer, the first programming language, the first operating system, the first mouse, and the first microprocessor. The teacher can easily change the thread of conversation to discuss the broader factors motivating the development of these "firsts," followed by their effect on different societies as they were introduced and how they eventually changed the culture in which people live.

As another curriculum example, suppose someone were teaching a computing course in programming. Irrespective of the language used, it is possible to provide interludes of history as the course progresses. The context of knowledge in this case might include events such as the evolution of an early programming language (say FORTRAN or ALGOL), the development of language paradigms, and the historical development of the language under discussion. The teacher can discuss how programming languages differ from natural languages and how programming affected different global societies in which it was applied.

In each of these two examples, we would encourage instructors to develop a "knowledge cluster" that focuses on a particular aspect of the subject. In this manner, instructors will be prepared (similar to having a lesson plan) to include the historical topic within their technical courses.

MAKING IT HAPPEN

The key to success is to seize historical opportunities within courses that can generate further interest in the topics of computing. Sometimes instructors plan these opportunities; sometimes they occur spontaneously. Ideally, all instructors of computing should possess a sufficient and scholarly background in computing history. In reality, only very few can legitimately claim to be computing historians. The lack of formal preparation in computing history, however, should not deter instructors from including history in their courses.

One approach is to develop knowledge clusters on particular areas of interest as mentioned in the previous section. Using the aforementioned models as a guide, instructors will find it easy to include the historical or social experience within areas of their technical interest. At the appropriate moment, instructors will be ready to include meaningful historical content in their courses.

Another approach is to have instructors enrich their own area of technical interest with computing history. They can do that in their own manner and in many different ways. One way is a time-categorical overview of the subject of interest by partitioning the evolution of the subject into categories over time. An obvious partitioning is as follows: early stages, developing era, modern events. By collecting historical information on their subject and organizing them in these categories, instructors would be ready to insert historical interludes within technical presentations in their courses.

Still another approach is to focus on the development of several important areas of a topic of interest. The subject of hardware, for example, contains many topics. One hardware topic is peripheral devices. Instructors may consider the development of this topic from a time perspective by tracing the development of, say disk drives, over time. They may even consider an industrial perspective on the subject by discussing corporate approaches to the manufacture of such devices. A business-oriented computing course may take advantage of this approach.

In special cases, it is possible to assign projects on the history of computing and to study the impact of computing on society. Instructors can accomplish these projects at all levels of study. The purpose of a project is to allow students to apply the methods of scholarship to the study of computing history. In this setting, students can undertake a significant self-directed historical inquiry. They can use historical sources effectively by locating and using primary, secondary, and tertiary sources, periodical literature, and electronic information. We caution that projects are not for everyone and instructors should use this approach judiciously.

Instructors can employ other interesting and exciting paradigms to make history happen in a curriculum. Indeed, we encourage faculty members to explore different ways to present computing history in their courses and to use the method that best suits their philosophy, their students, their institution, and their topic of discourse.

The crucial factors in making history happen in a course or curriculum are attitude and desire. Instructors need to focus not only on technical elements of the subject, but also on the historical flavors surrounding them. Weaving historical interludes within technical content makes courses exciting and real. Instructors can use this method to show how the dynamics of a topic or subject developed and continues to develop. Additionally, students enjoy the experience and often look forward to the social realities and the human side of the material they study. It also reinforces their interest in the subject and makes them better students.

ASSESSING PROGRESS

As with all educational experiences, some form of assessment is necessary to measure and evaluate performance. Using historical interludes in technical courses without a measure of student accountability causes an unspoken void and leaves students with the impression that the material is not important. It is essential that instructors assess the progress made by their students in all areas of their studies, including the interludes. If instructors assess students by examination, then they should include at least one question on the socio-historical content.

We would expect students emerging from an experience on the history of computing to be conversant on various topics of the field. They should be able to relate concepts and topics with people, time, and places and be able to have informed opinions on the social consequences of using computer in society. When that occurs, instructors will have achieved the goal of having students consider the social context of their technical abilities.

CONCLUSIONS

The intent of this paper is to provide instructors of computing with suggestions on how to integrate history in computing and how to make students more aware of the social context of the subject. The work has provided suggestions by which instructors who have not had formal education in computing history or the history of science and technology can still enrich their curriculum by including history in the subjects they teach. We hope that the use of history in computing will stimulate discussion and dialogue among students and render them more aware of the social consequences of the computer systems they will help design or create. In this spirit, our hope is that instructors will enrich the courses they now teach by integrating social and historical interludes within them. We believe that students and society will benefit from this experience.

ACKNOWLEDGEMENTS

The authors wish to acknowledge the members of the TC9 Committee for their review and input. They would also like to thank their students who have commented and benefited from using historical and societal issues in their studies.

REFERENCES

[ACM68] ACM Curriculum Committee on Computer Science. Curriculum '68 - Recommendations for Academic Programs in Computer Science. *Communications of the ACM 11* (3) (Mar. 1968): 151-197.

[ACM78] ACM Curriculum Committee on Computer Science. Curriculum '78 - Recommendations for the Undergraduate Program in Computer Science. *Communications of ACM 22* (3) (March 1979): 147-166.

[ACM93] ACM Two-Year College Computing Curricula Task Force. *Computing Curricula Guidelines for Associate-Degree Programs.* 4 vols. New York: ACM Press, 1993.

[IEEECS83] IEEE Computer Society Educational Activities Board / Model Program Committee. *The 1983 IEEE Computer Society Model Program in Computer Science and Engineering.* New York: IEEE Computer Society, 1983.

[IEEECS01] IEEE Computer Society and ACM, Computing Curricula 2001 – Computer Science, <http://computer.org/ education/cc2001/final/index.htm>, 2001

[Impagliazzo99] Impagliazzo, John, et al. History in the Computing Curriculum, IFIP (TC3-WG9.7 Task Group) Report. Task Group Chair. *IEEE Annals of the History of Computing*, January 1999.

[Leveson93] Leveson, Nancy and Clark S. Turner, An Investigation of the Therac-25 Accidents, *IEEE Computer*, Vol. 26, No. 7, July 1993, pp. 18-41.

[Longenecker97] Longenecker, Herbert E. Jr, David L. Feinstein, John T. Gorgone, Gordon B. Davis, J. Daniel Couger, co-chairs. *IS'97. Model Curriculum and Guidelines for Undergraduate Degree Programs in Information Systems.* ACM Press, 1997.

[Mulder00] Mulder, Fred, and Tom van Weert, IFIP/UNESCO's Informatics Curriculum Framework 2000 for Higher Education, *Proceedings of the IFIP World Computer Congress 2000*, International Federation for Information Processing, 2000.

[Tucker91] Tucker, Allen B., et al. *Computing Curricula 1991 - Report of the ACM/IEEE-Computer Society Joint Curriculum Task Force.* New York: ACM Press, 1991. Reprinted in summary in *Communications of the ACM 34* (6) (June 1991): 68-84.

APPENDIX

Appendix A

Some Institutions Dedicated to Computing History
1. Charles Babbage Institute (Minnesota)
2. Computer History Museum (California)
3. Deutsches Museum (Munich)
4. Heinz Nixdorf Museum (Paderborn)
5. IEEE History Center (New Jersey)
6. Museum of the History of Science (Oxford)
7. Smithsonian Institution (Washington, D.C.)

Appendix B

Some Journals, Textbooks, General Works, and Monographs on Computing History

Journals
IEEE Annals of the History of Computing; IEEE Computer Society, Los Alamitos, California.
Technology and Culture; Society for the History of Technology, Dearborn, Michigan.

Textbooks and General Works
Aspray, William (Ed.); *Computing Before Computers*, Iowa State University Press, 1990.
Augarten, Stan; *Bit by Bit: An Illustrated History of Computers*, Ticknor & Fields, 1984.
Campbell-Kelly, Martin and Aspray, William; *Computer: A History of the Information Machine*, Basic Books, 1996.
Lee, John A.N.; *Computer Pioneers*, IEEE Computer Society Press, 1995.
Randell, Brian (Ed.); *The Origins of Digital Computers*, Springer-Verlag, 1982.
Williams, Michael R.; *A History of Computing Technology*, Second Edition, IEEE Computer Society Press, 1997.

Specialist Monographs
Austrian, Geoffrey D.; *Herman Hollerith: Forgotten Giant of Information Processing*, Columbia University Press, 1982.
Bergin, T.J. and Gibson, R.G.; *History of Programming Languages*, ACM Press, New York, 1996.
Hodges, A.; *Alan Turing: The Enigma*, Simon and Schuster, New York 1983.
Pugh, Emerson W.; *Building IBM: Shaping an Industry and its Technology*, MIT Press, 1995.
Wexelblatt, R. (ed.); *History of Programming Languages*, Academic Press, 1981.

Appendix C

Websites Useful for Computing History

Some web sites useful in the computing curriculum
American Computer Museum in Bozeman, Montana: http://www.compustory.com
Charles Babbage Institute, Center for the History of Computing. University of Minnesota: http://www.cbi.umn.edu
Computer Conservation Society. British Computer Society and the Science Museum of London: http://www.cs.man.ac.uk/CCS
IEEE Annals of the History of Computing: http://www.computer.org/pubs/annals/annals.htm
Hobbes' Internet Timeline: http://info.isoc.org/guest/zakon/Internet/History/HIT.html
Impagliazzo History Site: http://www.CompHist.org
Lee history site: http://ei.cs.vt.edu/~history/index.html

Virtual Museum of Computing, Oxford University: http://www.comlab.ox.ac.uk/archive/other/museums/computing.html

Appendix D

Examples of Clusters Emphasizing Social Issues

Computing issues affecting society entwine themselves with many of the other broader issues facing society and with the development of the computer itself. The issues and their resolution can change with society's changing social, economic, and governmental priorities, as well as with advances in computer technology. Each cluster contains the historical background as well as the contemporary status and potential future development of the issue.

Cluster 1

Subject:
Government-related Issues

Description:
In the United States, federal funding helped foster computer technology and protect American interests. Examine the government's past role in the growth of this technology, and some of the issues relating to the impact of computing technology upon government functions.

Topics:
National issues: Government role in fostering computer technology–past and present.
Privacy issues: Previous and present privacy legislation, freedom of information
Defense issues: Role of the military in computer development, the "computer battlefield," origins of the Internet, and combating terrorism.
Political issues: Uses of computers in prior presidential election campaigns, citizen lobbying, freedom of speech

Activities:
Use the Internet to research early and more recent government defense and science initiatives relating to computer technology development of one or more countries. Find an abbreviated government budget report and the amounts allocated to various agencies for computer science and technology. Examine one or more of the resulting government uses of the new technology.

Discussion:
What has been the role of the national government in the development of computer science and technology? Why was the national government involved? Would computer technology be the same today without governmental support in the past and present? How has the new technology transformed government functions?

Cluster 2

Subject:
Free Market Issues

Description:
Consider several important anti-trust and copyright or patent infringement cases past and present, and how their outcomes have affected or will affect the computing industry.

Topics:
The Atari vs. Nintendo case
The Apple vs. Microsoft case

The United States government (and nine states) and the European Union vs. Microsoft

Activities:
Research each of these cases, the issues involved on both sides, the outcome in each case, and the impact or potential impact on the perceived problem.

Discussion:
Since governments have played a key role in promoting computer technology and its economic development, what role should it have, if any, in the computer marketplace. What has been the general complaint about Microsoft in the Microsoft-related cases? Do you think this is fair? What should be the role of businesses and corporations.

Cluster 3

Subject:
Computers in Education

Description:
Consider how educational institutions have utilized computers in the past and how they might better use them in the future.

Topics:
Computer assisted learning–pros and cons
Status of computers in elementary education,
Status of computers in higher education (e.g. science education)
Changing computer literacy
Filtering Internet and web content in schools and libraries

Activities:
Research how educational institutions have used, or not used, computers. Determine the impact of computing technology on students' learning. Examine the pros and cons of content filtering in schools and libraries.

Discussion:
People have said that more computers in the classroom and access to the Internet will enhance education. So far, have computers and the Internet really enhance education? What place have computers had in education, and should this change? What are the issues involved in filtering efforts?

Cluster 4

Subject:
Computers and Work

Description:
The office computer arose from a confluence of electronic technology and office machinery. Consider how the computer was introduced into the work place (office and non-office), how it has affected the work environment, worker productivity, and the issues that have arisen as a result.

Topics:
Changing nature of work
Changing employer-employee relationship (monitoring etc)
Health related issues
Impact on employment and unemployment

Activities:
Research how the introduction of computers has affected each of the above topics.

Discussion:

What place has the computer gained in the work place? How did employees receive it initially? Was computer technology largely responsible for the economic boom of the 1990s, as some claim? What issues have arisen for employees, employers, and the economy in general as a result?

Cluster 5

Subject:
Selected Legal Issues

Description:
Consider the impact of computer technology on crime, law enforcement, and such legal issues as protection of intellectual property

Topics:
Crime: transforming cases in hacking, viruses, forgery, theft
Law enforcement: defensive measures, response to terrorism, Federal computer crime units.
Intellectual property: copyright laws, the United States vs. Napster case, piracy vs. innovation and free speech

Activities:
Examine some of the transforming cases in computer crime and the law enforcement response to them. Examine some of the legal, economic, and ethical issues involved in the Napster case.

Discussion:
How has computer crime changed over the years, and the response to it? What are your views on the issues surrounding the Napster case and similar services?

Cluster 6

Subject:
Science and Medicine

Description:
Scientific research has been a driving force behind computer development in past and it still is. The new technology has also benefited basic research in other sciences and the development of new tools and technologies in fields such as medicine. Consider the relationship between basic research and computers and the impact on medical diagnostic devices.

Topics:
Early research computers and their uses
Impact of computers on computer science
Current large-scale modelling (e.g. climate)
Applications of computer technology in medical imaging equipment (MRI, PET, CT)

Activities:
Examine the interaction between basic research and computer development, past and present. Give an example of how basic research enhanced computer technology, and vice versa. Research the origin and workings of one or more of the new medical imaging devices.

Discussion:
What has been the relationship between science and technology? How has computer science benefited from the growth of computer technology? What is the role of computers in medical science?

Cluster 7

Subject:

Sociological Issues

Description:
Computers have also had a direct impact upon individuals, their relationships with others, and in the economic and social structure of society.

Topics:
Isolation and changing relationships
Women, minorities, and computers
Disabled persons and computers
Changing social attitudes toward computer technology
Impact of computers on economic and social stratification
Computers and the changing quality of life

Activities:
Find research reports and discussions on some of the various aspects of the sociological impact of computers listed above.

Discussion:
What has been the sociological impact of computers? Is this a necessary consequence of the introduction of computers? Alternatively, is the impact a consequence of the way society introduced computers? How might society used computers to have a positive benefit for its people?

Cluster 8

Subject:
Ethical Issues

Description:
Computers have profoundly affected our ability to access and utilize private information, to manipulate social, economic, and political affairs, and to create advantages and disadvantages for different individuals and groups of people. Examine some of the ethical and legal issues involved, and their influence in the past and present.

Topics:
Codes of ethics
Legal vs. ethical issues
Social impact of computer ethics and computer law

Activities:
Research the Code of Ethics of the ACM and the IEEE Computer Society. Find and analyze some previous case studies of important ethical and legal situations. Think of a situation, real or imagined, in which you are confronted with an issue in each of these areas, and analyze your response to the situation.

Discussion:
What are the legal, ethical, and moral obligations of a computer scientist in an environment driven by economic and technological advances? Are there similar obligations pertaining to a computer-related corporation?

Appendix E

Some Resources Related to Societal Issues and Computing

Printed Materials
Baird, Robert M., et al. (eds); *Cyberethics: Social & Moral Issues in the Computer Age*, (2000)
Bowyer, Kevin (Ed.); *Ethics and Computing: Living Responsibly in a Computerized World*, (2000)

Forester, Tom, Perry Morrison; *Computer Ethics: Cautionary Tales and Ethical Dilemmas in Computing*, (1993)

Hart, John; Ethics and Technology: *Innovation and Transformation in Community Contexts*, (1997)

Johnson, Deborah G.; *Computer Ethics*, 3rd ed., (2001)

Johnson, Deborah G. and Helen Nissenbaum (Eds); *Computers, Ethics and Social Values*, (1995)

Kallman, Ernest and John Grillo; *Ethical Decision Making and Information Technology: An Introduction With Cases* (1995)

Kizza, Joseph Migga, et al; *Ethical and Social Issues in the Information Age (Undergraduate Texts in Computer Science)*, (1997)

Ohler, Jason; *Taming the Beast: Choice & Control in the Electronic Jungle* (1999)

Schellenberg, Kathryn (Editor); *Computers in Society 00/01* (Computers in Society, 8th Ed)

Spinello, Richard A.; *CyberEthics: Morality and Law in Cyberspace*, (2000)

Spinello, Richard A.; *Case Studies in Information and Computer Ethics*, (1996)

Websites

Check <http://courses.cs.vt.edu/~cs3604/support/FrontEnd/> by John A.N. Lee)

Some Organizations

(From <http://courses.cs.vt.edu/~cs3604/support/FrontEnd/> by John A.N. Lee)
ACM Special Interest Group on Computers and Society (SIGCAS).
Centre for Computing and Social Responsibility (CCSR)
Computer Professionals for Social Responsibility (CPSR)
Cyberspace Policy Institute, George Washington University
Electronic Frontier Foundation
Ethics Center for Engineering and Science
IEEE Society on Social Implications of Technology.
Joint IEEE Computer Society and ACM Steering Committee for the Establishment of Software Engineering as a Profession
Joseph & Edna Josephson Institute of Ethics
Markkula Center for Applied Ethics
National Institute for Engineering Ethics
Poynter Center at Indiana University-Bloomington
U.S. Office of Government Ethics
Web Clearinghouse for Engineering and Computing Ethics

Appendix F

Chronologies of Historical Events in Computing

Many chronologies of historical events exist. Some of these include:

Chronology of Personal Computers: http://www.islandnet.com/~kpolsson/comphist/
Chronology of Digital Computing Machines: http://wilson.best.vwh.net/faq/chrono.html
Hobbes' Internet Timeline: http://info.isoc.org/guest/zakon/Internet/History/HIT.html
IFIP WG 9.7: http://www.CompHist.org/
Yahoo! Computers and Internet History:
http://dir.yahoo.com/Computers_and_Internet/History/

The Role of the Information Society Model in Education in the United States

Ronald E. ANDERSON
University of Minnesota, rea@umn.edu

> *"These lively debates over IT-related curriculum issues diverted the attention of educators from the challenge of investigating how best to apply the new technologies to helping students improve their learning."*

Abstract   This critical appraisal of the role and impact of the information society model in the United States educational system begins with a discussion of three dominant paradigms: automation, "information society," and "mind tools;" and then traces the history of information and communication technology (ICT)[1] in education in the United States, describing how ideas, intertwined with the conceptions of the information society, led to distractions that have impeded vigorous development of ICT to improve education. These distractions included the claim that schools should take up the responsibility of training all students in ICT for the so-called information workforce. Promoters of the information society model together with the marketing arms of the IT industry perpetuated the adoption of ICT as an end in itself rather than as a means toward improving the main business of education, learning. These pressures over the past three decades have left the ICT in education in a state of confusion, lacking adequate support and, in many instances, the infrastructure to adapt to the demands of the twenty-first century.

Key words: Education, information society, information literacy

---

[1]   Although the acronym ICT is used extensively around the world, it can scarcely be heard in the United States. While the acronym IT (information technology) is commonplace in American business and government, the term "technology" is generally used within the educational system to refer to ICT or IT. In a few educational circles the word "edtech" is used instead. In this paper all of these acronyms and terms will be used interchangeably.

INTRODUCTION

Compared with many other countries, the term "information society" is not often used in the United States and its publications, although ironically, the information society label is arguably more befitting North America than any other society today. Paradoxically, the United States pioneered the Internet and led most other countries in eCommerce, but it has been slower than many other technologically advanced countries in using the information society label. It would appear that the label "information society" could not be heard as much in the US because in the 1960s and 70s it came to be associated with those voices in the computer community emphasizing cautionary and negative implications of technology, namely the "computers and society" sub-community. In contrast, Japan fostered less negative voice on these issues and also pioneered use of the label [Kohyama, 1968]. Japan was the first country to use the information society as a justification in a major national policy document [Mashda, 1981]. The information society concept emerged in the USA primarily from analysis of economics and the nature of nonmaterial production. Outside the USA, e.g., Japan, there was more emphasis on the changing nature and role of media in society.

The information society metaphor is actually an archetype in that it captured the essence of an economy and culture dominated by ICT and associated information products, predating and anticipating the metaphor "knowledge society." The information society label was legitimated in the 1970s and 1980s when economists were able to confirm that a majority of the jobs in the United States were information oriented, in that they were designed to produce informational rather than material products. In subsequent years, as global networks made discernible a global information economy, the information society metaphor became compelling, but it still did not catch on in the US, perhaps because of the promotion of the knowledge society concept by new industries promoting knowledge products.

PARADIGMS OF ICT IN EDUCATION

Before tracing how the information society concept permeated education in the United States, paradigms will be discussed that embody the dominant clusters of rationales, promises, and goals for using ICT in learning and teaching. The field of ICT and education is so heterogeneous in purpose, as well as function, that any in-depth critique requires some kind of focusing on goals in order to do justice to the intent of particular practices.

Three largely competing paradigms are defined here, for the purposes of evaluating the state and impact of ICT in education. The three paradigms identified are (1) "automation," which seeks to reduce reliance on human teachers for the delivery of instruction using various types of machine-coded processes, (2) "information society," which subsumes all of the rationales for curriculum that relate to preparation of students for an evolving labor force oriented toward a global information economy, and (3) "mind tools," which refers to rationales that argue for technology applications that augment higher order intellectual functions and social or collaborative activity. While the three paradigms may sometimes overlap, they represent three distinct competing sets of priorities for ICT in education.

Automation

Programmed instruction (PI) began as an engineering discipline even prior to the emergence of the digital computer. With the guidance of stimulus-response learning theory, procedures were designed to produce rote learning more efficiently. While it could be argued that such technology could save the teacher for other, more humane functions, another expressed aim was to offer cheaper teachers. The invention of digital processors gave birth to the field of computer-assisted instruction (CAI), which initially consisted of little more than transferring PI to the computer.

As the CAI field expanded into testing and instructional management, the labels and acronyms proliferated, e.g., computer-managed instruction (CMI) and computer-based instruction (CBI), a label that still persists today. These various sub-fields all came to be associated with "tutorials" and "drill and practice," what is now a negatively charged label among educators. The adherents to developing these technologies have adapted to the latest technologies today including multimedia and the Internet. Multimedia CBI, distance education (DE), and online learning (OL) all have their roots in the earlier instructional techniques and all purport to provide cheaper teachers. A substantial number of elementary schools have purchased integrated learning systems (ILS) that utilize programmed instruction aligned with learning objectives and assessments. These systems give the teacher better ways to track individual student progress. This approach is particularly popular for remedial instruction in basic subjects.

While the automation paradigm in education preceded the information society archetype, it has continued to retain a solid, if controversial share, of the edtech (educational technology) industry, as well as maintaining a role within school technology programs. Its most recent variant, distance education (DE), is promoted as offering educational and training opportunities needed by information and knowledge workers.

Information Society (IS)

The information society (IS) paradigm is used here to refer to the goals, explicit and implicit, that impinge upon education in an information economy. Perhaps the greatest demand is the responsibility to train students for the information industry and other workforces utilizing information. This training encompasses ICT skills and other skills needed by workers in a global information economy. The IS paradigm is distinctive from the other paradigms in that its justification is not to improve student learning but to prepare the student for the workforce or the information economy outside of school.

In the 1960s and 70s the authors of computer-related texts were not likely to use the term "information society" but used the labels "information age" and "computerized society" instead [Martin and Norman, 1970]. The first textbook for the college-level "computers and society" course was published in 1972 [Rothman and Mosmann], but it did not mention the "information society". In 1979 Daniel Bell's "framework for the information society" gave academic legitimacy to the concept. In the early 1980s large-scale electronic networks rapidly expanded providing physical representations that make the notion of the information society more compelling. Not surprisingly, numerous IT textbooks during the 1980s discussed the information society concept. For instance, Rosenberg [1986] included an entire chapter on social issues and called the chapter "Information Society." When the information society rhetoric was used in academic works, it most frequently referred to a general trend in restructured social institutions and lifestyles throughout society, but in more popular publications in came to be largely synonymous with IT and its culture. In the 1990s the phrases National Information Infrastructure (NII) and Global Information Infrastructure (GII) were used in discourse arguing for an expanded role of the Internet, which implicitly made the concept of the information society less and less an abstraction.

For at least two decades educators have tried to translate these information society concerns into curricula and instruction that addressed prevailing notions of what the workforce needed. Initially the emphasis was on computer literacy, then computer programming, followed by general productivity tools. As many students came to learn to use word processors, emailers, and browsers, at home, work, or on their own at school, the curriculum shifted toward information literacy as the central preparation for the so-called information society. Information literacy came to be broadly defined as use of collaborative tools as well as the core skills of web and database searching, with some attention to the critical evaluation of information.

The topics most unique but central to the information society model are the social, legal, and ethical aspects of information work, but ironically they were often completely omitted from the ICT-related curricula or were mentioned briefly and discussed superficially. The one exception to this was the "computer and society" course that emerged in most university computer science programs, but was typically offered only for advanced majors in computer science.

As the IS paradigm was defined to be those objectives for ICT-related education intended to prepare students for life outside of school, this paradigm includes apprenticeships and other educational programs for particular occupations or tasks central to the information economy. Included here are computer science programs at both secondary and postsecondary institutions, management information system programs, and activities designed to prepare students to apply ICT tools in any number of occupational fields.

Mind Tools

The emphasis of this paradigm, like that of the automation paradigm, is upon using ICT for immediate in-school learning rather than for future jobs. But the emphasis is upon high-level thinking and problem solving on the one hand and upon teamwork and joint projects on the other. The roots of this paradigm lie in recent theory and empirical research in cognitive psychology, which concluded that learning environments should be student-focused, assessment-focused, and knowledge-centered [Bransford, et al. 1999]. These conclusions largely overlap with the philosophy of instruction, called constructivism, that many education and edtech leaders support. The objectives subsumed here have been greatly facilitated by the National Science Foundation (NSF), which funded a number of projects that designed technologies to scaffold existing learning strategies or provide for new means of learning using ICT. Typical strategies developed include new modelling and visualization tools for specific mathematics and science problem solving.

The mind tools paradigm should not be confused with that of Jonassen's [2000] approach called "mindtools," although there are many overlapping elements. Jonassen promotes the use of specialized, advanced computer tools for problem-solving, improving understanding, and otherwise augmenting intellectual processes. He would not consider a word processor as one of his mindtools, however the use of a word processor to improve writing or compositional skills would be consistent with our mind tools paradigm.

Empowerment is at the core of this paradigm and one of the earliest programs to embody this approach was ESCOT, which was sponsored by

Apple [Sandholts, Rignstaff, and Dwyer, 1997]. More recent variants of this philosophy have been espoused for higher education [Weigel, 2002] and life long learning [Shneiderman, 2002].

The mind tools paradigm is currently the most favored rationale for edtech among educational ICT leaders in the U.S.. The main argument for giving this paradigm priority is the growing body of cognitive research literature that confirms its superiority from the standpoint of pedagogy. Another argument used for this paradigm is that it is the most effective way to use scarce resources. Certain mind tools contain ICT-essential functions, e.g., dynamic modelling, that cannot be done in any other way. To the extent that their learning outcomes are pedagogically effective, mind tools add value to the educational process.

Word processing illustrates the distinctions among the three paradigms. Automation objectives foster the use of typing tutor programs and spelling drill software for giving students repetitive practice in basic skills of using a word processor. Information society objectives are fulfilled by vocational word processing training and by course work that gives students the ability to prepare documents in an ICT environment. Mind tool goals are achieved when students use a word processor to write papers for their classes or for producing intellectual products for other purposes. Even though any given ICT-based learning activity could be classified as predominantly intended to serve one of the three paradigms, it is also true that many learning activities could be seen as facilitating objectives associated with more than one paradigm.

A BRIEF HISTORY

Next the history of ICT in U.S. education is summarized in order to chart the emergence of these three paradigms and to show how some of the ideas of the information society infiltrated education.

The 1970s

The 1970s was the decade when the field of computers in education struggled to become established. In 1969 with funding from the NSF, the first general conference on digital technology and education was held. It was called Conference on Computers in Undergraduate Curricula (CCUC) and attracted an attendance of less than 100 persons. This conference was held annually for 10 years until 1979 when it was re-named the National Educational Computer Conference (NECC). By that time there were quite a few elementary and secondary educators active in supporting computer applications in education. It was not until the 1970s that timesharing and minicomputers became available and ultimately commonplace within the education sector. General productivity tools were scarce and so it was not surprising that the computer education or informatics curriculum, such as it was, consisted mostly of computer literacy and computer programming instruction.

This decade was the "hey-day" of automated approaches to edtech. Control Data started the Plato project that employed hundreds of software engineers pioneering techniques of CAI and CMI for the purpose of selling systems and system services, as well as courseware. The National Science Foundation gave enormous grants to Patrick Suppes to develop CAI, initially in mathematics and later in science and reading. This project spawned the start up of Computer Curriculum Corporation (CCC), which became one of the largest companies in the educational software and the ILS businesses. In addition to these two huge projects that dominated the field of CAI, there were numerous smaller scale projects in both business and academe to design, refine, and sell CAI and its variants. During this time many teachers and professors discovered that their educational expertise could be successfully marketed, obtaining consultant and full time employment in this new, volatile industry. As timesharing, minicomputers and microcomputers all became reality during this decade, excitement, optimism, and entrepreneurial spirit were rampant within the rapidly growing community of educational technology specialists.

The 1980s

The 1980s was the era of the microcomputer and the personal computer (PC). By the end of the decade microcomputers were often connected within local area networks (LANs) and into large-scale networks such as Bitnet. During this decade the number of computer units in schools grew rapidly and many teachers were newly persuaded to incorporate computing into their teaching. Fierce competition emerged among software companies over their proprietary productivity tools, and some instructors became wealthy writing texts teaching how to use the more popular tools. Many teachers and their students were trained in using these tools as it was considered critical to the future of the economy for the incoming labor force to be skilled in these tools. Although neither developers nor teachers used the information society terminology, the IS paradigm was the driving force shaping curriculum and classroom during this decade.

At the beginning of the decade the fierce debates (in both public and private) over the definition of computer literacy, led to a common understanding by the middle of the decade that computer literacy was passé. Initially the debate was over whether or not the introductory computing courses (or course units) should include computer programming in BASIC or LOGO. Several prominent educational technology leaders left teaching for full time authoring of programming textbooks. But within a few years, powerful application packages for word processing, spreadsheets, and databases were widely available on personal computers, leading to the replacement of programming language instruction with application packages and their control languages. Text book authors and publishers jumped very rapidly on the bandwagon as the number of microcomputers soared and the potential for enormous profits in trade and text books, as well as educational software, became obvious. School curriculum supervisors defined their primary responsibility for the emerging information workforce to be training students in productivity tools, and academics intensely debated the priorities of these new curricula. At the middle school level, the debates were effectively squelched when the Texas Education Department, the first and largest textbook adoption auction, selected their top computer literacy textbooks. From that point on, requirements for the information society were institutionalized into K-12 education. During this decade, at least, the IS metaphor appears to have been over-driven by authors of textbooks, software developers, and the computer industry more broadly. The synergy between these various groups became apparent as textbook sales were fuelled by expanded sales of IT and vice versa.

These lively debates over IT-related curriculum issues diverted the attention of educators from the challenge of investigating how best to apply the new technologies to helping students improve their learning. Simultaneously, software developers were becoming millionaires almost overnight, enticing many to leave teaching and research jobs to try their hand at software and related ventures. Not only was this a serious brain drain on the budding field of educational technology, but these trends were all shifting intellectual focus away from trying to apply ICT to improve learning.

The 1990s

The 1990s decade was the decade of the Internet. Politicians, as well as educational practitioners, claimed magical outcomes from the Internet, and promoted private initiatives like Net Day and new public policy, such as the E-rate grants to schools, to pay for the high costs of the Internet. In the early part of the decade the Internet became widely used for file sharing and email. In the later years the World Wide Web (WWW) became a routine place for teachers and their students at all grade levels to look for information and to construct web sites. Handheld devices, such as personal data assistants (PDAs) became available and educators began to explore their use in teaching. As new legal and ethical issues piled up, a majority of the schools at all levels adopted an acceptable use policy (AUP), which was generally a statement of what ICT-related ethical responsibilities staff or students were expected to follow. As many students came to learn to use word processors, emailers, and browsers, at home, work, or on their own at school, there were attempts to shift the curriculum toward information literacy as the central preparation for living in the information society. Information literacy was increasingly defined to encompass use of collaborative tools as well as the core skills of web and database searching, and the critical evaluation of information. For the most part information literacy did not achieve a place in the curricula. Instead teachers were expected to address, on an as-needed basis, how to critically evaluate Internet-based information, how to avoid inappropriate web-based material, as well as other social, legal, and ethical aspects of information work.

In many ways the 1990s were parallel to the 1980s in terms of radical transformation due to a new technology, this time the Internet instead of the PC. While the technology of interest shifted to the web, and ICT-related teaching shifted to web-site use and design, many of the best younger educators left for jobs in Internet and web businesses. The enormous cost of building an infrastructure for Internet access caused policy-makers and other stakeholders to question the payoff of technology in learning. They called for research that would show that payoff, but few researchers and evaluators were left. And the amount of funding available for research and accountability studies had been so low for many years, that answers were essentially impossible to produce.

TODAY'S IMPLEMENTATION REALITIES

Shifting from a historical focus to an understanding of the current state of education with respect to technology, we examine today's realities in terms of what we call "implementation goals," because they are relevant no matter which rationale or paradigm one subscribes to. These cross-cutting goals include: (1) access adequacy, relative to the infrastructure; (2) skilled ICT users, especially teachers and students; (3) supportive organizational climate (technical and instructional) for these users; (4) ethical climates that minimize unethical and illegal use of ICT; and (5) equity in digital benefits, which includes access and skill to use ICT. After reviewing contemporary fulfilment of these implementation goals, we will look at the future and return to the role and impact of the information society model on education.

Access Adequacy

The overall contemporary picture appears remarkable when viewed from an historical perspective. Whereas in 1970 only universities and some colleges had computers, within thirty years essentially all 150,000 schools had not only computers but Internet connections, and they were using and supporting ICT for instruction. By the year 2000 secondary schools had an average of 3 students for every instructional computer and essentially every school had access to the Internet. From this glimpse of the infrastructure growth, it would seem that the infrastructure is in good shape. To some extent that is true, however, K-12 schools still are a long way from providing adequate, up-to-date ICT for all teachers and students. Many teachers as well as students essentially lack access because the competition for resources is too great, the equipment is in disrepair or obsolete, the machine(s) have little usable software, no tech support is available to help them, they lack the skills to use the technology, or all of the above. Even for a large share of those who do have physical access to computers or the Internet, neither the human capital nor the social capital is sufficient to provide for effective utilization.

Obsolescence is still a major problem in schools, although it is less of a problem than 10 years ago when the majority of school computers were Apple II computers of 1970s vintage. Most business and governmental organizations currently have a computer replacement cycle of about 5 years, whereas for schools it is approximately 10 years. In 1998 as much as 40% of the installed base of computers consisted of units that could not run multimedia programs because they lacked both sound capability and a CDROM drive [Anderson and Ronnkvist, 1999].

There are a myriad of additional obstacles that result in low access and use. For instance, one school studied by Means et. al. [2002] and her associates could not acquire more computers for classrooms because security costs were so high. For any classroom with computers, they had to install bars on the windows, replace the door with a special, secure door, and install surveillance cameras. Anecdotes of this type from many sources [cf. Stoll, 1995] indicate that school administrators often do not have the knowledge or resources to deal with thefts and other security problems. Technical malfunctions (in either hardware or software) can produce a similar impasse when the school lacks adequate technical support. These are two of the major reasons for high rates of equipment non-use, which includes local networks and Internet connections.

Skilled ICT Users (Teachers and Students)

Little data are available on the skills of students, much less teachers, to adequately use ICT in their work. One exception is the IEA Computers in Education Study in 1992 [Anderson, 1993; Pelgrum et al, 1993]. They found that students in the USA performed significantly lower than those in Austria and the Netherlands in terms of "computer fitness," a fairly low-level test measuring what some would call "computer literacy" or IT "fluency". The US was relatively low compared to other technologically advanced countries on such indicators largely because its school system is highly decentralized. Countries with nationally centralized educational systems can generally establish and enforce curriculum changes more rapidly. The problem is not just that learning opportunities in ICT skills are generally not found in the curriculum, but it also is the case that many students who want or need the technology are not able to access it.

In 1998 the Teaching, Learning, and Computing (TLC) study conducted a national survey of over 4,000 randomly selected elementary and secondary teachers [Becker, 1999]. In that year 90% of the schools and a large share of the classrooms had Internet access. Nevertheless, the survey found that 27% of the teachers did not access the Internet at either home or school and only 39% reported classroom use of the Internet. Some groups of teachers, for example, math teachers, used computers and the Internet far less in or out of class than the average. While the share of teachers using the Internet reflected to some extent the lack of convenient equipment and network access, the survey found that the lack of skill in using the Internet was an important factor inhibiting its use [Becker, 1999].

Teachers need not only technical skills but skills in using ICT effectively pedagogically. The TIMMS Video Study in 1995 revealed how some teachers need guidance in this area. The TIMSS (Third International Mathematics and Science Study) classroom study videotaped over 150 8th grade mathematics classrooms in the US and Japan during the 1994–95 school year. They found that Japanese teachers, compared to American teachers, were more likely to use methods for teaching "deep understanding," as defined by the Authentic Achievement Project of Newmann and associates. The study also found that American classrooms had many more outside interruptions. The videotapes showed some American teachers giving their students trivial computer tasks, i.e., work that could be done more quickly with a calculator or an encyclopedia. One video showed the students stepping from one sheet of paper to another to illustrate how binary bits move around inside the computer microprocessor. This does not seem like a productive way to use classroom time in a middle school computer class, much less an algebra class. Some schools have reduced such limited classroom activities by setting up teacher mentoring programs dealing extensively with ICT issues.

Supportive Organizational Climates

Several reports from the TLC study have identified organizational attributes that played major roles in facilitating and inhibiting the integration of ICT into the classroom activities of a large share of a school's teachers

[Ronnkvist, Dexter, and Anderson, 2000; Anderson and Dexter, 2001; and Anderson and Becker, 2001]. These investigations found that schools' commitments to technology investments, strong technology leadership, and the widespread availability of technology support for teachers all were strongly associated with technology integration. Without these organizational climates, a school was not likely to have integrated technology, as measured by the use of a variety of technology applications by a large share of teachers. Furthermore, the study found that it wasn't just a commitment to any technology spending that made a difference, but spending on software and support services were the most important investments contributing to greater technology integration.

There are relatively few indicators and almost no data on these organizational climates: financial commitments for technology, technology leadership, and technology support. The most comprehensive national study of school technology financials was the TLC school-level study in 1998. The conclusion was that the average school spent only $113 per year per student on technology (including support services), which was 2.7% of total educational expenditures for that year. Of the total $113 per student, only $8 was spent on software, $22.50 on support, and the remainder on hardware. While about $30 per student was spent on software and support, the consensus of the technology coordinators themselves was that about twice that amount ($60/student) *should* be spent on software and support. We can infer from that set of findings that neither the technology support climate nor the technology leadership climate were adequate, as the hardware dollars have been over dominating the technology acquisitions and spending climate.

Ethical Climates

IT, and the Internet in particular, link students to the world outside the classroom and this poses one of the biggest problems. Students left to their own whims can access material on the Internet that most of their parents consider inappropriate or objectionable. Through the Internet, students can also break laws by using copyrighted material or by illegal entry into databases and computer systems. Many schools have responded to concerned parents by installing filtering or blocking software. Nevertheless, even schools that have such electronic mechanisms in place still must find effective ways to teach and encourage students and teachers to engage in responsible ICT behavior.

Most schools in the United States have responded to these challenges by instituting an Acceptable Use Policy (AUP). Often students, and sometimes parents, are asked to sign a version of the AUP which states that the signer agrees to follow acceptable uses and avoid unacceptable behaviors with respect to ICT, and the Internet in particular. In her study of school Internet activity, Schofield and Davidson [2002] found that many signers had not read the AUP and many students were aware of other students who had not followed the acceptable use guidelines.

Given that these mechanisms, both electronic and administrative, do not solve all of the emergent problems, it is important that a school organization creates a climate of ethical and social responsibility in general. While the administrative leadership of the school should address this challenge and take steps to create and develop supportive climates, involvement of the entire school community is needed to maintain the climate. Filters and AUPs are useful, but attitudes and values of all involved are important too, especially in adapting to new ethical issues that arise as the technology evolves and changes.

Equity in Digital Benefits

Many of America's 46 million public school students remain largely unaffected by the existing technological infrastructure. Huge numbers of teachers and students never touch a computer. Even while it is true that computers outnumber teachers, most teachers lack convenient access to them because student computer labs house the majority of the schools' equipment. Many schools have so few computers that they tend to be used only by small, elite groups of students or teachers.

During the last few years of the 1990s, considerable attention by both local and national policy-makers was given to reducing the so-called digital divide, which initially referred to gaps in access to digital technology, especially computers and the Internet. The Anderson and Becker national survey in 1998 found that average per student expenditures on technology were about twice as much at schools in high-income, as in low-income communities. Numerous surveys earlier had shown substantial digital divides: that students from low-income or high-minority communities were much less likely to have access to computers or the Internet from home than those in other communities. However, more recent surveys have detailed how such gaps have been declining but not disappearing. In fact, the general pattern is that digital gaps remain high for the initial period of diffusion of new digital technologies. The literature on the digital divide in the past two years has noted a variety of different types of digital divide, particularly those that have to do with the quality of technology use and the skills to use them.

TOMORROW'S REALITIES

The Beginning of the 21st Century

The remarkable patterns of repeated, major innovations in dominant ICTs for education during the past three decades necessarily leave us timid about predicting the future, even for five years in advance. What we have seen in the first few years of the current millennium is steady growth in the quantity and quality of educational applications, especially related to the Internet. A recent national survey by the Pew Internet and American Life Project [2002] found that 78% of children between the ages of 12 and 17 used the Internet and 98% of these had used it for a school research project.

The same Pew Internet study, using a very different methodology, probed focus groups of students in the 12 to17 age range on their thoughts about Internet use in school. The study found that Internet-savvy teenagers were saying that "educators often don't know how, don't want, or aren't able to use online tools to help them learn or enrich their studies." The report argued that the nation's multi-billion dollar effort to wire schools is at risk of being squandered because there is not a similar commitment "to improve connectivity in classrooms, help all students master computer skills, teach more sophisticated Internet literacy, make sure that high-quality information is available to them, and - most important of all - create assignments that take advantage of the wonderful Web resources they have found on their own." Most teens claimed that "their Internet use occurs mostly outside of the school day, outside of the school building, and outside of the direction of their teachers." Students even claim that more engaging Internet activities would improve learning.

It would appear that in many ways Internet utilization among children and adolescents is outpacing that of adults. If nothing else, these trends suggest rapidly growing pressures of children on teachers and schools for better accommodation of their ICT-related learning needs.

Twenty-First Century Standards

Another very different trend is a shift in what government policy-makers and industry representatives perceive as the needs of the evolving "information society" labor force. In the past five years a number of special study commissions such as The 21st Century Workforce Commission [2000] have issued white papers on "twenty-first century standards." These standards describe what students should be able to do upon graduation. They depart from earlier standards in that they no longer emphasize information and technology skills but instead stress skills in thinking, knowledge management, and communication. These new sets of standards suggest that greater value in the future likely will be placed upon abilities to construct knowledge and think creatively. These new standards also seem to reflect a relaxation of pressure upon schools to train students in ICT skills.

Goals for Effective Technology Use

Our earlier analysis demonstrated how the purposes for ICT have evolved in accord with the technological capabilities available, the conventional wisdom and other pressures on how best to utilize that capability, and the priorities given to alternative goals or paradigms. The twenty-first century white papers suggest that the future will experience less (or perhaps a different) influence by the information society model, and that there may well be greater focus on the approaches of the mind tools paradigm, especially greater emphasis on complex thinking and achieving deep understanding.

Critics such as Cuban [2002] and Hodas [1996] have objected to the high cost of the technology going into schools, to the neglect of other societal priorities. However, our portrayal of today's implementation realities has shown that while some policies have not been well thought out, the investment generally has not been nearly enough. If information-oriented industries and government agencies are taken as models for the role of ICT in schools, then schools fail miserably, especially in terms of IT support services. Ironically, education is one of the most information-oriented industries in modern society, and yet the expenditures for technology of about 2.5% of total expenses are about the lowest of all information industries.

Our critical analysis suggested that the information society model provided fuel, or an advocacy base, for a hegemony of diverse commercial interests steering education away from its prime mission of maximizing learning by technology and whatever other tools can best facilitate that process. This concert of forces also succeeded in duping education into sometimes treating ICT as an end in itself. Education will probably take some years to get over this corrupted sense of values.

The current popularity of distance education, which is heavily shaped by the tradition of the automation paradigm, indicates that education has been caught up in the fun and excitement of this new activity without taking adequate time to be accountable and investigate its social and educational impact. Brown and Duguid [2000] offer an exemplary analysis of the role of community in learning, which should serve as a framework guiding serious research in this area in the future.

CONCLUSIONS

Cuban [2002] attributes technologically oriented reform measures in education to a "coalition of corporate executives, public officials, parents, academics and educators." In general he claims that "computers for the classroom have been oversold by promoters and policymakers and underused by teachers and students." While there are traces of truth in his claim, a more appropriate conclusion is that educators have not been given a clear, compelling mission for technology nor have they received the support and, in many cases, the infrastructure to carry out that mission.

An historical analysis of the role of goal paradigms on the state of ICT in education has revealed some weaknesses associated with each. The automation tradition has over emphasized teacher displacement and failed to address advances that would facilitate the learning of highly complex cognitive tasks. The information society tradition became commercially entangled and has over-emphasized the training of students for information jobs, especially lower-level occupations. The mind tools tradition requires much more research and creative development than it now receives.

REFERENCES

Anderson, Ronald E. (1998), Human and social issues in the age of informatics. In Tinsley, David and Johnson, David C. (eds), *Information and Communications Technologies in School Mathematics* (IFIP TC3/WG3.1 Working Conference), pp. 237-246. London: Chapman and Hall.

Anderson, Ronald E. and Becker, Henry Jay (2001), *School Investments in Instructional Technology*, Report #8. Irvine, CA: Univ. of California [Available online at http://www.crito.uci.edu/TLC/findings.html]

Anderson and Ronnkvist, (1999), *The presence of computers in American schools.* Report #2 Irvine, CA: Univ. of California [Available online at http://www.crito.uci.edu/TLC/findings.html].

Anderson, Ronald E. and Dexter, Sara (2001), School technology leadership: Incidence and impact. (Teaching, Learning, and Computing, 1998, Report #6), Irvine, CA (http://www.crito.uci.edu/tlc/findings.html).

Becker, H. J. Ravitz, J. and Wong, Y. (1999), Computer and software use by teachers. [Available online at http://www.crito.uci.edu/TLC/findings.html]

Bell, Daniel (1979), The social framework of the information society, pp 163-211, in Dertouzos, Michael L. and Moses, Joel (eds), *The Computer Age: A Twenty-Year View*. Cambridge, MA: The MIT Press.

Bereiter, Carl (2000), *Education and Mind in the Knowledge Age.* (800 page manuscript at http://csile.oise.utoronto.ca/edmind/edmind.html).

Bransford, John D., Brown, Ann l. and Cocking, Rodney R. and Pellegrino, J. W.(1999), editors. *How People Learn – Bridging Research and Practice*, Washington DC: National Academy Press (www.nap.edu).

Brown, John Seely and Duguid, Paul (2000), *The Social Life of Information*. Cambridge, MA: Harvard University Business School Press.

Cuban, Larry (2001), *Oversold and Underused: Computers in the Classroom*. Cambridge, MA: Harvard University Press.

Hodas, Steven (1996), Technology refusal and the organizational culture of schools. pp 197-218, in Kling, Rob (ed), *Computerization and Controversy: Value Conflicts and Social Choices, 2nd edition.* San Diego, CA: Academic Press.

Jonassen, David H., *Computers as Mindtools for Schools – Engaging Critical Thinking,* 2nd Edition, Merrill, Prentice-Hall, Upper Saddle River, New Jersey, 2000.

Kohyama, Kenichi (1968), Introduction to information society theory, Chuo Koron (Winter 1968).

Martin, James and Norman, Adrian R. D. (1970), *The Computerized Society*. Englewood Cliffs, NJ: Prentice-Hall, Inc.

Masuda, Yoneji (1981), *The Information Society as Post-Industrial Society.* Bethesda, MD: World Future Society.

Means, Barbara, Penuel, William R. & Padilla, C. (2001), *The Connected School - Technology and Learning in High School.* San Francisco: Jossey-Bass.

National Research Council. *Being Fluent with Information Technology.* Computer Science and Telecommunications Board, Washington DC: National Academy Press (www.nap.edu), 1999c.

Newmann, Fred M. and Associates (1996), *Authentic Achievement – Restructuring Schools for Intellectual Quality.* San Francisco, Jossey-Bass Publishers.

Norris, Cathleen, Elliot Soloway, and Terry Sullivan (2002), Examining 25 years of technology in U. S. education, *Communications of the ACM* 45, 8 (August), pp 15-18.

Panel on Educational Technology. (1997), *Report to the President on the Use of Technology to Strengthen K-12 Education in the United States.* Washington DC: President's Committee of Advisors on Science and Technology.

Pellegrino, James, Chudowsky, Naomi, and Glaser, Robert (Editors), *Knowing What Students Know: The Science and Design of Educational Assessment.* Washington DC: National Academy Press.

Pew Internet and American Life Project (2002), *Digital Disconnect*: The widening gap between Internet-savvy students and their schools. http://www.pewinternet.org/reports/pdfs/PIP_Schools_Internet_Report.pdf

Quality Education Data. (1999), *Technology in public schools 1998-99.* Denver, Colorado: Quality Education Data, Inc. (QED).

Rosenberg, Richard S. (1986), *Computers and the Information Society.* New York, NY: Wiley.

Rothman, Stanley and Mosmann, Charles (1976), *Computers and Society.* Chicago, IL: Science Research Associates. Inc.

Sandholtz, J. H., Rignstaff, C., and Dwyer, D. C. (1997), *Teaching with Technology: Creating Student-Centered Classrooms.* New York: Teachers College Press.

Schofield, Janet W. and Davidson, Ann L. (2002), *Bring the Internet to School.* San Francisco, CA: Jossey-Bass.

Shneiderman, Ben (2002), *Leonardo's Laptop - Human Needs and the New Computing Technologies.* Cambridge, MA: The MIT Press.

Soloway, Elliot et. al. (2000), K-12 and the Internet, *Communications of the ACM* 43,1 (January, 2000), 19-24.

Spitzer, K. L., Eisenberg, M. B. Lowe, C. A., *Information Literacy – Essential Skills for the Information Age*, ERIC Clearinghouse on Information and Technology, Syracuse, New York, 1998.

Stoll, Clifford (1995), *Silicon Snake Oil - Second Thoughts on the Information Highway*. New York, NY: Anchor Books.

Twenty-First Century Workforce Commission. (2000), A Nation of Opportunity. National Alliance for Business, Washington DC (www.workforce21.org)

Weigel, Van B. (2002), *Deep Learning for a Digital Age: Technology's Untapped Potential to Enrich Higher Education*. San Francisco: Jossey-Bass.

Working with Information Systems - the Role of the Professional

Richard SIZER
CEng FIEE FBCS CITP
Chairman, Ethics Expert Panel, British Computer Society
Richardtsz@aol.com

Key words: Information Systems, professionalism, personnel, codes of conduct, regulation, powers of sanction.

INTRODUCTION

The integrity of personnel, their 'professionalism', is a key requirement in working with Information Systems (IS). One way of achieving a measure of professionalism is by means of codes governing behaviour in terms of conduct (how the individual behaves in moral or ethical terms) and practice (how the individual carries out work in technological terms): both should be backed by disciplinary procedures.

PERSONNEL

Few, if any, systems are immune to misuse by personnel whose professionalism, at all levels, is a significant requirement for achieving the state of 'fitness for the purpose' for which the use of a given IS is intended. Codes of conduct and practice are one way of achieving professionalism but their effectiveness is dependent on powers of sanction (disciplinary procedures). However, the term 'professional' is often used ambiguously. Thus, for present purposes, definitions [1] of the terms which are associated with 'professionalism and professional status' are given first to make clear its meaning in the remainder of the chapter.

DEFINITION OF TERMS ASSOCIATED WITH PROFESSIONAL STATUS

It is meaningful to start with 'amateur' - one who engages in a pursuit, sport, study or science for love, not remuneration. In a sense, the opposite of 'amateur' is 'professional', which has two definitions - (i) one who takes remuneration for participating in an activity or field of endeavour often engaged in by amateurs; (ii) one who conforms to the technical and/or ethical standards of a profession. 'Profession' is: a calling requiring specialised knowledge and often long and intensive academic preparation.

Professionals are, by implication, subject to regulation. 'Regulation' has two definitions - (i) an authoritative rule dealing with details of procedure; (ii) a rule or order having the force of law. Broadly, there are three forms of regulation[2] - (i) state regulation; (ii) regulation of a given group of professionals by a higher, independent body (sometimes referred to as devolved self-regulation); (iii) self-regulation by a body involved in, and comprised of members, of the activity being regulated. Control is effected in the case of State regulation by statute, by disciplinary procedures in the case of chartered bodies and, with self-regulation, by, for example, public reprimand, a monetary fine, withdrawal of registration and the law.

The regulated professions may be characterised by groups - one group provides a service based on confidence or trust such as barristers, solicitors and patent agents. A second group provides a vital service such as medicine, pharmacy, nursing and midwifery whilst a third group is identified with public safety such as airline pilots, captains of ships and mine managers.

It is convenient in this chapter to refer to regulated professionals as 'chartered'; a 'charter' is a grant or guarantee of rights, franchises or privileges from the sovereign power of a state or country. Such chartered professionals (devolved) are regulated by 'sanction' - (i) a principle or influence that impels to moral action or determines moral judgement; (ii) a mechanism of social control for enforcing a society's standards. Moore[3] and Saunders, Carr and Wilson[4] show that the professional, as defined above, is loosely descended from the European craftsmen's Guilds and Inns of medieval times. Interestingly, clerics formed the first identifiable intellectual professional group, membership of which required the achievement and maintenance of personal criteria which excluded virtually all other members of contemporary society. There was elitism in its purest form!

In the definition of 'professional' given above, reference is made to 'ethical standards'. We need, now, to define 'ethic': there are three definitions - (i) the discipline dealing with what is good and bad and with moral duty and obligation; (ii) a set of moral principals or values; (iii) the principles of conduct governing an individual or group.

PROFESSIONALISM IN THE CONTEXT OF IS

It is difficult to fit IS *per se* into the groups of regulated professionals given above, a point recognised by Parker [5]

Individual practitioners of the three professions of law, religion and medicine can do a great deal of harm, but, in general terms, only to one person at a time. Engineers can harm many people at one crack, but this is less likely because engineers tend to have their work checked and.....work as a team. The possibilities of information processing doing great harm to society are increasing rapidly, however, and it tends to be very difficult to check an individual's work in detail.

Parker wrote the above words before the proliferation of personal computers and mass communication. It is likely, too, that all he had in mind was the lack of good engineering practice of work-checking in the IS fraternity. In today's wide-spread environment of malicious attacks on, and exploitation of, IS, coupled with a general lack of standards, his words are particularly germane.

THE APPROACH OF THE BRITISH COMPUTER SOCIETY (BCS)

The BCS is the only chartered body in the UK concerned specifically with IS. A brief description of the BCS is given at Appendix 1.

An apparent conflict in the 1992 version of the BCS Code of Conduct between what is desirable (in ethical terms) and what is enforceable had become a matter for public debate[8]. The Ethics Expert Panel was tasked with examining the apparent conflict and concluded that there was, indeed, a problem presented by the, then, Rule 1:

'Members shall in their professional practice safeguard public health and safety and have regard to the protection of the environment.'

Whilst in a general social context few would argue that the rule represented an altruistic aim, it was recognised that, in reality, where what is ethically right or wrong in given circumstances is often highly subjective, the rule was inappropriate in the context of a professional body whose members practised in virtually all sectors of industry, commerce and education: taken literally, the rule's application would require the BCS both to expel many existing members and not to accept new members from a wide variety of industrial sectors. This was, clearly, an untenable position and showed the need for an urgent review of the codes.

The review looked first at codes published by other bodies [9], [10], [11], [12], [13] as well as the 1992 version of the BCS code. It was noted that Bye-law 18 of the BCS Regulations requires that:

> Every member .... shall exercise his professional skill and judgement to the best of his ability and discharge his professional responsibilities with integrity. He shall at all times order his conduct to safeguard the public interest and to the best of his ability uphold the reputation and dignity of the profession.

The dichotomy between Bye-law 18 and the 1992 version of the Code of Conduct referred to above was, in essence, an inherent conflict between what is desirable and what is enforceable in the Code in terms of a member's *personal* responsibility stated in Bye-law 18. To clarify matters in professional terms, the Introduction to the new version of the Code of Conduct states:

> The Code governs your personal conduct as an individual member of the BCS and not the nature of business or ethics of the relevant authority. It will, therefore, be a matter of your exercising your personal judgement in meeting the Code's requirements.

Relevant authority is defined earlier in the Introduction as:

> The person or organisation which has authority over your activity as an individual. If you are a practising professional, this is normally an employer or client. If you are a student, this is normally an academic institution.

The new code is now in the public domain on www.bcs.org/codes

CONCLUSION

The BCS Code of Conduct represents one method of achieving a measure of professionalism. However, like any code of conduct, or ethics or practice, its effectiveness is dependent on an associated power of sanction. Such powers cannot exist in isolation because their ultimate enforcement depends broadly on two organisational attributes - (i) the power of sanction must reside in, and be administered by, a body relevant to a given professional field, such that there is a manifest result applying directly to a given individual and (ii) a third party has to 'trigger' the application of the power of sanction by laying a complaint against the individual to whom, in given circumstances, the code applies.

REFERENCES

1. *Webster's Seventh New Collegiate Dictionary.*
2. *Alternatives to State Regulation* - Better Regulation Task Force 2000, UK Dept. of Trade and Industry.
3. Moore WE, *The Professions: Roles and Rules,* Russell Sage Foundation 1970.
4. Saunders A, Carr M. and Wilson P. A., *The Professions,* London Frank Cass 1964.
5. Should Computer Professionals be Licensed? *Communications of the ACM,* May 1971 Vol. 14 No 5.
6. Combating Computer Pornography - Guidance Notes for BCS Members.
7. Written evidence to a BCS Working Party.
8. How high-principled should BCS members be?, Richard Jennings *Computer Bulletin,* November 2000.
9. Professional Association Research Network (PARN), *Code of Conduct* 2000.
10. *Software Engineering Code of Ethics and Professional Practice,* ACM/IEEE Joint Task Force 1999.
11. IEEE, *Code of Ethics* 1990.
12. *Foundation of Professional Ethics,* Richard Jennings, 2000.
13. *Guidelines for Institution Codes of Conduct,* UK Engineering Council 2000.

APPENDIX: THE BRITISH COMPUTER SOCIETY (BCS)

The BCS is the Chartered Institution for Information Systems Engineering. It enables individuals, organisations and society to maximise the benefits from Information Systems (IS), by setting and maintaining professional standards for IS professionals and initiating and informing debate on IS issues with Government, Industry, and Academia.

As the BCS is a professional body and a learned society, supporting the IS community in the UK and overseas, it recognises individual and organisational professional integrity and technical competence through the award of its professional qualifications. It also sets standards for education and training through its examination, and by inspection and accreditation of university courses and company training schemes. It defines standards for professional conduct through its codes of conduct and good practice and advises the UK Government and its agencies on IS-related matters included in proposed legislation, including sponsoring important legislation itself - for example the Computer Misuse Act 1990.

In its pursuit of supporting society at large, the BCS also examines and initiates debate on topical IS issues such as safety critical systems, software certification, intellectual property rights and computer pornography.

The BCS offers a wide range of services for individuals and business, among them numerous membership benefits, a network of branches and specialist groups also open to non-members, and on-line discussion forums. The BCS provides professional qualifications that cover all major areas of the IS discipline, and provides models for a recognised set of training standards and methods for maintaining and awarding best practice in IS staff development. It also provides a wide range of knowledge services through its publishing operation, events, competitions and awards, providing a Professional Advice Service and general IS, security and expert witness consultancy services.

The BCS also manages the highly successful European Computer Driving Licence (ECDL) – the international computer skills qualification. More information is available on http://www.bcs.org or call 01793 417424 for more information.

Collaboration and Research Methods

Pertti JÄRVINEN
Department of Computer Sciences, University of Tampere, Finland
mailto:pj@cs.uta.fi

Key words: Research method, design science, cooperation, theory, consensus/dissent.

INTRODUCTION

The problems in practice are seldom solved by applying knowledge from one science only. The co-operation and collaboration between experts from different sciences are then needed. Customer relationships management (CRM) and supply chain management (SCM) systems strongly show that information technology (IT) is helping and supporting the collaboration needed. But the problems related with co-operation and collaboration can be different. I shall in this paper perform a small survey on the recent literature to demonstrate the variety of problems. The presented examples refer to different research methods required. The methods are structured into the new taxonomy in order to help a researcher to find a suitable research method for a certain research problem.

COLLABORATION

Collaboration is needed in many information technology (IT) efforts. To give some light to different opportunities, we give some examples below. We shall name them by letters A, B, ..., H and later use those letters in referring to our categories of research methods in the next section. Collaboration can be successful or unsuccessful. We start with the latter case.

Example A: The requirements specification plays a key role in building the new IT application. To my mind, Davidson [2002] nicely described her longitudinal case study with eight episodes. The project focused on defining requirements for a new marketing and sales system to replace an existing legacy system. The real project leader or the opinion leader changed at least eight times during the Davidson's follow up period. Depending on who was guiding the project work both the goals of the project and the sketches of specifications changed At the end of the study period any accepted specifications did not yet exist. Davidson applied the principles of interpretive field study presented by Klein and Myers [1999] to her case. If she would use Deetz's [1996] classification of four discourses, she would not call her study as interpretive but *dialogic* one, because there were not only one view on requirements but many.

Example B: Virkkunen and Kuutti [2000] studied a certain organisation at the public sector. They described inspectors' work in a labour-protection. They found many conflicting parties in the organisation, and therefore they selected the cultural historical activity theory to study organisational learning. On the basis of the historical analysis, the researchers prepared the model of the inspectors' activity system and its inner contradictions. This historical analysis really gave an important information. By using term, historical analysis it was no need to say anything bad about participants, and it psychologically laid a more sound basis for the development work than speaking about conflicts between some persons or between some collectives.

Example C: Lamb and Kling [2003] considered that a concept of the user is fundamental to much of the research and practice of information systems design, development, and evaluation. User-centered information studies have relied on individualistic cognitive models to carefully examine the criteria that influence the selection of information and communication technologies (ICTs) that people make. In many ways, these studies have improved our understanding of how a good information resource fits the people who use it. However, research approaches based on an individualistic user concept are limited. In their paper, they examined the theoretical constructs that shape this user concept and contrast these with alternative views that help to reconceptualize the user as a social actor. Despite pervasive ICT use, social actors are not primarily users of ICTs. Most people who use ICT applications utilize multiple applications, in various roles, and as part of their efforts to produce goods and services while interacting with a variety of other people, and often in multiple social contexts. Moreover, the socially thin user construct limits our understanding of information selection, manipulation, communication, and exchange within complex social contexts. Using the grounded theory approach [Glaser and Strauss 1967] in analyses from a recent study of online information service use, they developed an institutionalist concept of a social actor whose everyday interactions are infused with ICT use.

Example D: Jarvenpaa and Staples [2000] reported an exploratory investigation of individual perceptions of factors that underlie the use of collaborative electronic media (electronic mail, World Wide Web, list serves, and other collaborative systems) for sharing information in a large state university in Australia. The model builds on the Constant et al.'s [1994] theory of information sharing. The authors propose that perceptions of information culture, attitudes regarding information ownership and propensity to share, as well as task and personal factors influence people's use of collaborative media. Jarvenpaa and Staples found that task characteristics (task interdependence), perceived information usefulness and the user's computer comfort were most strongly associated with the person's use of collaborative media. Consistent with Constant et al.'s [1994] earlier findings, views of information ownership and propensity to share were significantly related to use. Interestingly, use of electronic media for sharing information and contacting people was weakly associated with a more structured, closed information culture. This implies that heavy users and sharers want more structured information flow in place, possibly due to their need to have reliable access to other individual's knowledge and information. Contrary to suggestions in the literature, a fully open, organic information culture may not always be most desirable.

Example E: van Aken [2004] studied approaches in design science. Concerning outcomes of design science studies he emphasises design knowledge, especially prescriptions as an important category. The logic of a prescription is 'if you want to achieve Y in situation Z, then perform action X'. There are algorithmic prescriptions, which operate like a recipe. However, many prescriptions in a design science are of a heuristic nature. They can rather be described as 'if you want to achieve Y in situation Z, then something like action X will help'. 'Something like action X' means that the prescription is to be used as a *design exemplar*. A design exemplar is a general prescription which has to be translated to the specific problem at hand; in solving that problem, one has to design a specific variant of that design exemplar." [van Aken, 2004]

"In the design sciences the research object is a '*mutandum*'; these sciences are not too much interested in what *is*, but more in what *can be*. The typical research product is the prescription discussed above or in terms of Bunge [1967b, p. 132] a technological rule: 'an instruction to perform a finite number of acts in a given order and with a given aim'. A *technological rule* is defined as *a chunk of general knowledge, linking an intervention or artefact with a desired outcome or performance in a certain field of application*. A major breakthrough occurred with the systematic testing of technological rules. The *tested* technological rule is one whose effectiveness has been systematically tested within the context of its intended use. The real breakthrough came when tested technological rules could be *grounded* on scientific knowledge [Bunge 1967b, 132], including law-like relationships from natural sciences. The typical research design to study and test technological rules is the multiple case: a series of problems of the same class is solved, each by applying the problem solving cycle. By borrowing concepts from software development one can say research on technological rules typically goes through a stage of *α-testing*, i.e. testing and further development by the originator of the rule, to be followed by a stage of *β-testing*, i.e. the testing of the rule by third parties."

As said earlier multiple case studies are valid for the extracting and the developing case study. The *extracting* multiple case-study [van Aken 2004] "is a kind of best-practice research and is aimed at uncovering technological rules as already used in practice. A good example of such research is the classical study of Womack et al [1990] of the automotive industry and especially of Japanese practices. This research has produced, among other things, a number of very powerful technological rules, like the Kanban-system and Just-in-Time delivery for driving a supply chain.

Example F: Lindgren et al. [2004] claimed that even though the literature on competence in organizations recognizes the need to align organization level core competence with individual level job competence, it does not consider the role of information technology in managing competence across the macro and micro levels. To address this shortcoming, we embarked on an action research study that develops and tests design principles for competence management systems. This research develops an integrative model of competence that outlines the interaction between organizational and individual level competence and the role of technology in this process. Six Swedish organizations participated in their research project, which took 30 months and consisted of two action research cycles involving numerous data collection strategies and interventions such as *prototypes*, and developing a set of design principles.

Lindgren et al. [2004] describe how it is possible to find out the competences of a certain worker by utilizing search engines and recommender systems with the document repository. This is a really new domain to apply IT, and March and Smith [1995], and Hevner et al. [2004] recommend that this kind of application should be included into the knowledge base of design science. The *evaluation* of two prototypes made by Lindgren et al. highlighted that their design principles generated not only anticipated but also unanticipated consequences. In light of these findings, they revised and refined their initial design principles.

Example G: Aulin [1982, 115] derived the Law of Requisite Hierarchy from the Law of Requisite Variety [Ashby, 1956] by supposing that a regulator R1 is incapable of reducing the variety of original disturbance $H(D)$ to the required level of survival, $H(E_0)$. The situation may be saved, if we have another regulator R2 that can be put to regulate further the outcome

Y1 of the first regulator. This may be still insufficient. But then, if we have a third regulator to handle the outcome Y2 we can proceed and go until a regulator of order m will yield a satisfactory result. In general case, the uncertainty term $H_D(R)$ for m regulators in the sequence will reduce the effective regulatory ability. Some controllers Gj, or a hierarchy of controllers to guide regulators Ri are then needed.

The Law of Requisite Hierarchy can be expressed as follows:
The weaker in average are the regulatory abilities and the larger the uncertainties of available regulators, the more hierarchy is needed in the organization of regulation and control to attain the same result of regulation, if possible at all.

Example H: Gefen et al. [2003] performed a literature survey and found that a separate and distinct interaction with both the actual e-vendor and with its IT Web site interface is at the heart of online shopping. Previous research has established, accordingly, that online purchase intentions are the product of both consumer assessments of the IT itself – specifically its perceived usefulness and ease-of-use (TAM) – and trust in the e-vendor. But these perspectives have been examined independently by IS researchers. Integrating these two perspectives and examining the factors that build online trust in an environment that lacks the typical human interaction that often leads to trust in other circumstances advances our understanding of these constructs and their linkages to behaviour.

THE NEW TAXONOMY OF RESEARCH METHODS

In this section we present our taxonomy (Figure 1) and argumentation for it. We firstly differentiate mathematical methods from other methods, because they concern formal languages, algebraic units etc., in other words, symbol systems not having any direct reference to objects in reality. From the remaining methods concerning reality we then use research questions in differentiation. Two classes are based on whether the research question concerns a) what is a (part of) reality or b) does the question stress on utility of an innovation (artefact) [cf. March and Smith, 1995]. From the former we differentiate conceptual-analytical approaches, i.e. methods for theoretical development, from empirical research approaches.

When empirically studying the past and present, we can use theory-testing or theory-creating methods depending on whether we have a theory, model or framework guiding our research or whether we are developing a new theory grounded on the raw data gathered. In the theory-testing studies we can a priori assume either dissent or consensus [Deetz 1996]. In the theory-creating studies we recognize whether dissent or consensus holds in the research site. Concerning innovations, we can either build or evaluate them. - Above we have tried to apply the Bunge's [1967a, 75] guidelines to the taxonomy.

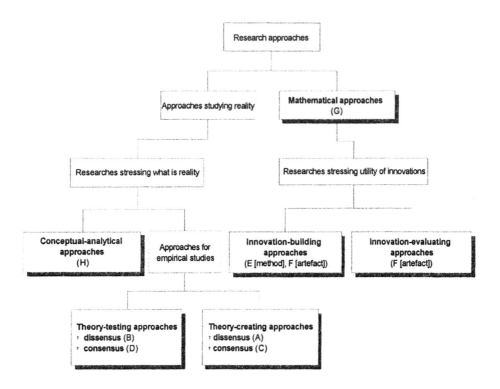

Figure 1. Our taxonomy of research methods [Järvinen, 2004]

March and Smith [1995] placed much emphasis on design science with two activities, *build* and *evaluate*. It is interesting to note that Susman and Evered [1978] described *action research* as a repetitive performance of the following cycle: Diagnose, plan, implement, evaluate and learn. The three first phases in the cycle (diagnose, plan and implement) are similar to the information systems development method, when the so-called phase approach is applied, i.e. when a new system is built. Hence, action research seems to contain both the build and evaluate activities.

Hence, our new taxonomy seems to give advice for researchers on how to select a suitable research method, and correct and improve earlier views on research methods.

REFERENCES:

Ashby R.W. (1956), *An introduction to cybernetics,* Chapman & Hall, London.

Aulin A. (1982), *The cybernetic laws of social progress*, Pergamon Press, Oxford.

Bunge M. (1967a), *Scientific Research I. The Search for System*, Springer-Verlag, Berlin.

Bunge M. (1967b), *Scientific Research II. The Search for truth*, Springer-Verlag, Berlin.

Constant D., S. Kiesler and L. Sproull (1994) What's mine is ours, or is it? A study of attitudes about information sharing, *Information Systems Research* 5, No. 4, 400-421.

Davidson E.J. (2002), Technology frames and framing: A socio-cognitive investigation of requirements determination, *MIS Quarterly* 26, No 4, 329-358.

Deetz S. (1996), Describing differences in approaches to organization science: Rethinking Burrell and Morgan and their legacy, *Organization Science* 7, No 2, 191-207.

Gefen D., E. Karahanna and D.W. Straub (2003), Trust and TAM in online shopping: An integrated model, *MIS Quarterly* 27, No 1, 51-90.

Glaser B. and A. Strauss (1967), *The discovery of grounded theory: Strategies of qualitative research*, Wiedenfeld and Nicholson, London.

Hevner A.R., S.T. March, J. Park and S. Ram (2004), Design science in information systems research, *MIS Quarterly* 28, No 1, 75-105.

Jarvenpaa S.L. and D.S. Staples (2000), The use of collaborative electronic media for information sharing: An exploratory study of determinants, *Journal of Strategic Information Systems* 9, No 2-3, 129-154.

Järvinen P. (2004), On research methods, *Opinpajan kirja*, Tampere, Finland.

Klein H.K. and M.D. Myers (1999), A set of principles for conducting and evaluating interpretive field studies in information systems, *MIS Quarterly* 23, No 1, 67-94.

Lamb R. and R. Kling (2003), Reconceptualizing Users as Social Actors in Information Systems Research, *MIS Quarterly* 27, No 2, 197-235.

Lindgren R., Henfridsson O. and U. Schultze (2004), Design Principles for Competence Management Systems: A Synthesis of an Action Research Study, *MIS Quarterly* 28, No 3, 435-472.

March S.T. and G.F. Smith (1995), Design and natural science research on information technology, *Decision Support Systems* 15, 251-266.

van Aken J.E. (2004), Management research based on the paradigm of the design sciences: The quest for field-tested and grounded technological rules, *Journal of Management Studies* 41, No 2, 219-246.

Virkkunen J. and K. Kuutti (2000), Understanding organizational learning by focusing on "activity systems", *Accounting, Management & Information Technology* 10, No 4, 291-319.

Womack J.P., D.J. Jones and D. Roos (1990), The machine that changed the world: How Japan's secret weapon in the global auto wars will revolutionize Western industry: The story of lean production, Harper Perennial, New York.

Subject Index

Printed in the United Kingdom
by Lightning Source UK Ltd.
133633UK00007B/109-111/P